RECLAIMING the OLD TESTAMENT for CHRISTIAN PREACHING

EDITED BY

Grenville J. R. Kent, Paul J. Kissling and Laurence A. Turner

WITH CONTRIBUTIONS BY

Daniel I. Block, David G. Firth, Alison Lo, Tremper Longman III,

Ernest C. Lucas, R. W. L. Moberly, Federico G. Villanueva,

Gordon J. Wenham, H. G. M. Williamson and Christopher J. H. Wright

IVP Academic

An imprint of InterVarsity Press
Downers Grove, Illinois

InterVarsity Press
P.O. Box 1400, Downers Grove, IL 60515-1426
Internet: www.ivpress.com
E-mail: email@ivpress.com

InterVarsity Press® is the book-publishing division of InterVarsity Christian Fellowship/USA®, a movement of students and faculty active on campus at hundreds of universities, colleges and schools of nursing in the United States of America, and a member movement of the International Fellowship of Evangelical Students. For information about local and regional activities, write Public Relations Dept., InterVarsity Christian Fellowship/USA, 6400 Schroeder Rd., P.O. Box 7895, Madison, WI 53707-7895, or visit the IVCF website at <www.intervarsity.org>.

ISBN 978-0-8308-3887-5
Printed in the United States of America ∞

British Library Cataloguing in Publication Data
Reclaiming the Old Testament for Christian preaching / edited by
Grenville J.R. Kent, Paul J. Kissling, Laurence A. Turner.
    p. cm.
  Includes bibliographical references and index.
  ISBN 978-0-8308-3887-5 (USA: paper: alk. paper)—ISBN
978-1-84474-448-0 (UK: paper: alk. paper)
  1. Bible O.T.—Homiletical use. I. Kent, Grenville J.R. II.
Kissling, Paul J. III. Turner, Laurence A.
  BS1191.5.R42 2010
  221.601—dc22
                                                              201019897

P	23	22	21	20	19	18	17	16	15	14	13	12	11	10	9	8	7	6	5	4	3	2	1
Y	30	29	28	27	26	25	24	23	22	21	20	19	18	17	16	15	14	13	12	11	10		

CONTENTS

CONTRIBUTORS

Daniel I. Block is Gunther H. Knoedler Professor of Old Testament, Wheaton College, Illinois, USA.

David G. Firth is Lecturer in Old Testament and BA Course Leader, Cliff College, Derbyshire, UK.

Grenville J. R. Kent is Lecturer in Old Testament, Wesley Institute, Sydney, Australia.

Paul J. Kissling is Professor of Old Testament and Biblical Languages and Director of Research, TCMI Institute, Austria.

Alison Lo is Lecturer in Old Testament, London School of Theology, Northwood, UK.

Tremper Longman III is Robert H. Gundry Professor of Biblical Studies, Westmont College, USA.

Ernest C. Lucas is Vice-Principal and Tutor in Biblical Studies, Bristol Baptist College, UK.

Walter Moberly is Professor of Theology and Biblical Interpretation, Durham University, UK.

Laurence A. Turner is Principal Lecturer in Old Testament and Research Degrees Director, Newbold College, Bracknell, UK.

Federico G. Villanueva is Assistant Professor of Old Testament, Alliance Graduate School, Manila, Philippines.

Gordon J. Wenham is Professor Emeritus of the University of Gloucestershire and Tutor in Old Testament, Trinity College, Bristol, UK.

H. G. M. Williamson FBA is Regius Professor of Hebrew, University of Oxford, UK.

Christopher J. H. Wright is International Director, Langham Partnership International.

ABBREVIATIONS

ABD	*Anchor Bible Dictionary*
AOTC	Apollos Old Testament Commentary
BCOTWP	Baker Commentary on the Old Testament Wisdom and Psalms
BST	The Bible Speaks Today series
CCLI	Christian Copyright Licensing International
CPNIVOTC	College Press NIV Old Testament Commentary series
CSCD	Cambridge Studies in Christian Doctrine
ESV	English Standard Version of the Bible
ET	English translation
HUCA	*Hebrew Union College Annual*
IBCTP	Interpretation Bible Commentary for Teaching and Preaching
ICC	International Critical Commentary
IDB	*The Interpreter's Dictionary of the Bible*
JNSL	*Journal of Northwest Semitic Languages*
JSOT	*Journal for the Study of the Old Testament*
LHBOTS	Library of Hebrew Bible/Old Testament Studies
MT	Masoretic Text
NCB	New Century Bible
NT	New Testament

NIB	*New Interpreter's Bible*
NIBC	New International Biblical Commentary
NICOT	New International Commentary on the Old Testament
NIDOTTE	*New International Dictionary of Old Testament Theology and Exegesis*
NIV	New International Version of the Bible
NLT	New Living Translation of the Bible
NRSV	New Revised Standard Version of the Bible
NTS	*New Testament Studies*
OT	Old Testament
OTL	Old Testament Library
SBLMS	Society of Biblical Literature Monograph Series
SBLSP	Society of Biblical Literature Seminar Papers
TDOT	*Theological Dictionary of the Old Testament*
TOTC	Tyndale Old Testament Commentaries
WBC	Westminster Bible Companion

INTRODUCTION

Grenville J. R. Kent, Paul J. Kissling and Laurence A. Turner

Don't waste time on an introduction. . .

And isn't that why some people skip the Old Testament?

Yet Jesus, walking with confused friends, started at Moses and the Prophets and explained all the things in the Hebrew Scriptures about himself. Contemporary audiences too can find their hearts burning within them as they hear his voice in the diversity of this ancient, exotic, endlessly fascinating and supremely challenging part of the Bible.

If you are a busy pastor, lay preacher or teacher, we hope this book will encourage you to use the Bible's often-neglected 78%, and to demonstrate its usefulness and relevance to the life of faith today.

This book offers solid scholarship in an accessible form. It does not try to make you fight in someone else's armour, but offers reflections on approaches you might use and issues you might consider in preparing an Old Testament sermon. It offers practical suggestions on how to understand the message of OT texts, paying attention to the features of various genres of literature, and how to bring their themes to a contemporary audience. Chapters include a discussion of the theory and then a practical example of a sermon (in summary form).

This is not another OT commentary that reads texts carefully but stays in the BC world; and it is not another book on general preaching techniques that is content with simple, surface readings of texts. Its contributors were chosen because they are not only OT scholars but also preachers who regularly experience the challenges and joys of bringing OT messages to contemporary audiences. They are passionate about faithfulness to what the ancient text is doing, and also care deeply about how it preaches today. They preach and teach in North America, Africa, Australia, South America, Great Britain, Europe, Hong Kong, the Philippines and the Middle East – basically every continent except Antarctica – and have also served across a wide range of church traditions – Anglican, Baptist, charismatic, Congregational, independent evangelical, Methodist, Seventh-day Adventist and Uniting – and so may offer you fresh perspectives.

The OT is presented within an overarching story, and so we begin with two chapters on understanding narrative, both plot and character. We then look at how to preach *torah* texts. We consider preaching from Wisdom literature, examining Proverbs, Job and especially Ecclesiastes. We also unseal the Song of Solomon as a unique kind of wisdom. We consider preaching Psalms: praise psalms, of course, but also sadly neglected lament psalms. The Prophets receive attention: classical prophets like Isaiah, apocalyptic prophets like Daniel and Ezekiel and minor prophets like Zephaniah. We then examine two special topics: how to preach 'difficult' texts, and how to preach Christ from the OT.

The chapters are based on papers presented at the Tyndale Fellowship Old Testament Study Group at the University of Cambridge in July 2009.

One of the great spiritual revivals of history was when Ezra and the Levites 'read from the book of the *torah* of God, making the meanings clear and helping people understand what they read' (Neh. 8:8, lit.). The result was men and women gratefully celebrating that they had heard and understood God's words, and finding joy and strength in a fresh connection with God. Our prayer is that readers like you will use all the rich resources of the Bible in the power of the Spirit to contribute to another revival, so that the good news of the kingdom can be preached worldwide and we can see Christ come.

1. PREACHING NARRATIVE: PLOT

Laurence A. Turner

Introduction

From a literary point of view, OT narratives are among the greatest ever told. Yet these biblical stories which communicate directly and immediately, lodging in the memory for a lifetime, have traditionally not been preached well. Preachers' lack of sensitivity to the ways in which narratives work has resulted in sermons which have less impact than the stories they seek to expound. For example, a sermon which retells the biblical account blow by blow and then appends a general moral obligation will always be less successful than a simple reading of the narrative itself. A similar fate awaits the preacher who latches on to this or that point from somewhere in the narrative, impales it 'upon the frame of Aristotelian logic',[1] and then expands on its timeless truth.

Successful preaching on OT narrative requires an understanding of its characteristics, a major element of which is plot. Our understanding of plots and the dynamics of narrative have been enhanced in recent years by the discipline of narrative criticism. Unfortunately, however, this approach to the

---

1. Fred B. Craddock, *As One Without Authority*, rev. ed. (St Louis: Chalice Press, 2001), p. 45.

text has often received a guarded, not to say hostile, reception in evangelical circles.

Throughout much of the twentieth century conservative evangelical OT scholarship fought a rearguard action against liberal 'historical-critical' denigration of the historical value of the biblical text. If a text did not accurately reflect real historical circumstances, so it was argued, then how could its theology be trusted? Consequently, evangelical engagement with the OT emphasized history and theology. Narrative criticism, with its emphasis on the text's literary art, seemed to many evangelicals to work independently of history, with little interest in theology. Reactions ranged from outright rejection,[2] or very guarded interest,[3] to reasoned acceptance of its potential for interpretation.[4] Any evangelical writing from a narrative-critical perspective seemed duty bound to affirm that the events narrated actually happened, because an interest in the text's aesthetics was often taken to be a denial of its historicity.[5] More recently, however, narrative criticism, shorn of its more extreme postmodern presuppositions, has entered the evangelical mainstream.[6] Once one accepts that narrative is the major way in which biblical authors address matters of first importance, and that historical interests do not need to dictate every engagement with Scripture, it follows that understanding the dynamics of narrative leads to theological and spiritual gains. The following approach to narrative plot is based on the conviction not only that narrative criticism is compatible with a high view of Scripture, but also that preachers who are non-specialists can enrich their preaching by utilizing its insights.

---

2. Carl F. H. Henry, 'Narrative Theology: An Evangelical Appraisal', *Trinity Journal*, 8 (1987), p. 19, cited in J. Daniel Hays, 'An Evangelical Approach to Old Testament Narrative Criticism', *Bibliotheca Sacra*, 166 (2009), pp. 3–18 (p. 4).

3. Grant R. Osborne, *The Hermeneutical Spiral: A Comprehensive Introduction to Biblical Interpretation*, rev. and expanded 2nd ed. (Downers Grove, Ill: InterVarsity Press, 2006), pp. 212–215.

4. e.g. Tremper Longman III, *Literary Approaches to Biblical Interpretation*, Foundations of Contemporary Interpretation (Grand Rapids, MI: Academie Books, 1987), p. 3.

5. e.g. Leland Ryken, 'And It Came to Pass: The Bible as God's Storybook', *Bibliotheca Sacra*, 147 (1990), pp. 131–142 (p. 134).

6. For a recent survey of this development, see Hays, 'An Evangelical Approach to Old Testament Narrative Criticism', pp. 3–18.

Plot in Old Testament narrative

In common parlance the terms 'narrative' and 'plot' have overlapping meanings. Narrative can be defined as an 'account of connected events', and plot as 'the main sequence of events' in written or oral literature.[7] These similar definitions indicate the intimate relationship between narratives and plots, but they are not synonymous.

It is generally agreed that a narrative has four major characteristics. First, a sequence of events which punctuate a timeline. Second, a major character or characters whose actions or motives drive the narrated events towards a conclusion. Third, a plot which provides an overarching coherence to the individual events. Fourth, the structuring of the plot in such a way as to imply cause and effect between events.[8] Note that the third and fourth criteria make explicit reference to plot, and the first and second are to some degree related to it. Much more could be said, but this preliminary definition of narrative is enough to provide a basis for considering plot.

Plots have an intimate relationship with narratives. 'Plot is, first of all, a constant of all written and oral narrative, in that a narrative without at least a minimal plot would be incomprehensible.'[9] Plot provides the 'main organising principle'[10] which brings order to the chaos of narrated human actions and experiences so that a coherent, though not necessarily straightforward, narrative emerges. But how does a plot achieve these functions, and why should readers and preachers of the OT appreciate it?

A classical plot has a fivefold, or 'quinary', structure. On this there is general agreement, though there is some variety in the terminology used for each element. Here, I use the vocabulary of Marguerat and Bourquin,[11] illustrating the analysis from the narrative of 2 Samuel 11.

---

7. *The Concise Oxford Dictionary*, ed. Judy Pearsall, 10th ed. (Oxford: Oxford University Press, 1999).

8. For a more detailed discussion of these points, based on the work of J. M. Adam, see Daniel Marguerat and Yvan Bourquin, *How to Read Bible Stories: An Introduction to Narrative Criticism*, trans. John Bowden (London: SCM Press, 1999), p. 16.

9. P. Brooks, *Reading for the Plot: Design and Intention in Narrative* (New York: Knopf, 1984), p. 5.

10. Jan P. Fokkelman, *Reading Biblical Narrative: An Introductory Guide* (Philadelphia: Westminster John Knox Press, 2000), p. 76.

11. Marguerat and Bourquin, *How to Read Bible Stories*, p. 43.

1. Initial situation (or exposition)

Information concerning characters, their situation and sometimes hints concerning their motives, so that readers may understand subsequent developments in the narrative. The initial situation requires development or destabilization for the plot to progress. (*While the army is out on a campaign against the Ammonites, King David is at ease in his palace in Jerusalem, v. 1*).

2. Complication

This begins the trajectory of the narrative from its initial status quo. The movement may be initiated by a speech, action, revelation of a problem, in fact anything which introduces enough tension into the situation to indicate that matters cannot remain at rest. (*He falls for the gorgeous Bathsheba, wife of the absent Uriah the Hittite, and she tells him she is pregnant, vv. 2–5.*)

3. Transforming action

The transforming action introduces the (potential) means of removing, overcoming, managing or in some way responding to the complication. This clearly stands at the heart of the plot and marks the initial move towards resolution. (*David calls for Uriah and tries to persuade him to go down to his house. Uriah resolutely refuses, so David plots his demise, vv. 6–15.*)

4. Dénouement (or resolution)

This brings to a conclusion the move begun by the transforming action and (at least partially) resolves the issues introduced by the complication. (*Uriah is killed and David is informed of his death, vv. 16–25.*)

5. Final situation

This brings the narrative to a resting place by showing how the situation has returned to that in the initial situation, or moved on to a new stage of equilibrium. (*Bathsheba mourns for Uriah, marries David and gives birth to a son. God is not pleased, vv. 26–27.*)

In any plotted narrative the transitions from one movement to the next are likely to be gradual rather than abrupt, so there might be a difference of opinion as to where exactly to draw the line between them. For example, in 2 Samuel 11, at which precise point does *transforming action* merge into *resolution*? Nevertheless, the narrative's general progression through its fivefold plot is clear. While a full-fledged plot has a quinary structure, it is not mandatory to have all five elements. However, *initial situation, complication* and *resolution* are almost always present.

On the one hand, therefore, the plot of any narrative has a predetermined trajectory. What prevents a good narrative descending into the utterly predictable, however, is the creativity of the narrator in including certain details and omitting others. For example, in 2 Samuel 11 the narrator could have chosen to bring Bathsheba's emotions into the foreground. But apart from one brief mention of her mourning, right at the end, we are never told how she reacts to these tragic events. These potential elements are omitted, while others, such as David's 'sending' all and sundry to do his will, or Uriah's refusal to go down to his house, are repeated throughout. These omissions and inclusions indicate to interpreters what the narrative's emphases are, and where to dwell in expounding its meaning. The end result is a narrative whose general plotted structure can be predicted before it is read, but a story which is full of surprise.

There are numerous variations on the basic plot structure. For example, in Genesis 18:16–33 we move from the *initial situation* in verse 16 (Abraham's visitors depart for Sodom and he sets them on their way) to the *complication* of verses 17–21 (Abraham learns of possible divine judgment falling on Sodom – home of his nephew Lot). This leads to Abraham's daring *transforming action* of challenging God to act justly and save the whole city if it contains fifty righteous people (vv. 23–25). God's response, that he accepts Abraham's plea (v. 26), appears to be the *resolution*, and a reader might assume we are now set for the *final situation*. However, Abraham repeats his plea, this time reducing the threshold to forty-five (vv. 27–28a), thus reverting to *transforming action*, and God's positive response (v. 28b) is another potential *resolution*. This oscillation between *transforming action* and *resolution* is repeated no fewer than four more times, until God agrees to a minimum of ten righteous people (vv. 29–32). The interest of the hearer is thus increased, as the threshold is decreased one step at a time: have we now reached *resolution*, or have we not? Abraham's bargaining is brought to an end by God, who abruptly 'went his way', while Abraham 'returned to his place' (v. 33 NRSV), thus producing a brief *final situation*.

Narrators also utilize different kinds of resolutions, which might not be full, but rather partial or open ended. A classic example is that of Jonah, where the book concludes with God's question: 'And should I not be concerned about Nineveh, that great city, in which there are more than a hundred and twenty thousand people who do not know their right hand from their left, and also many animals?' (Jon. 4:11 NRSV). While the question concerns God's own attitudes, it also challenges Jonah and the reader and is left hanging with no answer. This open-ended 'resolution' means that the narrative of Jonah never achieves a true final situation – at least not one provided by the narrator. How Jonah might have answered, or how the reader might respond, are surrendered by the narrator to those who hear his narrative.

An important feature of the way in which narrators manipulate the basic template of plot development is the distinction between 'narrative time' and 'narration time'. 'Narrative time' refers to the temporal space taken up by actions within the world of the narrative. 'Narration time' describes the actual time taken by the narrative to convey those actions to the world of the hearer or reader. Twenty years in the life of a character ('narrative time') could be covered in the space of five verses ('narration time'), followed by one day taking up ten verses. The varying amounts of narrative space accorded to different elements in the plot are indications of the narrative's emphases. For example, in 2 Samuel 11, the *initial situation* and *complication* (vv. 1–5) cover a period of weeks, while the *transforming action* (vv. 6–15) takes up a week or so. However, the *resolution* (vv. 16–25) covers even less narrative time, comprised largely of comparatively verbose direct speech (vv. 19–21, 23–25). The *final situation* (vv. 26–27) covers several months. The disparity between narrative time and narration time is at its lowest in the *resolution*, delaying David's climactic response to Uriah's death (v. 25). Keeping the reader waiting for David's speech underlines its significance in the plot.

OT narratives tend to be surrounded by larger narrative blocks. This means that while plots structure their own micro-narratives, these plots themselves become part of the larger macro-narrative. An individual plot might come to its *final situation*, only for that equilibrium to provide the *initial situation* for complication in the succeeding episode. For example, Daniel 2 concludes with King Nebuchadnezzar's acknowledgment of Daniel and his God, as the consequence of Daniel's successful interpretation of the royal dream in which the king is represented as a head of gold. Daniel 3 begins, 'King Nebuchadnezzar made a golden statue. . .', an *initial situation* which disturbs the *final situation* of the preceding episode.

Serious misunderstanding can occur when individual episodes are viewed in isolation, rather than as part of their larger plot. An example of this is Genesis 38, which has been treated by many commentators as an intrusion into the story of Jacob's family, inserted by a dull-witted editor. Yet, far from being largely unrelated to its context, the plot of this narrative develops elements of the previous account and prepares the way for what follows. For example, in chapter 37, Judah's suggestion that the brothers profit from selling Joseph contributes to the *transforming action* which sets in motion the brothers' deception of Jacob concerning the fate of Joseph. In chapter 38, Tamar's dressing as a prostitute is the transforming action which deceives Judah into having sex with her. This in turn anticipates the *complication* of chapter 39 in which Potiphar's wife deceives her husband into thinking Joseph guilty of attempted rape. All three episodes utilize items of clothing as catalysts for deception: Joseph's bloodstained robe, Tamar's veil and Joseph's garment. At the very least, the contrast between Judah's easy seduction and Joseph's spirited rebuff indicate how the plots of these episodes are intertwined. Understanding the role of Genesis 38 in its macro-narrative enhances our understanding not only of that chapter, but also of the other episodes to which it is related.

An understanding of plot also affects our re-reading of narratives. As first-time readers of a biblical narrative, not knowing the end from the beginning, we are drawn to an unknown resolution, with escalating unresolved tension, until the final decisive moves. We put the narrative to one side with a sense of fulfilment. But what about the next time we read that narrative? As second-time readers we already know the conclusion, so the resolution, as such, no longer comes as a surprise. We can always read *as if* for the first time, that is, holding our privileged information in abeyance and adopting the perspective of the characters in the plot who remain eternal first-time participants. And I would maintain that some element of surprise should remain in any reading of a biblical narrative if we are to appreciate its narrative genius. For example, Genesis 22:1 informs us that 'After these things God tested Abraham' (NRSV). Commentators regularly state that since what follows is *only* a test, the reader realizes that Isaac is safe and will not die. However, such is not the case for the first-time reader, who knows merely that Abraham is being tested. Perhaps the test is to see whether Abraham actually will dispatch his son. Nonetheless, while reading *as if* for the first time is a helpful strategy for rediscovering the emotional impact of a narrative, we cannot, nor should we, avoid second-time reading. So reading Genesis 22 with a knowledge of how its complications are resolved allows us to revisit the constituent parts of the plot with fresh eyes. A first-time reading, of necessity, works its way through the plot from *initial situation* to *resolution* and *final situation*. A second-time reading begins by knowing this conclusion. Thus it can revisit initial situation and transforming action with new eyes. What on a first-time reading might be seen as enigmatic – e.g. Abraham's statement to his servants that he and Isaac 'will worship, and then we will come back to you' (v. 5 NRSV) – might now be seen as a significant (unconscious?) foreshadowing of later plot developments. Such a second-time reading complements a first-time reading by reconsidering the interrelationships between plot elements and demonstrating a truism of OT narratives: they are always more complex than a first-time reading suggests.

This brief and necessarily selective outline of plot is hopefully sufficient to demonstrate how a knowledge of it helps in appreciating the dynamics of narratives in general and those found in the OT in particular. Analysing plot structure gives insight not only into what a narrative presents, but also into how it does so and where its emphases lie. Variations on a theme are also easier to identify and appreciate. Seeing the plots of individual episodes also forces one to ask how these relate to one another and contribute to the overarching plot of the macro-narrative, so that one does not lose sight of the wood for the trees.

Plot in preaching Old Testament narrative

Since plot provides the structural framework for narrative, let us consider initially the relationship between the structure of a particular narrative's plot and that of a sermon expounding the same narrative. The proverbial three-point sermon structure might be well suited to – or rather, do less damage in – a thematic/topical presentation, or an exposition of a dense Pauline passage. But it can give the kiss of death to an exposition on a narrative, by substituting a logically deductive and synthetic sermon for the aesthetically crafted and inductive narrative original. Regardless of whether we think plot structure is culturally determined or hard-wired into the human psyche, its ubiquity across human societies, in expressions ranging from ancestral epic to the last episode of your favourite soap opera,[12] shows that people understand and respond to plotted narratives even if they are unaware of why they do. A typical plot structure maintains interest. Witness the ebbing away of curiosity in the congregation when the preacher moves from his or her 'illustrative story' to the real topic of the sermon. There is a narrative-shaped space in most people's minds, into which a well-crafted plot fits with no resistance. Consequently, preachers should not 'de-plot' an OT narrative in order to reconstitute it into acceptable sermonic form. Narratives are not theses supported by logically subordinate arguments leading to practical implications. Any sermon based on a narrative which is structured in this manner has failed to engage with the literary essence of the story.

In order to avoid this problem, one obvious strategy is for the structure of the sermon to replicate that of the narrative it expounds. A sermon on Daniel 3, for example, could follow the contours of its plot: beginning with the *initial situation* of Nebuchadnezzar erecting his golden statue/idol and commanding all to bow before it (vv. 1–7), then the *complication* of the three friends who refuse to do so (vv. 8–18), Nebuchadnezzar's attempted *transforming action* of throwing the three friends into the furnace (vv. 19–23), the dramatic *resolution* of their being unharmed in the flames while accompanied by a fourth divine

---

12. Christopher Booker, *The Seven Basic Plots: Why We Tell Stories* (London: Continuum, 2004).

figure, and Nebuchadnezzar's acknowledgment of the true God (vv. 24–29), and concluded by the *final situation* of the king promoting the three friends (v. 30).

With this general structure the sermon could proceed in any one of several ways. For example, each element of the plot (the world of the text) allows for a connection with the world of the congregation. The sermon could move between these two worlds, each step determined by the structure of the plot: from the *initial situation* of the text, to the situation of the congregation; from the *complication* in the narrative to the conflicts in the lives of the hearers, etc. This would produce two 'stories' presented in parallel: the biblical story and the worshippers' story. Thus the biblical narrative is not simply one heard by the congregation, but one in which they participate. Another possibility is for a first-person sermon in which the preacher adopts the persona of a character in the narrative – perhaps one of the three friends, or Nebuchadnezzar – and the sermon *is* a plotted narrative, the biblical account lived through the eyes of the character, not just an exposition of it. Sermons like these *work through* the plot of the biblical narrative and are inherently inductive in form.

However, sermons may also *work with* biblical plots and be more deductive in approach. Using this strategy, the plot of the narrative needs to be understood, but is not replicated in the sermon's structure. The critical element in any plot is its *resolution* – the climax towards which the whole narrative moves. So the sermon could begin here, followed by a flashback to what has preceded, from initial situation to transforming action, until once again we re-encounter the resolution, this time with new eyes because it is the lens through which the whole plot is viewed, not simply the climax at which we arrive. This might be particularly effective with a well-known biblical narrative, where the resolution as such might not be a surprise, but the preacher wishes to shed new light on it. So a sermon on Daniel 3 could begin with a brief summary or setting of context and then go straight to the *resolution* in verses 24–29. Among its significant details are its listing of the witnesses of this amazing event, 'the satraps, the prefects, the governors, and the king's counsellors' (v. 27 NRSV). Also, the king's doxology praises God whose angel has 'delivered his servants' (v. 28 NRSV). Moving back to the beginning of the narrative, we discover that the witnesses of God's deliverance in the *resolution* are also present in the *initial situation* as those summoned to worship the idol (vv. 2–3), and the same vocabulary of deliverance in the *resolution* is found on the lips of both the threatening king and the defiant friends in the *complication* (vv. 15–17). This retrospective reading of the plot respects its structure without reproducing it sequentially, and acknowledges that this is a sermon for second-time hearers of the narrative. For such hearers the resolution's emphases can dictate the trajectory of the sermon from the outset, with stress on social pressure and the nature of deliverance.

Another way for a sermon to use the resolution to work with, rather than simply through, the plot is to identify the heart of the resolution and use that as the organizing principle or 'big idea' for the sermon. For example, one might conclude that the king's words in verse 28 express the essence of the resolution: *God delivers those who resist earthly powers and trust in him.* This then becomes the compass which the preacher uses to navigate through the chapter, the sermon's 'single, narrow, dominant thought'. The sermon then expounds the truth of the statement, filtering the narrative's details through this interpretative grid, without necessarily explicating each step of the plot. However, there are elements in the narrative which suggest that Nebuchadnezzar's assessment, while true at one level, might be too simplistic. For example, the three friends before being thrown into the flames (vv. 17–18) do not appear to be as dogmatic about deliverance as the king is afterwards. Such tensions allow for subtle applications for those in the congregation struggling to know how to live faithfully in a complex world.

'Big idea' preaching has a number of significant evangelical proponents – pre-eminently the highly influential Haddon Robinson.[13] It has also been criticized as being reductionistic, narrowing every complex biblical passage to a 'timeless truth', thus encouraging superficial exposition. One would certainly not want to condense the rich subtlety of a Hebrew narrative to a bumper-sticker slogan. However, what I am suggesting is that we allow the narrative's own plot structure to indicate the heart of the matter, and then allow the narrative itself to indicate the shades of meaning and thus nuanced application. Any sermon must focus on matters of central importance if it is to communicate with a congregation in a relatively brief time. A preacher who tries to reproduce every narrative twist and turn is doomed to failure.

Preaching an OT narrative often requires a sermon to embrace a relatively large block of text. This is because a sermon on a narrative text needs ideally to encompass everything from initial situation to final situation. Also, as noted earlier, the interrelationship between the plot of a micro-narrative and that of the larger macro-narrative in which it is embedded results in the larger context remaining in view. This has implications for the preacher. For example, the relatively brief narrative of Genesis 11:27 – 12:9 is structured as: the *initial situation* of Terah and his family settling in Haran (11:27–32); the *complication* of

---

13. See, for example, Haddon W. Robinson, *Expository Preaching: Principles and Practice*, rev. and updated ed. (Leicester: Inter-Varsity Press, 2001).

the Lord's command to Abraham to leave, with contingent blessings (12:1–3); Abraham's response – moving on as commanded – provides the *transforming action* (12:4–6); the Lord's promise of the land is the (partial) *resolution* (12:7), while Abraham's nomadic existence within the land is the *final situation* (12:8–9). The divine command to leave Haran for another land, accompanied by promises of nationhood and blessings extending to the whole world (12:1–3), might well catch the preacher's eye. Here, surely, is a text to expound. However, verses 1–3 represent only the *complication* of the plot; subsequent plot elements focus on only one of its details, that of land. The *transforming action* is a move to the land; the *resolution* is a land promise, and the *final situation* concerns Abraham's wanderings within the land. The promises of nationhood and blessing are not developed in this episode. Land is centre stage. Initially, in 12:1, its role is unclear. Why is Abraham going to another land? This question is not answered until we encounter the resolution in the Lord's announcement, 'To your offspring I will give this land' (12:7 NRSV). While this resolves the question in the reader's mind about the reason for Abraham's moving there, the promise itself is not fulfilled yet. That will be taken up by the macro-narrative, as will the two other elements in the *complication*, those of nationhood and blessing extending to all the families of the earth. Here they are introduced, but not developed. And an expository sermon on this micro-narrative needs to reflect that.

As a consequence, wherever possible, individual micro-narratives should be preached as part of their macro-narrative. While a 'profiles of faith' type of series on one key episode each from the narratives of Abraham, Moses, Gideon and David might have some merit, far better to demonstrate the coherence of OT narrative blocks by preaching a sermon series on consecutive, contiguous episodes in the lives of just one of these characters. This makes the interdependence and overarching plot of large blocks of Scripture much easier for a congregation to understand, and much easier for a preacher to exploit. Seeing this larger picture also has pastoral implications. Preaching a succession of disparate sermons on narrative highlights from the OT makes each a self-contained experience, in which *complication* moves to *resolution*. On the one hand, this appeals to the human craving for coherence, affirming that we live in a meaningful world. On the other hand, however, repeated week after week, with no larger narrative perspective, such sermons will cause some in the congregation to question whether they ring true to their experience. Complications, spiritual or otherwise, are not always resolved permanently in the short term. This fact of life is the stock-in-trade of the OT's narrative blocks, discernible only when their larger picture is exploited. For example, Genesis 11:27 – 12:9 comes to rest with Abraham living in the land promised to his descendants. That equilibrium is disturbed by the complication of the next episode, 12:10–16, in which famine in the same land of promise forces Abraham to migrate to Egypt, yet culminates in his being materially blessed by Pharaoh . . . only for the next episode, 12:17 – 13:1, to show Abraham's ruse of passing his wife off as his sister exposed, resulting in his expulsion from Egypt. Nevertheless, all is well by the conclusion, with Abraham's family and Lot back in the Negeb. Until. . . And so on. Preaching such a series of episodes, a preacher of necessity would have to show that seeming resolutions are often just temporary resting places in the narrative. Thus, over time, a larger perspective would emerge.

That larger perspective, however, can sometimes be attempted in a single sermon. As we have already seen, Genesis 12:1–3 forms the *complication* of its own micro-narrative, but only the element of land, rather than those of nationhood or blessing, is explicitly developed immediately. Yet every episode in the Abraham story, right up to chapter 25, can be related to one or other of those initial promises. They act as anticipatory announcements of plot development and can be traced throughout the macro-narrative.[14] For example, a thematic sermon on the promise of nationhood could encompass this larger plot, providing a bird's-eye view of the whole Abraham narrative. Such a sermon would take the congregation on a roller-coaster ride of multiple complications and temporary resolutions. In very simplified outline, from the initial promise to Abraham that he would become a great nation (Gen. 12:2), we see him taking Lot (possibly as an adoptive heir, 12:4–5), only to be told that he must be the biological father of his heir (15:4), thus eliminating Lot. Then he fathers Ishmael (16:15), an apparent fulfilment of the divine promise, only to have him removed by God as the son of promise (17:18–19). This coincides with the revelation that Sarah must be the mother of the child (17:15–16), a possibility apparently dismissed by Abraham when he again passes Sarah off as his sister (20:2). And when, against all the odds, Isaac finally arrives and this narrative thread appears to have reached its resolution (21:2), God gives Abraham the crushing command to offer him as a sacrifice (22:2). And only in his being rescued from that fate (22:12) do we arrive at the full resolution of the matter – but only for this particular generation. Taking in this broad picture in a single sermon not only counters a simplistic understanding of the Abraham story, but also ministers pastorally to those in the congregation

---

14. Laurence A. Turner, *Announcements of Plot in Genesis*, *JSOT* Supplement Series (Sheffield: JSOT Press, 1990; republished Eugene, OR: Wipf & Stock, 2008), pp. 53–114.

whose experience of life matches the punctuated disequilibrium reflected in these narrative episodes. This quality, as much as anything else, makes these convoluted narratives eminently preachable. The nationhood promise will be further complicated and temporarily resolved in multiple episodes stretching to the end of Genesis and beyond. These developments, however, await further sermons!

While a knowledge of plot structure can help a preacher to work *through* or *with* a narrative, it is equally important to know the limits of homiletical manipulation of the text in order to avoid moving *beyond* the plot. OT narratives communicate indirectly, with infrequent comments or summaries from the narrator, which to a modern Western reader seems to leave a number of loose ends. Some of these could well be addressed by the preacher, so that oddities and problems are not left to rankle the congregation. However, some loose ends are best left as they are if the plot is to do its work. There is a big difference between clarifying incidental problems and 'solving' inherent ambiguities. When preaching Jonah 4, for example, one would be wise to embrace the absence of an explicit resolution, rather than constructing one to fill the gap in an ill-advised attempt to give the congregation pastoral guidance. God's final question causes a reader to ponder how Jonah might have answered; a sensitive sermon will allow the congregation the same freedom.

Plot and explicitly Christian proclamation

The history of Christian exposition of the OT is littered with unfortunate examples of preachers who prooftext their way to dubious and predetermined applications. Space prohibits a comprehensive treatment of appropriate guidelines for interpretation here. However, an appreciation of narrative plot does help in preaching OT narratives so that they have an authentic Christian voice.

At the risk of oversimplification, the overarching Christian biblical-theological perspective has a narrative quality with a basic plot. Starting with God's good creation (*initial situation*), which was disrupted by the fall (*complication*), God responds initially with the call of Israel (*transforming action*) and ultimately with the death and resurrection of Christ (*resolution*). We now live in the tension between the 'already' and the 'not yet', awaiting the climactic eschatological scenes (*final situation*).

Just as individual micro-narratives need to be read in the context of their OT macro-narrative, so Christian proclamation must read OT narratives in the context provided by the whole 'plot' of Christian Scripture. However, the individual and distinctive voices of OT narratives must not be muted by processing them through a theological grid in which they serve simply as illustrations for the larger synthetic Christian biblical theology. Rather, this larger theological perspective enriches our understanding of OT plotted narratives, so that their literary charm remains and their narrative genius as vehicles for profound theology is enhanced. For example, the sermon suggested above, which focuses on how the nationhood promise in Genesis 12:1–3 moves falteringly and confusingly through repeated complications to a provisional and partial resolution by the end of the Abraham narrative, can legitimately reflect on the larger canvas provided not only by the rest of the OT, but also by the NT. The nation promised to Abraham will be the source of blessing for the whole world. So the arrival and fate of Abraham's 'seed' has implications which transcend this individual narrative. This potential is picked up by Paul, for example, who avers that Christ is the ultimate seed of Abraham and that all who accept Christ are his true descendants and heirs of the promise of universal blessing (Gal. 3; Rom. 4:13–25). A Christian exposition of the narrative in Genesis cannot ignore such NT reflections on the significance of the OT story. Incorporating these insights requires a homiletical strategy which understands the plot of the Abraham narrative, with its repeated complications, as meeting its ultimate resolution in the NT. The unpromising beginning in Genesis really does climax with a blessing for all the nations of the world. This results in a sermon in which the OT narratives shed light on the NT fulfilment as much as vice versa.

Conclusion

Plot is a major element in any understanding of OT narrative, and appreciating it will enhance homiletical exposition. Benefits range from sermon structure and focus of message, to the pastoral potential of multiple complications and resolutions presented in an expository series. Perhaps most significantly, sermons which utilize insights gained from plot analysis can work with the grain of the text so that their exposition of the text from the pulpit will be as memorable as the unforgettable narratives they seek to apply. Grasping the potential of plot analysis will enable a preacher to work through and with, rather than against or beyond, Scripture expressed as narrative.

But plot is not everything, not even in preaching narrative. Preachers shall not live by plot alone, but by every word which proceeds from the mouth of God. Plots provide structure and progression, the skeleton of the narrative and the bare bones for the sermon, but we also need flesh to make the sermon live. For that we need an understanding of other narrative elements, such as character – and beyond that, the larger framework of biblical theology in which these narratives live and move and have their being.

Sermon outline on 2 Samuel 11

The following sermon outline works with the plot of 2 Samuel 11, but does not begin at the beginning. The rationale is to establish the main theme of the sermon from the climax of the narrative's resolution, in which David responds to the death of Uriah by saying, 'Do not let this matter trouble you, for the sword devours now one and now another' (v. 25 NRSV). In other words, 'Don't worry, these things happen.' This is an example of a 'big idea' sermon, with David's words providing the focus for the sermon's exploitation of the narrative's plot.

Introduction
This establishes the focus of the sermon with contemporary illustrations of those who have used the excuse, 'These things happen.' Then it turns to 2 Samuel 11.

Resolution
David receives the report from Joab concerning the death of Uriah. His response (v. 25) absolves anyone of blame, because 'these things happen'. The sermon then picks up this statement by asking how indeed these things have happened, which provides the transition to the narrative's initial situation.

Initial situation
David's life of ease in Jerusalem (v. 1) leads quickly to the complication.

Complication
David sees Bathsheba. The narrative emphasizes David's conscious reactions: he sees her; enquires about her; gets her; sleeps with her. This is underlined by the repeated use of the phrase 'David sent'. Narrative events happen because David is in control and achieves his desires. That is, things do not just happen, but arise out of conscious choices and plans. Bathsheba's pregnancy does not just happen either. There is scope here to illustrate our moral responsibility. While on occasions we may be victims of events, more often than not our lives are the result of our conscious decisions and actions. That is, most of the time, 'things *do not* just happen'. As Paul explains in Galatians 6:7–8, morally

and spiritually we reap what we sow. David's harvest here bears testimony to that. Bathsheba's pregnancy necessitates transforming action.

Transforming action

David calls Uriah back from the military campaign. We might expect some form of confession from David, but rather we witness a series of attempts to cover his tracks. There are three well-thought-out steps:

Plan A: David tells Uriah to go down to his house. (What could his
          motivation be, we wonder.) But Uriah's integrity means he refuses to
          do so. So we move on to:
Plan B: David gets Uriah drunk, and again tells him to go down to his house,
          but Uriah maintains his integrity and does not go down. David's
          failure here requires:
Plan C: David plots Uriah's death.

All of David's actions show foresight and planning. The whole train of events going back to David's first glimpse of Bathsheba could have been stopped in its tracks by David choosing an alternative course of action. But he chooses not to. That is, David exemplifies the sinful human condition. We are morally responsible beings, and our choices have consequences. Since all of us sin and fall short of the glory of God (Rom. 3:23), we see our own dilemma reflected in David's crisis.

Resolution

Uriah is killed (v. 17). In what is otherwise a tersely written account, we have to wait until verse 25 for David's response. We are given details we already know and others that are not essential, rather than getting to the conclusion as soon as possible. This delay highlights David's concluding speech: 'These things happen' (v. 25). Mulling over these words now, having seen the course of events in the main narrative, means that we fundamentally disagree with David. Nothing in this account has 'just' happened. David unconsciously passes judgment on himself.

Final situation

The narrator provides a sting in the tail with a final comment which draws us back to David's dismissive 'these things happen'. A literal translation of David's words would be, 'Do not let this matter *be evil in your eyes*' (v. 25). The final sentence of the episode, translated literally is, 'The thing David had done *was evil in the eyes of the Lord*' (v. 27). This divine appraisal echoes David's speech and coincides with the congregation's assessment of David's callous words. These things *did not* just happen. No more here than they do in our lives. We have little choice but to identify with David and confess our sin in order to be forgiven (1 John 1:9), as David himself finally does: 'Have mercy on me, O God, according to your steadfast love' (Ps. 51:1 NRSV).

Further Reading

BAR-EFRAT, SHIMON, *Narrative Art in the Bible*, Bible and Literature Series (Sheffield: Almond, 1989).

MARGUERAT, DANIEL, and YVAN BOURQUIN, *How to Read Bible Stories: An Introduction to Narrative Criticism*, trans. John Bowden (London: SCM Press, 1999).

MATHEWSON, STEVEN D., *The Art of Preaching Old Testament Narrative* (Grand Rapids, MI: Baker Academic, 2002).

2. PREACHING NARRATIVE: CHARACTERS

Paul J. Kissling

Readers have failed to hear the narrator's subtle insurgent voice because they are so attuned to hear and accept the clamorous pieties of the human characters of the Bible, with whose existential predicament and religious sentiments they can so easily identify.[1]

[David is a] man with much more ambiguity in his life than the plaster saint portrayals usually allow.[2]

Introduction

When one considers the way that Christian sermons on 'Bible characters' can degenerate into simplistic moralizing or heroic misreadings, one can only responsibly advise when it comes to preaching from the narratives of the OT's human characters, 'Use with Caution!' The 'What would Abraham do?' approach founders on the question, 'Which Abraham: the one who

---

1. L. Eslinger, *Into the Hands of the Living God*, Bible and Literature Series 24 (Sheffield: Almond, 1989), pp. 228–229.
2. John Goldingay, *Walk On*, rev. ed. (Grand Rapids: Baker, 2002), p. 115.

twice lied about his wife being his sister to save his own life, or the one who got up early in the morning to obey a command to sacrifice his son Isaac?'

There are several reasons for using caution: (a) the tradition of reading the human characters of the Bible heroically; (b) the tradition of oversimplifying the narrative portrayal of characters, sometimes with the assumption of the relative simplicity of ancient literature in contrast to allegedly more sophisticated modern literature; (c) a tradition of reading biblical characters as moral models for contemporary behaviour – 'Dare to be a Daniel'; (d) a tradition of literature which focuses on detailed descriptions of human characters and in particular detailed descriptions of the inner workings of their minds and psyches, which leads to frustration with OT narratives and/or the temptation to speculate about the inner workings of a biblical character's mind, in what might be termed 'psychologizing'.

On the other hand, we, and our audiences, are quite naturally drawn to the characters of the Bible and the potential those narratives seem to have to illuminate our own struggles and situations. We must, nevertheless, take seriously the tradition of oversimplifying Hebrew narrative.

Can and should we preach from the Bible's narratives about human characters?

While plot and characterization are inseparably intertwined,[3] most regard the Bible generally to be plot-dominated rather than character-dominated literature. To focus on the human characters is potentially to endanger the interpretative process by majoring on the minor. Another way to say this is to affirm the truism that God is the only character in the Hebrew Bible who should be the focus of interpretation. Certainly only God can be affirmed to be truly and absolutely reliable in the narratological sense.

A second concern is the way that much traditional interpretation, whether historical-critical, evangelical or popular, operates (unconsciously?) with simplistic notions about biblical characterization. This often involves an unsophisticated confusion between the narrator's point of view and that of the characters depicted in the narrative.

---

3. Note Henry James's proverbial remark, 'What is character but the determination of incident? What is incident but the illustration of character?' (H. James, *Selected Literary Criticism*, ed. M. Shapira, Harmondsworth: Penguin, 1963, p. 88).

One cause for this confusion is what we might call the reticence of Hebrew narrative. For whatever reasons, Hebrew narrators rarely give explicit moral evaluation of characters. When this is coupled with the fact that more contemporary means of hinting at the narrator's point of view on a character are also rare, the preacher is sometimes left in a quandary. Hebrew narrators rarely give any physical description of human characters, much less the detailed description to which contemporary readers are accustomed. There is also little information which would hint at social location. Perhaps even more significantly, there is sparse interior monologue and psychological description. Because we lack the typical contemporary clues to the narrator's point of view of characters, we tend to supply the gap through speculation and psychologizing as though what I imagine I would do or feel if I faced a situation like the one portrayed in biblical narratives were a reliable guide to how the narrator is steering the audience to read the characters in the narrative.

A third concern is not unique to the narrative genre, but is a more general problem in preaching any text from the so-called 'Old Testament', or 'New Testament' for that matter: the problem of historical, cultural and religious distance between the world of the text and the worlds of its contemporary interpreters.

A final concern is our tendency to miss the point of OT narratives and the depiction of characters within them. OT depictions of human characters are generally not given to vilify Israel's enemies or to heroize her ancestors.[4] Ellen Davis, after noting the intertextual echoing between the situation of Hagar and Israel enslaved in Egypt on the one hand, and Sarai and Egypt and its Pharaoh on the other, helpfully observes how the narrative of Sarai's treatment of Hagar stands as a rebuke to Israel:

> Hagar the Egyptian slave looks eerily like Israel in Egypt, that is, paradigmatic Israel, Israel when it is afflicted, endangered, desperate. Hagar looks like Israel oppressed, and Sarah, the mother of all Israel, is her oppressor. This is stunning. With this story Israel goes on record that from the beginning it has an identity as oppressor as well as oppressed.[5]

---

4. It may be that Daniel and his friends and Ezra are exceptions. For the case that Nehemiah is not an exception, see Tamara Cohn Eskenazi, *In an Age of Prose*, SBLMS 36 (Atlanta: Scholars Press, 1989).

5. Ellen F. Davis, *Wondrous Depth: Preaching the Old Testament* (Louisville: Westminster John Knox, 2005), pp. 133–134.

The OT's narratives refuse to hide the weaknesses, failings, sins and foibles of its human characters because their character and example is not the focal point. In fact their weaknesses point to the remarkable fact that the Lord chooses to use them anyway.

But preach from the OT's narratives about human characters we will and should. The only question is how to do so responsibly.

If we can and should, how should we approach the text?

Choosing the right characters
Since the time of E. M. Forster it has been traditional in the literary analysis of character to distinguish between 'flat' characters who have no inner life and do not change and are subordinate to the plot and 'round' characters who are complex and do change. But, as has often been noted, there are intermediate gradations between these extremes. Genuinely flat characters like the builders of Babel are difficult to preach on as characters since the plot is the predominant focus of the narratives in which they appear. But even relatively minor characters like Hagar[6] or Dinah or Eve[7] often bear sermonic fruit if their stories are read closely.

Carefully distinguishing between the point of view of the narrator and the seeming 'heroes' and 'villains' in the narrative
There is a tendency for contemporary interpreters to accept the claims of biblical characters at face value unless explicitly contradicted by the narrator.[8] This sometimes results in a form of superficial harmonization or the positing of divergent sources. For example, the Amalekite who informs David of Saul's death in 2 Samuel 1:1–16 claims to have personally killed Saul. The narrator, however, informs us that Saul killed himself. Whom does the reader trust? The

---

6. Davis, *Wondrous Depth*, pp. 131–137. Her sermon on Hagar in Genesis 21 is a classic example of taking a relatively minor character in the broader narrative and engaging it with a close reading.

7. John Goldingay gives a suggestive, if playful, first-person sermon on Eve as an old woman reflecting back on the narrative of the 'fall'. See *After Eating the Apricot* (Carlisle: Solway, 1996), pp. 33–45.

8. For the argument that biblical narrators are always reliable in literary terms, see Yairah Amit, *Reading Biblical Narratives: Literary Criticism and the Hebrew Bible* (Minneapolis: Fortress, 2001), pp. 93–102.

Bible's reliable narrator leads the reader to conclude that the Amalekite is lying, and the overall context leads the reader to infer that this is probably because he thinks he will ingratiate himself to David by having killed his enemy Saul, a fatal miscalculation as it turns out. Abraham's claim that in fact Sarah is his half-sister during the second narrative of his lying about her to a foreign king is suspicious because the narrator's genealogy of him does not mention this fact, even though it does mention another endogamous marriage in his family. Also Abram himself does not mention this when he sets the scheme up the first time in Genesis 12:11–13.

It is especially when a character is a protagonist in literary terms that the reader must be very careful to distinguish between what a character claims for himself or herself and what the narrator affirms about that character. Jacob, for example, promises to tithe what God blesses him with while away from the Promised Land, but never is said to have done so. Because Jacob is often regarded as a protagonist, there is a tendency to assume that he must have fulfilled this vow even though it is not mentioned. But the narrator is more wary of Jacob than many contemporary interpreters.

For example, in Genesis 32:9–12 Jacob, confronted with the prospect of having to face what he presumes to be his still angry brother, prays. How does the reader evaluate this prayer? Jacob refers back to God's previous words to him, but with slight adjustments. When Jacob speaks with self-deprecation in verse 10, is he only feigning it to curry God's favour, or has he come to a new appreciation of God's guidance and protection? Notice the ambiguities the reader senses in Jacob's prayer. When Jacob prays for God's deliverance he refers to Esau as his 'brother'. This may be a way of reminding God of the injustice of Esau's intended violence – it would be one brother killing another. He adds the killing of the mothers with the children as a potential consequence of Esau's anger. But Jacob fails to mention that the reader knows that Esau's anger primarily came from Jacob's own scheming. It seems as though Jacob uses an emotional appeal for God to protect the vulnerable (notice it is mothers – not women – and sons) as a means of trying to manipulate God to protect him. The final rationale which Jacob gives is the ultimate destiny of God's promise. If Esau kills Jacob, how will God's promise of innumerable descendants ever be fulfilled? His addition to God's words, 'I will surely do you good' (vv. 9, 12 NRSV), with the use of the emphatic form seems to be another way Jacob amplifies the promise, and therefore God's obligation. Jacob receives no immediate response from God and consequently sets about his own strategizing to ameliorate Esau's anger. This may be an indication to the reader that Jacob's prayer has already been answered. Esau has no intention to harm Jacob. But Jacob seems to assume in his ensuing actions that since

God had not explicitly answered his prayer he must, in typical Jacob fashion, take matters into his own hands.

Since biblical narrators rarely provide explicit evaluation, moral and otherwise, the reader is left to evaluate a character on the general norms of the work and by carefully comparing and contrasting the words and actions with the norms established by the work. Robert Alter suggests a scale of certainty of means which biblical narrators use to convey information about a character. From the least certain to the most certain they are:

1. Aspects of showing through the actions and his or her physical appearance.
2. A character's direct speech or what other characters say about him or her.
3. A character's inward speech where we enter the 'realm of relative certainty about character'.
4. Narrator's comments on the motives, feelings, intentions and desires of characters.[9]

Helpful though this scale might be, however, this often leaves us with uncertainty since the OT's narratives are rather reserved when it comes to numbers 3 and 4 of the above. Many times we are left with ambiguity or the necessity to tease out the narrator's perspective carefully by the clues which are left in the text. If the character's speech and actions are the basis for much of the characterization, how does one find the narrator's point of view?

One technique that I have found to be helpful is to place side by side the words and actions of characters as reported by the narrator, by other characters and by the character herself or himself.[10] The way that characters retell events and conversations from the past is often decisive. Is their version of events exactly the same as the narrator's or some other character's version of events? When they quote earlier conversations, do they quote them with strict accuracy, or do they paraphrase? If there are differences between the various versions of events and conversations, are they substantive differences? If substantive, what narrative-based explanation is there for them?

For example, Elijah's words to Yahweh at Horeb in 1 Kings 19 before and

---

9. Robert Alter, *The Art of Biblical Narrative* (New York: Basic Books, 1981), pp. 116–117.

10. If I am using PowerPoint with my sermon, I sometimes find it helpful to put the texts side by side with italics showing the differences.

after the earthquake, wind and fire experience are identical to the vowel point. Why? This seems to indicate that Elijah's perspective on what is happening in Israel is just as skewed after the revelation of Yahweh's presence as it was before it. In the previous chapter Obadiah's account of what he had done in hiding the 100 prophets of Yahweh is so close to the narrator's that the reader trusts Obadiah even more than Elijah.

An example from the Joseph narrative might clarify this point.[11] If one compares the narrator's version of events and what Joseph actually said to them during his brothers' first trip to Egypt to buy grain with the story they tell Jacob, the differences are striking and significant.

What Joseph actually said (Gen. 42:18b–20a NIV)	What the brothers claim Joseph said (Gen. 42:33–34 NIV)
'Do this and you will live, for I fear God: If you are honest men, let one of your brothers stay here in prison, while the rest of you go and take grain back for your starving households. But you must bring your youngest brother to me, so that your words may be verified and that you may not die.'	'Then the man who is lord over the land said to us, "This is how I will know whether you are honest men: Leave one of your brothers here with me, and take food for your starving households and go. But bring your youngest brother to me so I will know that you are not spies but honest men. Then I will give your brother back to you, and you can trade in the land."'

A close comparison between these two texts and the narratives in which they are found might lead to the following observations. The brothers do not mention that they were all held in prison for three days before the man who was lord over the land changed his mind and decided to release them. They do not mention that Simeon was to be kept in prison. More importantly, they fail to mention that one of them found the money for the grain in his sack on the return trip. All of these facts would presumably contribute a more ominous tone to the events that had transpired, something they evidently wanted to avoid in narrating these events to Jacob. They also add an inducement which

---

11. For other examples of this technique of close comparison of different versions of previous words and actions and the potential implications of the differences, see my *Genesis Volume 2*, CPNIVOTC (Joplin, MO: College Press, 2009), pp. 138, 224, 273, 335, 505, 527, 572.

Joseph had not mentioned. Once they returned with Benjamin and had established trust with the Egyptian man, they would have business opportunities which might be quite lucrative. The brothers do not lie to Jacob so much as narrate the events in such a way as to increase the chances that Jacob would allow them to take Benjamin back to Egypt with them. This sort of analysis helps the interpreter to arrive at a thicker description of the family dynamics and a more nuanced appreciation of the subtlety of Hebrew narrative.

The order of the telling

In Hebrew narrative, not only what is said, but how it is said is crucial. The *order* of the narrative is often important. Genesis 22:1 informs its readers that the Lord had no intention of allowing Abraham to sacrifice Isaac; it was a test. This information is given to the reader before the reader has an opportunity even to entertain the notion that the Lord would actually want a child to be sacrificed to him. Obadiah's risky faithfulness in hiding 100 prophets from Jezebel's clutches and feeding them from the pantry of the royal court is confirmed by the narrator *before* he tells Elijah that this is true in their verbal battle over who Obadiah's real Lord was. Sternberg sees great significance in the fact that Simeon and Levi are given the last word in their argument with Jacob over the appropriateness of their actions against Shechem and kin.[12]

Ambiguity as a narrative technique

Sometimes the most careful narrative analysis comes up with uncertainty as the only certain conclusion. But this can be the preacher's best friend if handled properly. We do not know why Jacob was unable to see that he had been given Leah instead of Rachel. Was it the wine? Was it a genetic eye disease? Was it the darkness or the veils? We do not know. But the audience can be invited to consider the alternatives with the preacher as I attempt to do in the sample sermon below. This involves the audience in the act of interpretation and cautions them against coming to overly simplistic conclusions in their own readings of the Bible. It also gives them permission to say 'I don't know', often a sign of a growing spiritual maturity.

Close attention to narrative naming

Adele Berlin originally pointed out how close attention to the way that the narrator, God and human characters within the narrative refer to or address

---

12. Meir Sternberg, *Poetics of Biblical Narrative* (Bloomington, IN: Indiana University Press, 1985), p. 448.

others is a vital, though sometimes subtle, clue to the perspective of a reticent narrator. An example is the Dinah narrative in Genesis 34. The narrator in verse 1 calls Dinah 'the daughter Leah had borne to Jacob' (NIV). Leah is the despised wife and Dinah is a daughter, not a son. The narrator repeatedly refers to Dinah as Jacob's daughter (vv. 3, 5, 7, 19), and the narrator and Jacob's sons refer to her relationship to them as 'sister' and 'brother' (vv. 13, 25, 27, 31) and surprisingly 'daughter' (v. 17 NIV mg., NRSV). Jacob never directly refers to Dinah and shows no emotion regarding what has been done to her. It may well be significant that while the other voices in the narrative speak of familial relationships, Jacob does not. The narrator seems to share the point of view of the brothers more than that of Jacob.

Another example is the way that Elijah and Ahab's servant Obadiah refer to each other and to Ahab during their meeting in 1 Kings 18:1–16.[13] Elijah wants to pigeonhole Obadiah as Ahab's servant. Obadiah regards himself as Elijah's servant as well as having Ahab as his lord. The narrator and Obadiah regard Obadiah as a faithful servant of the Lord and loyal to his prophet Elijah. But Elijah will have none of it. For Elijah, Obadiah, like everyone else in Israel at the time excepting himself, is compromised.

An exercise that I sometimes find helpful is to make a list of the named and unnamed people in a narrative and note the various ways the narrator, the person herself or himself and other characters refer to each person. This sort of list can be used in preaching to emphasize the narrative naming when reading the text.

Parallel and opposite situations

The similarities and the differences between two situations in Hebrew narratives invite the reader to compare and contrast them. Both Moses and Joshua send spies into Canaan, but Joshua only sends two, not twelve. Jacob twice receives news that something horrible has happened to one of his children. In the case of Dinah he shows no emotion. In the case of Joseph he grieves and refuses to be comforted. The children of the unfavoured wife get very different responses from their father compared with the children of Rachel.[14]

---

13. See Paul J. Kissling, *Reliable Characters in the Primary History*, *JSOT* Supplement Series 224 (Sheffield: Sheffield Academic Press, 1996), pp. 121–122.

14. Sternberg notes that Leah was the unfavoured wife and Simeon and Levi, along with Reuben and Judah and Dinah, were also her children. He says, referring to news of Joseph's tragedy (*Poetics*, p. 462), 'No wonder, then, that Jacob reacts so differently to the catastrophe that befalls Rachel's child.'

Often one's hearers can be reminded of the other story which is paralleled in the sermon text and perform the comparison and contrast with the preacher.

Intertextuality, textual echoing and typology

Repetition of words, phrases, concepts, situations and roles from textually earlier portions of the Hebrew Bible is common. In terms of characters, there are often numbers of parallels between characters which set the latter character up as a sort of new version of the earlier. Noah is a new Adam, as is Abram; Joshua and Elijah are both the new Moses for their generation, while Elisha is a new Joshua. Ezra leads a sort of new exodus from slavery, being careful to leave at Passover, and leads in the public proclamation of the Torah, a sort of new Moses.

While the distance between allegory and typology can be overdrawn, the latter arises out of close reading within the context of the wider macro-narrative, is something inherent to the text and is not imposed from the outside. When typological connections are in the text, they should be mined in the proclamation of that text. In the case of biblical characters, it is later characters who are a new version of an earlier character or characters.

Careful attention to the macro-narrative context

Perhaps the biggest failing of popular-level preaching on biblical characters is the failure to relate the specific text in view to the wider narrative context or macro-narrative. The result of ignoring the macro-narrative is often enough the reduction of the message of a subtle and complex narrative to fodder for simplistic moralizing.

Abraham's willingness to sacrifice Isaac is only comprehensible when one understands the historical and religious context and when one recalls the earlier tendency of Abraham, like many of the flawed characters in the Bible, to try to do God's work for him. In Genesis 22 Abraham's faith reaches its apex as he gives up on all attempts to help God fulfil his promises.

In the book of Genesis, for example, it must constantly be kept in mind that the stories are told for the benefit of the nation of Israel. The narratives of the ancestors are to be read as implicitly expressing the social and religious identity of the nation as a whole. Jacob is Israel *in nuce* and the sons of Jacob are the tribes of Israel *in nuce*. The tensions between the sons anticipate the tensions between the tribes. When Isaac is nearly sacrificed, the future of the nation is at stake.

Another thing the macro-narrative helps us to remember is that the Bible's characters are not to be viewed in unsophisticated black-and-white terms. While I would certainly not want to endorse much of his overall project, Joel

Kaminsky's recent study of election[15] gives salutary counsel when he reminds us that in the Hebrew Bible human beings fall into three categories, elect, non-elect and dis-elect, rather than merely two. Heard's recent work[16] reminds us of the ambiguous and not merely negative portrayal of those not chosen.

J. G. McConville[17] has written helpfully about the suspicion of the biblical macro-narrative in regard to earthly power brokers – particularly kings. He did not go quite far enough in my view to note that even Moses, Joshua, Elijah and Elisha have their failings laid out before the reader in plain view.[18] It is not merely kings and other power brokers who fall under the Bible's critical gaze, but even, at times, its prophets. Hero and villain alike and everyone in between with rare exception have their weaknesses displayed in the full glare of the Bible's wider narrative. This cautions us against simplistic readings in individual texts.

Character development

OT narratives in which longer stretches of the text are dominated by a single character are not to be viewed as modern novels. The ultimate focus of the text is not upon any human being but upon God. But are there characters who develop? Do characters change over time? I have argued that this does sometimes happen. Joshua goes from a person who receives divine encouragement to one who gives the same sort of encouragement to Israel near the end of his life (Josh. 1:5–9; 17:14–18; 18:3; 23:6). Abraham develops from a person who is tempted to come up with his own plans to see the promises of God find fulfilment to one who willingly allows the Lord to take responsibility for those promises. As I suggest in the sample sermon, the wrestling match with the divine man seems to change Jacob, and it is a changed Jacob who finds a form of reconciliation with Esau.

Reading over Israel's shoulder

Rein Bos suggests a new take on the fourfold meaning of Scripture: *Sensus Israeliticus*, Christological sense, Ecclesiological sense, Eschatological sense.[19]

---

15. Joel S. Kaminsky, *Yet I Loved Jacob: Reclaiming the Biblical Concept of Election* (Nashville: Abingdon Press, 2007).

16. R. Christopher Heard, *Dynamics of Diselection: Ambiguity in Genesis 12 – 36 and Ethnic Boundaries in Post-Exilic Judah, Semeia* 39 (Atlanta: Society of Biblical Literature, 2001).

17. J. G. McConville, *God and Earthly Power: An Old Testament Political Theology: Genesis– Kings*, LHBOTS 454 (London/New York: T & T Clark, 2006).

18. See my *Reliable Characters in the Primary History*.

19. Rein Bos, *We Have Heard that God Is with You: Preaching the Old Testament* (Grand Rapids: Eerdmans, 2008), pp. 166–184.

Using the analogy of holograms and other security measures on euro notes, Bos suggests that 'the multiple layers are actually a sign of trustworthiness'.[20] Often there is much homiletical mileage found in taking one's audience through the process of reading over Israel's shoulder (*Sensus Israeliticus*). Israel sees its own identity in the patriarchs and matriarchs. What would this have meant for Israel? How would they have responded to this? For example, in the sermon précis at the end of this chapter it is noted that the Bible's very first mention of the children of Israel occurs in a seemingly obscure allusion to the nation's practice of not eating the hip tendon because of her ancestor Jacob being struck there in his wrestling match with the divine person. Reading over Israel's shoulder enables one to see more clearly the significance of this seemingly obscure custom. Jacob the person becomes Israel and achieves a form of reconciliation with Esau the person whose descendants are some of Israel's fiercest rivals. But this only happens when he has received a form of divine crippling. The Israelite readers see themselves in this narrative.

How can/should we structure sermons from the characters of Hebrew narrative?

Using the arc of tension in the narrative to maintain interest and flow

The simplest way to structure a sermon on a character in the Bible is to use the order of the story to control the structure. Narratives biblical or otherwise create and maintain interest by pursuing the arc of tension, the suspense over what will happen. How will the problem be resolved? Even a narrative with which we are intimately familiar has this quality. We know at one level how things will work themselves out. We have read the story before. But in the re-reading of it we experience this tension yet again. While sermons on characters can be structured inductively or deductively, if the latter approach is used then the order of the points should usually be presented in their story order so as not to disrupt the flow of the narrative. The arc of tension is what makes or breaks a narrative and the power of biblical narratives should be used to enhance communication and not be discarded as some unnecessary husk for one's theological corn. With contemporary audiences in the West at least, I also find that it is naïve to assume that all or most of the audience is familiar with the story. For them this may be the first time they have read or even heard about the narrative. Use the story's narrative structure. We humans

---

20. ibid., p. 166.

are story-structured in our thinking and the Bible's narratives about human beings in their struggles with God speak naturally to our own stories and our way of thinking about the world.

Explain how the text fits into the larger narrative context and especially the macro-narrative context of the Bible

Assuming that contemporary audiences know the wider narrative context of specific OT narratives is usually naïve. Even audiences who know the facts of the Bible quite well struggle to put the narrative together. If the text is to be understood well, it must be read in light of its wider narrative context. This involves the texts before and after the sermon text. Ultimately this also means reading the text 'backwards' from the NT. This ensures that we help our audiences make the connection to their own lives and circumstances. Many times the typological connections within the OT itself serve as a guide to extending such connections into the NT. The use of the NT readings paired with your text in the standard lectionaries can be a real aid here, even if your tradition, like mine, does not ordinarily follow a lectionary.

My seminary homiletics professor's maxim, 'If it does not mention Jesus or the church, it is not Christian preaching', is a helpful reminder even if the maxim should not be turned into an unalterable law. But explaining how the narrative in view fits into the Bible's macro-narrative helps the audience to make the transference to how it speaks afresh in our present situations.

First-person narrative sermons

In working on a commentary on Genesis 12 – 50 recently, I found it amusing that I was unconsciously slipping into the historical present even though I was describing past events. The OT's narratives often seem to have a life of their own which overcomes often great gulfs of cultural and religious difference. The use of the present tense as though 'we are there' is often helpful in sermons on characters. Sometimes sermons can be recrafted into first-person monologues where the preacher takes on the personality of the character. I remember fondly a retired pastor's wife who had a 'makeover' and delivered a first-person narrative of Esther looking back on her life when she was Miss Babylonia. While this can be overdone and the preacher should be warned that it takes more preparation, not less,[21] to do this well, first-person narrative

---

21. See Stephen Chapin Garner, *Getting into Character: The Art of First-Person Narrative Preaching* (Grand Rapids: Brazos, 2008), for helpful advice on preparing such sermons.

sermons can bring the text alive in new ways. While a certain sort of literary licence attends to such sermons, we must be careful that our filling in of unmentioned details does not distract from the message of the text.

Conclusion

The portrayals of the human characters of the OT come to life before our very eyes and the eyes of our listeners. We will either guide them to read their stories responsibly, or they will continue to decontextualize them and turn them into fodder for simplistic moralizing. Nehemiah the Christian CEO and Abraham that fine Christian man will still fill the imaginations of our congregations until and unless their pastors show them a better way. We will either point them to the God and Father of our Lord Jesus Christ who used such broken human vessels to do his work, or our people will turn them into plaster saints who have nothing to say to us that is not a little bit naïve and a little bit dangerous.

Sermon outline on Genesis 32:22–32: 'Crippled to be Healed'

It happened that very night

What night was that? It all began some sixty years previously in the womb where Jacob grabbed Esau's heel and Rebekah was given the enigmatic promise-cum-prophecy regarding the two nations who would descend from her twins with the greater serving the lesser. Apparently Rebekah thought it was her responsibility to see to it that the 'prophecy' came true and she could imagine no way for it to come true if it did not come true in the lifetime of her sons, not among their distant descendants. Jacob must have the birthright and the blessing by hook or, as it turns out, by crook. And so the game is on.

We next hear of the twins when the red-haired, earthy Esau returns from an unsuccessful hunting trip famished and Jacob the domestic opportunist supposedly buys Esau's birthright for a bowl of that red stuff.

With the birthright 'secured', we next meet the twins at the age of forty, with Isaac nearly blind and apparently on his deathbed. He actually lives another eighty years, but neither Rebekah nor Jacob nor Esau nor Isaac himself expected that. Dressed in Esau's clothing and bearing his aroma, with skin so hairy it could not be his own, Jacob somehow, implausibly, fools his nearly blind father.

Jacob's and Rebekah's crookery begins to receive its recompense when Rebekah, ever the strategizer, fears Esau's violent revenge and with apparently phony piety expresses concern to Isaac over Jacob's future marriage partner being a Canaanite. She suggests a marriage within the extended family, like the one Isaac enjoyed with her. This will require a trip to the home country of Paddan-Aram, away from Esau's wrath.

Isaac is shrewder than he at first seems. He agrees to send Jacob back to the extended family to get a wife, but sends him with nothing to use as a bride price. This will be no short trip.

When Jacob arrives penniless in Paddan-Aram he falls for a young shepherdess named Rachel. Three shepherds are unable or unwilling to lift the heavy stone lid from the well. But when Jacob sees the eye-popping Rachel, his masculine bravado takes over and he lifts the stone off all by himself. To his delight Rachel is from his extended family and a suitable marriage partner. If only he had the bride price!

Jacob the grabber meets his match when he negotiates with Laban over Rachel. Seven years of free labour is a high, if not exorbitant, bride price. But the seven years of free labour seemed like only a few days as Jacob anticipated his marriage bed (Gen. 29:20–21) with the beautiful Rachel.

Jacob, who took advantage of his father Isaac's failing eyesight, experiences the ultimate payback. He wakes up from his honeymoon night to discover that he has married the wrong girl. No one is that blind. I do not know if it was the wine, the veils or the darkness, or all of these things, or something or Someone else. But no one is that blind. Laban's defence, while improbable or at least questionable on the truth-o-meter, digs at Jacob's past with biting irony: 'In our country [unlike yours] it is not done to give the lesser before the firstborn' (Gen. 29:26, lit.). Jacob may have tricked Isaac into doing this, but Laban would not allow it. Jacob's trickery receives its comeuppance with interest and penalties.

Seven years turns into fourteen and then into twenty as Jacob receives three more wives than he wanted. Ironically, the hated Leah (29:31) has no difficulty producing children, while the much-loved Rachel is infertile and desperate about this. The years and the four wives produce a large but fractured family and eventually enough material blessings to support them. Jacob, with a mixture of divine blessing and crafty practice, grabs enough of Laban's flocks and herds to ensure, he thinks, his family's future.

Not wanting to suffer a surprise attack from his brother, Jacob sends messengers to inform Esau of his return. He matter-of-factly offers an enormous bribe of servants and valuable animals in abundance as a gift to find favour in Esau's (tellingly referred to here as his lord's) eyes. The repetition of 'lord' for Esau and 'servant' for Jacob strikes us. I thought the greater (Esau) was to serve the lesser (Jacob)? Not, apparently, in their lifetimes. Jacob strategizes that by slowing Esau down with gift after gift and using overly deferential language and dividing his family into two groups and praying, he might just assuage Esau's wrath from twenty years earlier.

It was that very night that Jacob moved his family to the other side of the river and awaited his fate. Esau was coming with 400 men and Jacob must get himself and his family ready. *It was that night* that Jacob found himself wrestling with an unknown man who turns out to be a divine person. In an act of condescension, the man allows Jacob to battle him to a draw, but not before Jacob is blessed and crippled in the process. Ever the grabber, Jacob struggles to weasel a blessing from his divine opponent. The blessing is the giving of a new name, Israel. The name means either God fights (for or with Israel) or (Israel) fights with God. All of these connotations are true. God fights for Israel. God fights with Israel. And Israel fights with God.

That very night Jacob becomes God's struggle and receives divine crippling.

Speculation about river demons notwithstanding, the most natural explanation for why the divine man must leave by daylight is that Esau is about to arrive. And painful though the preparation for that meeting is for Jacob, that meeting is the primary reason for this one-sided wrestling match. If Jacob is to persist in trying to wrestle the blessing out of his brother, father and even God himself, so be it. He will only succeed in crippling himself – economically, spiritually and, yes, even physically. But perhaps the crippling is a hidden form of blessing, or at least hidden in the crippling is a form of blessing.

When Jacob finally faces the dreaded meeting with his presumed-to-be-still-angry brother, he is changed. After arranging his family in groups from least favoured in the front to most favoured at the back, he limps *in front of* his family to face the music. He does so crippled by his encounter with the Divine. He who presumed himself to be the lesser, who would be served by the greater according to the divine word given before their birth, now limps up and painfully bows seven times before Esau, his lord. He must give up as a bribe much of the material blessing which he has gained through hard labour and God's blessing. He is militarily defenceless before his brother and his army of 400 men. And with the fresh wound of a dislocated hip reminding him of his vulnerability, he bows painfully before his 'lord' (brother), whom he had previously presumed was to serve him.

This text is the very first time that the 'sons of Israel' are mentioned in the Bible. At first it seems rather odd to have the very first mention of them relating to a rather obscure food taboo (Gen. 32:32). Up to the very present the descendants of the man whose name became Israel have not eaten the tendon in the hip socket because of this event. But maybe there is more here than historical curiosity or impenetrable dietary prohibitions. For them this was a holy thing, a significant thing, and the taboo was a way to remember this holy thing. The man who gave the nation its name was a cripple and in his crippled condition he limped up to his presumably angry brother and in pain bowed to the ground seven times. More significantly, in that humbled and broken condition he found a form of reconciliation with his brother. The last time Jacob and Esau are together, they meet peacefully to bury their father.

Sometimes we must be crippled in order to be healed.

Israel did not tell this story about their origins because they were motivated by some ethnocentric pride. In the Bible's macro-narrative, Israel is that deaf and blind servant whom the Lord nevertheless used as the channel of his blessing to the entire world. The reality of Israel's rather ambiguous origins is the black canvas upon which the bright colours of God's grace are painted. The story is not told in this way to puff up the nation with pride, but to remind Israel and all who read her story that nevertheless God used her, sinful and broken though she might be.

We who have been privileged to read the rest of the story know that the one final elect servant of the Lord, the remnant of Israel, the new Israel himself, Jesus Christ, did his greatest work in his humble, broken state. By his humility and humiliation we are saved. By his crippling we are healed.

And as followers of that humble and broken servant of God, we know that sometimes we too must be crippled in order to be healed.

Suggested further reading

AMIT, YAIRAH, *Reading Biblical Narratives: Literary Criticism and the Hebrew Bible* (Minneapolis: Fortress, 2001).

DAVIS, ELLEN F., *Wondrous Depth: Preaching the Old Testament* (Louisville: Westminster John Knox, 2005).

KISSLING, PAUL J., *Genesis Volume 1* and *Genesis Volume 2*, CPNIVOTC (Joplin, MO: College Press, 2004, 2009).

3. PREACHING FROM THE LAW

Christopher J. H. Wright

Introduction

Before thinking about how we should preach OT law, it is worth reminding ourselves of *why* we should do so. On what theological foundation do we build a homiletic that includes these books? I will take it as foundational, rather than seeking to argue for it, that 2 Timothy 3:15–16 applies to the Law as much as to all the rest of the OT. When Paul said 'all scripture', he was thinking of the canon of Law, Prophets and Writings that we now know as the OT. OT law, therefore, is *included* among that which leads us to salvation through faith in Christ, is breathed out by God, and is relevant and useful for teaching, training and ethical instruction – as much for Gentile Christian believers as for Jews like Paul himself and Timothy. If that was the conviction that undergirded Paul's own preaching of the Scriptures, it should motivate us not to neglect the OT law in our own preaching.

Of course, it is one thing to affirm this text as an article of doctrine. It is another thing to have confidence in it when our heads are down in the task of understanding an OT legal text with a view to preaching from it. And yet, there seems little point in boldly declaring, '*All* scripture is inspired by God and is useful. . .' (NRSV) unless one is willing to write above every chapter in an OT book, including the law, '*This* scripture is inspired by God and is useful. . .' So my point in starting here is to say that I am not going to argue *that* OT law is authoritative and relevant, but rather to explore *how* we can make its authority and relevance living and active and sharp in our preaching.

The law was founded on grace

We need to start by seeing the importance of the *narrative* context of the law in the Torah. The law comes within a story. Before we reach the legal texts of the Torah, we have had a book and a half of preceding narrative. This is the story of creation, fall, election, promise and redemption. This great narrative and its theological significance is the context of the law, and it should always form the context of our preaching of law – whether explicitly or implicitly.

The law is given by *this* God – the God who created the whole earth and all nations, the God who made a covenant with Abraham that included a promise for all nations, the God who had just delivered the Israelites out of slavery as an act of faithfulness to that promise, the God whose law thus mirrors his own demonstration of compassion and justice.

So before we preach law to people, we need to make sure they know the God who stands behind it and the story that goes before it. It is the God of grace and the story of grace. This foundational theological assumption may be illustrated from several very preachable texts.

Exodus 19:4–6: The law was given to people whom God had already redeemed

No sooner has God got Israel to himself at Mount Sinai than he points them back to his own initiative of saving grace: 'You have seen what I have done . . . now then, if you obey me fully. . .' (vv. 4–5, author's translation). Grace comes before the law. There are eighteen chapters of salvation before we get to Sinai and the Ten Commandments. So the structure of the book supports the fundamental theology.

I stress this because the idea that the difference between the Old and New Testaments is that in the OT salvation was by obeying the law, whereas in the NT it is by grace, is a terrible distortion of the Scripture. It is a distortion that Paul was combating, but has somehow crept into common Christian assumption. We need to preach rigorously against it. It is sad that in so many churches that have the Ten Commandments on the wall, they leave out the opening words of God, 'I am the LORD your God, who brought you up out of slavery. . .' (author's translation). That is posting the law without the gospel that grounds it. Paul makes it clear that salvation came through faith in God's promise, and that obedience was a response to God's saving grace.

Deuteronomy 6:20–25: Gratitude – a major motivation for obedience

The same theological order and point is found in the answer that the father is told to give to his son when he asks, 'What is the meaning [or point] of all this law?' The father could have gone straight to verse 24, 'The LORD *commanded* us to obey' (NIV). That is enough, surely. But no: when the son asks about the meaning of the law, the father is to answer with the story of salvation, Israel's redemption out of slavery in Egypt. The very meaning of the law is found in the gospel – the good news of God's saving righteousness. Obedience, therefore, is a matter of a right response on our part to what God has done – which is what the phrase 'that will be our righteousness' (v. 25 NIV) means; not some kind of righteousness earned or deserved by obedience. Obedience, here as elsewhere in Deuteronomy, is the only right response to having been saved, and the way to enjoy the fruits of redemption, not to earn them.

Examples: Exodus 23:9; Leviticus 19:33–36; Deuteronomy 15:12–15

The effect of this grace foundation of OT law can be seen in the many places where Israel were commanded to do something, motivated by what God had done for them in rescuing them from Egypt. This typically affected the attitude and actions they were to adopt towards aliens, but it also extended to generosity to released slaves, etc. Deuteronomy 15:12–15 is the clearest example of this dynamic at work. Generosity to the needy is rooted in the experience of God's historic redemption.

The upshot of this foundational point, then, is that we should always preach OT law on the foundation of God's saving grace. Anything else will lead people to legalism, or to despair, or to pride. It is as if, as we preach the law, God points to the cross, as he pointed to the exodus in Exodus 19:4, and says, 'You have seen what I have done.' Only then should we tackle specific commandments and start asking about how we ought to respond to them today. We should not preach the law without the gospel – but recognize that the gospel begins with Abraham (as Paul affirmed in Gal. 3:6–8).

The law was motivated by the 'mission' of God through Israel

To say that the law was founded on grace is to see it from a perspective that looks back to what God had already done in historical redemption. To say that it was motivated by God's mission puts it in a perspective that looks in the opposite direction, towards the future purpose of God for the whole world. For when Christians down the ages have asked the question, 'Why the law?' it might have saved a lot of theological blood, sweat and tears if they had paused to ask the prior question, 'Why Israel?' – to whom the law was actually given.

Genesis 12:1–3; 18:18–19: God's mission – to bless all nations through Israel

The answer, of course, lies in the Abrahamic covenant and its universal perspective. All nations would in some sense be involved in the blessing that God promised to Abraham, even if the precise mechanism is unclear in the earliest texts.[1] So foundational is this promise that Paul actually calls it 'the gospel' in Galatians 3:8. The good news is that, in spite of human sin, God still plans to bless the nations, and has kept that promise in and through Christ. And Israel, the descendants of Abraham, would be the people through whom that promise would proceed.

But what has this got to do with OT law? Genesis 18:18–19 answers by showing God, in conversation with himself, linking together his election of Abraham (at the beginning of the verse) and its missional purpose (at the end of the verse), with the ethical requirement that such an identity and role placed upon Abraham and his descendants (in the middle of the verse).

> For I have chosen him [election], so that he will direct his children and his household after him to keep the way of the LORD by doing what is right and just [ethics], so that the LORD will bring about for Abraham what he has promised him [mission – blessing all nations]. (v. 19, NIV)

God wanted Abraham to be the starting point of a community that would be different from the world of Sodom (in which this chapter is set). God wanted people committed to his ways, character and values, as the means of accomplishing his purpose extending blessing to all nations (see v. 18).

'The way of the LORD' and 'righteousness and justice' are among the most prominent concepts in the Law (and in the whole OT). And here they are the middle term between election and mission. God's purpose for Israel includes a moral agenda, which the law later fills out in detail.

So the law, then, which embodies the way of the LORD and the doing of righteousness and justice, is foreshadowed in this text, as part of the essential

---

1. I am well aware of the exegetical issues in the verbal forms of *brk* in the promise texts of Genesis, and have explored them in depth in Christopher J. H. Wright, *The Mission of God: Unlocking the Bible's Grand Narrative* (Nottingham: Inter-Varsity Press; Downers Grove: InterVarsity Press, 2006), ch. 6.

mechanism by which God intends to fulfil his goal of bringing all nations within the sphere of redemptive blessing. When we preach it, we need to remember this part of its function – to shape God's people to be the agents of God's mission to the nations.

Exodus 19:6: Israel to be a priesthood in the midst of the nations

In the context of 'the whole earth' and 'all nations' (Exod. 19:5–6 NIV), Israel as a nation was to be God's priesthood. Priests in Israel stood between God and the people, operating in both directions. They were to teach God's law to the people (Lev. 10:11; Deut. 33:10) and bring the people's sacrifices to God. That is, through the priests God would be known to the people and through the priests the people would be brought to God. So, says God to Israel as a whole community, you will be for the nations of the world what your priests are for you. Through you I will teach the nations my law (ways, character), and through you I will ultimately draw the nations to myself in redemption and covenant.

But that priestly role could only happen as Israel were also a holy people and lived in obedience to the covenant law. Holiness meant being distinctive – from the idolatry of imperial power in Egypt, and from the idolatry of fertility, sex and success in Canaan (Lev. 18:3), and reflecting the character of God in everyday ordinary social life (Lev. 19). In other words, the law had the function of shaping Israel to be that representative people, making the character and requirements of God known to the nations. That is a missional function. The law itself constitutes revelation of God; so do those who live it out in loving, grace-filled obedience.

Deuteronomy 4:6–8: Israel's obedience to the law would make them a visible model

Many are the motivations in Deuteronomy – it is one of the noted features of the book (as it should be of our preaching). Most of the motivation clauses are to do with Israel herself and her security and long life in the land. This one, standing in the powerful opening chapter of the great hortatory section 4 – 11, is remarkable in suddenly bringing *the nations* into view. They will observe Israel's society, the nearness of their God and the justice of their laws, and will ask questions. This is another interesting hint at the purpose of the law – to make Israel visibly different, in such a way that would draw interest and comment, and essentially bear witness to the God they worshipped.[2]

---

2. I have discussed this text much further in *The Mission of God*, pp. 375–387, and at a more popular level in *The Mission of God's People* (Grand Rapids: Zondervan, 2010), ch. 8.

The New Testament preaches the same principle – Matthew 5:14–16; Luke 22:25; 1 Peter 2:12

The principle that obedience to God makes us visible to the world around is not confined to the OT. In the NT too we find a missional function for ethical obedience. Disciples of Jesus are to be distinctive in such a way that people notice, and ultimately come to glorify God.

If we put our first two main sections together, we can see the law as if it were suspended like a hammock between two poles: the past grace of God's historical redemption, and the future grace of God's missional promise. Between those two poles Israel, and ourselves, are called to live in the present as those who know where we have come from and where we are going. The law, in other words, makes sense within the whole story of redemption, past and future.

So then, we should preach OT law in such a way as to remind Christians not only of the grace of God to which they must respond, but also of their mission responsibility: to live distinctively as God's people among the nations. The ethical challenge of the gospel is essentially the same as faced Israel. Those whom God has redeemed are to live for God's glory in the world. God's people are created for his praise and honour, so that the nations may know who the living God is: that was the mandate of Israel and it remains ours in Christ.

The law of Israel was meant to be a model, or paradigm, for the nations[3]

Putting the earlier points together, we can see that all God did for and in Israel is relevant to the nations. As we read the OT, we can discern two great related fields of God's action – within creation and within Israel. The outer triangle in our diagram is the basic pattern of relationships established at creation. The earth was created by God and belongs to him. But the earth is also given to humanity, to rule and care for. And of course human beings, made in the image of God, are created to love and worship him. Every one of these three fundamental relationships of creation has been distorted and fractured, of course, by our sin and rebellion, but the basic framework is

---

3. I have developed this 'paradigmatic approach' in much greater theological and ethical detail in *Old Testament Ethics for the People of God* (Leicester: Inter-Varsity Press; Downers Grove: InterVarsity Press, 2004).

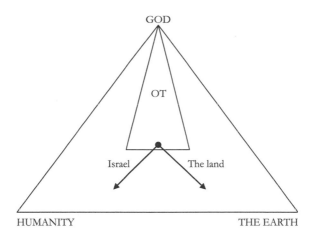

still there and is still the sphere of God's sovereignty and ultimate redemptive mission.

When God begins the great biblical story of redemption (portrayed in the inner triangle), it starts with one man who becomes one nation (Israel), to whom God gives one particular land (the land of Canaan). Yet it becomes clear that what God does in that one nation was intended to bring blessing and salvation to all nations of humanity, and that the land of Israel becomes a microcosm of God's will for life on earth in a wider economic sense and in ultimate eschatological vision (the new creation).

This inner triangle, then, of God, Israel and the land, becomes a model or paradigm of God's wider intention for the rest of the nations in all the earth. Israel was meant to be 'a light to the nations', in the totality of their covenantal relationship to God in worship and their social ethics – in economic, political, social, familial and personal spheres.

This means that OT law, as part of that inner triangle of God's redemptive work in OT Israel, was intended to have, and can be seen to have, a relevance to other cultural and historical contexts – including our own.

So we can preach OT law, not seeking to enforce it literalistically, but looking for what it taught and required within that inner triangle (OT Israel) that still addresses and challenges the context in which we live in the outer triangle – wherever that may be. It still has the capacity, rightly handled, to challenge church and society on issues of social ethics and justice. We stand, as it were, among the observing nations of Deuteronomy 4:6–8, asking questions not only about the kind of God Israel worshipped and the kind of society they were meant to be, but also about how the answers to those questions can help us in engaging our own contexts in our preaching within the community of faith.

The law was based on the character of God

Another feature of OT law that is an encouragement to us to preach from it is that it reflected the character of God himself. That is why one of the commonest expressions for obeying the law is 'to walk in the ways of the LORD'.

Now of course there were a lot of laws. But Jesus was not the first to propose that they could be reduced to certain basic simplicities. Deuteronomy presents Moses asking the question, 'So now, O Israel, what does the LORD your God require of you?' (Deut. 10:12–13 NRSV). He answers with five fundamental requirements: to fear God, walk in his way, love him, serve him and obey him.

But if somebody had been inclined to ask, 'What does it *mean* to walk in the way of the LORD?' Moses had his answer ready to that also.

> The LORD your God . . . shows no partiality and accepts no bribes. He defends the cause of the fatherless and the widow, and loves the foreigners residing among you, giving them food and clothing. And you are to love those who are foreigners, for you yourselves were foreigners in Egypt. (Deut. 10:17–19, author's translation)

That is, Israel was to reflect the integrity, justice, compassion and love of God in their own dealings with others. This strong motivation in OT law can also be seen in the way Leviticus 19 punctuates its demands for Israel's ethical life – on the farm, in the family, in the court, in the neighbourhood, in business, in ethnic relations – with the simple statement, 'I am the LORD; I am holy, so you must be holy.'

Imitation of God is a strong theme in OT law, but it does not stop there. It is the same basic principle that undergirds the teaching of Jesus about our behaviour. We are to model what we do on what we know God is and does (Matt. 5:45–48; Luke 6:27–36).

So our preaching of OT law should not merely be moralistic – focusing on the minutiae of behaviour and burdening people, as the Pharisees did. Rather we preach the law in such a way as to point to the God who stands behind it, asking what it reveals of his character, values and priorities. That seems to have been the thrust of Christ's preaching too.

In other words, as with all Scripture, the question we need to ask before preaching it is not just 'What does this mean to me?' or 'What does this tell me to do?' Starting there can often lead to rather slim results in more obscure passages from Israelite life and culture. Rather we start by asking, 'What does this show of the character, action and will of God? How is God revealed through this text and the surrounding context?' And then we go on to ask (and to preach), 'If that is what God is like, what God values, what God prioritizes, what God has done – what sort of response is appropriate in the circumstances in which we now live?'

The law was given for human benefit

When Jesus said, 'The Sabbath was made for man, not man for the Sabbath' (Mark 2:27 NIV), he could have been speaking about the whole law. God gave his law to Israel, not to keep himself happy, nor to take pleasure in finding fault with Israel's failures, but for their own good. This is the repeated message of Deuteronomy (e.g. Deut. 4:40; 5:29; 6:24; 10:13, etc.).

It is also the testimony of the psalmists:

> The law of the LORD is perfect,
>   reviving the soul.
> The statutes of the LORD are trustworthy,
>   making wise the simple. . .
> They are more precious than gold,
>   than much pure gold;
> they are sweeter than honey,
>   than honey from the comb.
> (Ps. 19:7, 10 NIV)

> I will walk about in freedom,
>   for I have sought out your precepts. . .
> I delight in your commands
>   because I love them.
> (Ps. 119:45, 47 NIV)

The least one can say about people who express such enthusiastic sentiments for the law is that they were certainly not grovelling along under a heavy burden of legalism. They were not anxiously striving to earn their way into salvation and a relationship with God through punctilious law-keeping. They were not puffed up with the claims of self-righteousness or exhausted with the efforts of works-righteousness. They did not, in short, fit into any of the caricatures which have been inflicted upon the OT law by those who, misunderstanding Paul's arguments with opponents who had *distorted* the law, attribute to the law itself the very distortions from which Paul was seeking to exonerate it.

On the contrary, people who could frame such paeans of praise for the law knew that it was a national treasure greater than any museum could boast. Such devout Israelites delighted in the law as a gift of God's grace and a token of God's love, given to them for their own good (Deut. 4:1, 40; 6:1–3, 24, etc.). They saw it as a blessing in itself, and the means of enjoying God's continued blessing (Deut. 28:1–14). They recalled that the revelation of the law to Israel was a unique privilege, granted to no other nation (Deut. 4:32–34; Ps. 147:19–20). They urged one another to obey it, not in order to get saved, but because God had already saved them (Deut. 6:20–25). They delighted in it as the road to life (Lev. 18:5; Deut. 30:15–20), and as the river of fruitfulness (Ps. 1:1–3).

Elsewhere I have outlined some examples to illustrate this principle from the way that OT law typically tends to prioritize human *need* over strict legal rights and claims. This is another aspect of the general principle that people matter more than things, but it is more subtle. It is saying that some people's needs and circumstances matter more (i.e. generate a greater moral urgency) than some other people's legitimate claims. I quote (from myself):

- *The need of a refugee slave, as against the claims of his owner (Dt. 23:15–16).* This is a very counter-cultural law. In all other societies where slavery has operated, the legal rights and claim of the slave-owner take priority. Running away is an offence. Harbouring a runaway is an offence. Israel, however, not only *prohibits* sending the slave back, but *commands* that the slave be allowed to find refuge in any place of his own choosing. The need of the weaker party is given priority over the legal right of the stronger.

- *The need of a female prisoner, as against the rights of a soldier (Dt. 21:10–14).* Here is another law, which at first reading wrinkles our noses. We want to say that there should not be wars, and there should not be prisoners, and women should not be captured. Doubtless. But Deuteronomy's legal and pastoral strategy is to deal with the world where such things were realities, and then to mitigate the worst effects for those caught up in them. So the law permitted the victorious soldier to take a woman from among the captives. However, first of all he may only take her as his fully legal wife with all the responsibilities that gave him and the rights it gave her. That might make him pause. Rape or slavery are ruled out. Secondly, even having made her his wife, he is to give her a full month of adjustment after her traumatic experience before he may exercise the normal sexual right of a bridegroom. It seems that the law, in the midst of the nastiness of war, is trying to privilege the needs of the vulnerable (a woman, a foreigner, a captive), over the customary rights of the powerful (a man, a soldier, a victor and a husband).

- *The need of a debtor, as against the legal claims of a creditor (Dt. 24:6, 10–13)* . . . Yet again, the law seems to align itself with the weaker party by requiring the creditor to respect the needs of the debtor. On the one hand, there is his need for daily bread, so the creditor must not deprive him of the means of making it (the domestic mill-stone). On the other hand there is his need for shelter and warmth, so the creditor must not take basic clothing as security. And even the need of the poor for dignity and privacy is to be respected: the creditor is not to barge into the debtor's home, but remain outside and allow the debtor the free choice of what he will offer in pledge. . .

- *The need of the landless, as against the legal property of the landowner (Dt. 24:19–22).* The law concerning gleaning in the fields, olive groves and vineyards is also found in Leviticus 19:9–10. Those who possessed land, and had done all the hard work of clearing, ploughing, sowing and harvesting, might feel entitled to 100% of the produce of their own labour. But these instructions counteract such an attitude and remind the Israelite land-holder that actually Yahweh is the ultimate landlord and reserves the right to insist that all Israelites should 'eat and be satisfied'. So the needs of the landless poor are also upheld by granting them freedom to glean, and insisting that the harvesters make sure that there are plenty of gleanings left to be gathered. Once again, human need is brought to the forefront as a moral priority that relativizes the personal benefits of land ownership. . .[4]

Against this background of the values inherent in the law itself, we can understand why Jesus became angry when the law was turned into a burden, instead of a benefit to the needy (e.g. Matt. 23:23; Mark 7:9–13). Many of his parables teach mercy, compassion and care, as against justice, rights or expectations. In this he reflects the inner spirit and thrust of the law itself.

So then, we should preach OT law for human benefit. We should highlight the law's own priorities for the weak and needy and ask our people to reflect on what these could mean in today's society – not least within the church itself. There is plenty of material in the law that shows the heart of God for the needs of human beings, especially the vulnerable, those who are socially, economically, ethnically or sexually disadvantaged in our fallen world. Such material can be preached with powerful ethical impact – so long as (to repeat) it is connected to the character and saving grace of God, so that it does not merely become an exercise in legalistic guilt or sentimental idealism.

Old Testament law anticipates failure, judgment and future grace

We should not imagine that the failure of OT Israel to keep God's law somehow surprised God so much that he was forced to come up with a Plan B.

---

4. ibid., pp. 312–314.

On the contrary, the ending of Deuteronomy clearly anticipates the failure of successive generations of Israel, to the point that God would act in covenant judgment. But beyond that judgment lay the hope and promise of restoration and covenant renewal.

We cannot expound the depths of Deuteronomy 29 – 32 now, but suffice it to say that it makes clear that the fault is not in the law itself, but in us. It is not that we *cannot* obey God, but that we *will not and choose not to*. The emphasis is the same as Paul takes up in Romans, where he reflects on texts like Deuteronomy 30:11–14. This is a key passage – of realism and hope.

There is an open future and an open choice in Deuteronomy 30, along with a powerful evangelistic appeal to return to God. This too should form part of our preaching, for it is an integral part of the law – coming as it does as part of the climactic chapters that bring the whole Torah to a conclusion.

So then, we can preach OT law, not to drive people only to despair at their failure, but to lead them from the realization of failure back to the love and promises of God – as contained in the law itself. Failure is a fact. Failure is foreseen. But failure can be forgiven through the grace of God. The law itself expresses all three great gospel truths and can be preached accordingly.

Finding the message of the law for today

How then do we go about finding a message for today within particular passages of OT law? In principle the method is no different from our exegetical and hermeneutical task anywhere else in Scripture. We should not ask, 'What does this mean for me now?' until we have worked hard to find out, 'What did it mean for them then?'

One of the most effective keys, it seems to me, is to seek the social objective of any given law or set of laws. Again, I can say it no better than I did once before:

> Laws in any society are made for a purpose. Laws protect interests. Laws restrict power. Laws try to balance the rights of different and possibly competing groups in society. Laws promote social objectives according to the legislators' vision of what kind of ideal society they would like to see. So, in the light of our understanding of Israelite society, we need to articulate as precisely as possible the objective of any specific law. In other words, we are trying to understand, 'Why was this law there?' This can best be done by addressing a number of questions to the laws we are studying and trying to identify and articulate plausible answers. Remembering to keep ancient biblical Israel in focus, such questions might include:

- What kind of situation was this law trying to promote, or prevent?
- Whose interests was this law aiming to protect?
- Who would have benefited from this law and why?
- Whose power was this law trying to restrict and how did it do so?
- What rights and responsibilities were embodied in this law?
- What kind of behaviour did this law encourage or discourage?
- What vision of society motivated this law?
- What moral principles, values or priorities did this law embody or instantiate?
- What motivation did this law appeal to?
- What sanction or penalty (if any) was attached to this law, and what does that show regarding its relative seriousness or moral priority?

Now of course there are times when the obscurity of some laws defeats even such questioning. We may remain doubtful if we have really uncovered the objectives or rationale of certain laws. But again that does not greatly matter in the relatively few cases where it may be true. More often the sheer exercise of asking such questions and thinking through the possible answers generates a more nuanced understanding of the purpose of Israel's laws in their own context. And that then enables a much more targeted application of them when we move to the final step.[5]

And that final step, from a preacher's point of view, is to move back from all the study and reflection in the biblical world into the world of today – into the context of the preacher and his or her audience. As we make that move, we can ask a parallel set of questions about our own context. In the light of the issues we have observed in Israel's social context and how their laws addressed them, we can seek to identify comparable situations, interests, needs, powers, rights, behaviours, etc. that need to be addressed in our own society. Then in that new context, i.e. our own contemporary world, we ask how the objectives of OT laws can be achieved.

- What kind of situations or people in our society are comparable to those in the OT laws?
- What should be our objectives?
- How should the principles found in OT laws be applied in practical life today – in my own life, in the church, in wider society?
- What, in Christian terms, is our motivation now for responding to God's law in obedience?

---

5. ibid., pp. 322–323.

- How, then, can I preach this part of Scripture in a way that is faithful to its original context and purpose, but also relevant to my own people now? How can I make this text 'speak again', so that people today see its relevance and are moved to obey God in response?

As I work towards a preachable sermon from the legal text with such questions in mind, I keep in mind also the above core principles: God's grace as the starting point; the need for God's people to live for the sake of God's mission; the paradigmatic function of Israel's law for future generations; what the text teaches about the character of God and the demands of human well-being; the realities of sin and failure and the need to preach all God's Word with the profound sense of preacher and audience alike being sinners in need of forgiving grace.

Sermon outline on Deuteronomy 15:1–18: 'The Economics of Generosity'

Introduction

Our generosity should reflect God's generosity, just as the generosity of the righteous person in Psalm 112:3–5 mirrors the generosity of God in the parallel Psalm 111:4–5. Deuteronomy resonates with such reflective generosity, based on God's grace and redemption, yet it builds this into a clear legal framework of economic practice that has a lot to teach us.

The structure of the passage helps us to understand its message. It reminds us of two laws from the book of Exodus (vv. 1–3, 12–18), and then in between it preaches some strong motivation for generosity that should encourage people to obey them. So here we have obedience motivated by grace – as is the pattern throughout the Bible.

Generosity as a brake on economic forces
Release from debt (vv. 1–3)
These verses expand the law of Exodus 23:10–11, requiring that the land should be 'released' every seventh year. Deuteronomy extends the principle from land to people, especially poor people burdened with debt, and requires that they be released from it. The OT recognized that people sometimes need to borrow to survive, and lending to the needy is commended. But such lending should be responsible and properly scheduled – *and finite*. Debt should not be for ever. We do not believe in the eternal life of money. Such principles challenge the small-scale offence of unscrupulous loan-

sharks, but also the global scandal of international debt that goes on for generations.

Release from slavery (vv. 12–18)

These verses are an extension of Exodus 21:1–11. 'Hebrew slaves' should serve six-year contracts and then be free to change employment or stay on. If they are set free, verses 12–15 insist that then they should receive a generous gift – a substantial redundancy package to tide them over for a fresh start. In other words, warm generosity is added to legal compliance with contract. And verse 18 tells the owner to do his sums and realize that he has got far better value than from a hired worker, and should not begrudge releasing the 'Hebrew' or behaving generously when he does so.

These two laws then show how generosity can be connected to a legal framework, to counteract the relentless forces of impoverishment, especially as related to debt. Debt and poverty are still huge realities and scandals in today's world. They need to be addressed with systemic and legal instruments, allied to a change of heart that inculcates generosity to the needy.

Generosity as a bridge between economic ideal and reality (vv. 4–11)

Verse 4 is an obvious *ideal*. Verse 11 is an equally obvious *reality*. How can we handle the tension between these texts? They seem contradictory, and yet the tension must have been as obvious to the author of Deuteronomy as it is to us. How can we build a bridge between them – bridge the gap between the economic ideal of verse 4 and the economic reality of verse 11?

God's ideal, and its essential conditions (vv. 4–6)

God's desire for his people is sufficiency for all, not extremes of poverty for some. That is, we must read Deuteronomy 15:4 as a statement not about individual prosperity, but about social equality. 'There should be no poor among you' (NIV) is not about the kind of bank balance God promises to individuals, but about the kind of economic balance that God wants in society. *Time* magazine on 18 September 2006 headlined an article, 'Does God want *you* to be rich?' Maybe, maybe not. What verse 4 says is that God does not want a society where some are poor while others luxuriate in selfish surplus.

But note the *condition* in verse 5: *obedience to the Lord*. That is, if only Israel would follow God's economic laws, then there need be no such glaring inequality and poverty. *Time* got the question all wrong. What God *wants* is for us to be obedient, to be holy, to do justice, to love mercy and walk humbly with God.

And *if* God's people live that way, there need be no poverty among them – a point that Luke was keen to exemplify in his portrayal of the church in Acts, which matched their Spirit-filled unity with Spirit-led economic equality. And he saw it as a fulfilment of the ideal of Deuteronomy. Acts 4:34 is virtually a quotation of Deuteronomy 15:4 (in the Greek translation of the OT).

What would such Spirit-led obedience look like if practised across the world church today? What an enormously powerful and prophetic sign it would be of the reign of God in the hearts (and pockets) of his people.

Human reality, and the response that God commands (vv. 7–11)

So verses 4–6 present the only condition in which the laws about release of debt and slaves would *not* be necessary – that is, complete obedience to God's ways. But then verses 7–11 bring us down to reality, with the sad but true assumption that because of our disobedience, such laws will *always* be necessary, along with the generosity that should accompany them.

There will always be poor people in the land (or in the earth). *But then what? What response is called for to this tragic fact?*

There are some really rich features of *generosity* in response to poverty in verses 7–11. Generosity is to be:

Emphatic: When Hebrew wants to emphasize something, it just doubles the verb. In English this is caught by adverbs like 'richly' (v. 4), 'fully' (v. 5), 'freely' (v. 8), 'generously' (v. 10 NIV). But in Hebrew, the doubled-up verbs occur in chapter 15 more than in any other chapter in the book. God is saying, 'I really care about this, and you must really do something about it.' Does God want you to be rich? Maybe, maybe not. Does God want you to be generous? Emphatically *yes*!

Personal: There is a great deal of body language in these verses, not always clear either in English. Hands, hearts and eyes occur often in the original idioms: hand in verses 2, 7, 8 and 11; heart in verses 7, 9 and 10; eye in verses 9 and 18. Deuteronomy is saying that our response to the needs of others is to touch every part of our person: our practical behaviour (hands), our motives and intentions (hearts), and our attitudes (eyes). We are challenged as to how we think, feel and act towards the poor.

Relational: The word 'brother' is used repeatedly (vv. 7, twice, 9, 11), for this is a covenant relationship. And the word 'your' occurs far more often in Hebrew than in translations (v. 11 speaks of '*your* poor and *your* needy in *your* land'). They are not just '*the* poor' as a social category. Deuteronomy insists on relating, not just classifying. Poor people need to belong, not just to be counted.

Imperative: Generosity is *commanded* (vv. 11, 15). This is even more strongly seen in Deuteronomy 26:12–15, where a person could only claim to have kept

God's law *when* he had obeyed the laws for the poor. The law had not been kept if the poor remained uncared for. We could illustrate this from several of Jesus' parables (based on the Law and Prophets, Luke 16:9–13), and notice that it is just as much commanded in the NT also (1 Tim. 6:17–19). Generosity to the poor is not a matter of charity, but of obedience – to the teaching of God in the Law, the Prophets, the Gospels and the Epistles. Are we getting the message?

Imitative: As we said at the start, our generosity is to reflect God's own saving generosity (vv. 14, 15). All our giving is only a response to the grace of God. David knew this too (1 Chr. 29:14–16). And the principle is echoed by Jesus, Paul and John.

Summary and conclusion

God's ideal is that if only people would live according to the principles, standards and values he has given us in Scripture, there need not be extremes of poverty. *But*, in a world where such things are the reality, we are called to *both* justice *and* generosity, in a way that is emphatic, personal, relational, obedient to God's law and reflective of God's grace.

Further reading

In addition to my own works cited in the footnotes, I recommend:

DAVIS, ELLEN F, *Wondrous Depth: Preaching the Old Testament* (Louisville: Westminster John Knox, 2005).

GOLDINGAY, JOHN, *Old Testament Theology III: Israel's Life* (Downers Grove: InterVarsity Press, 2009).

LALLEMAN, HETTY, *Celebrating the Law? Rethinking Old Testament Ethics* (Milton Keynes: Paternoster, 2004).

4. PREACHING LAMENT

Federico G. Villanueva

Introduction

A few years ago, a fire broke out in a hotel in Manila, killing more than seventy people and injuring a hundred others. It was the worst hotel fire in my country. Most of the guests were pastors and lay workers from the provinces. They came to Manila to attend a conference organized by an American evangelical group. One of those who attended was a former church member of mine. He died along with the others, leaving his wife and three children. I immediately called one of the organizers, a pastor. I asked him about the situation. His response came crushing like the fire that killed my fellow workers. He lamented, 'They [referring to the loved ones] are reacting like they are not Christians, weeping and agonizing like they have no God!'

Such a response shows how Christianity has become an emotionless religion – or, more accurately, how anti-negative emotion it has become. Christians are not supposed to show anger or despair, even in extremely difficult situations, including the death of a loved one.[1] 'The Lord giveth and he taketh away,'

---

1. Speaking from a Western background, David Runcorn, in 'Tears have been my food: Loss, lament and protest', in D. Runcorn, *Choice, Desire and the Will of God – What More do You Want?* (London: SPCK, 2003), p. 107, remarks: 'By contrast

we often say. God is in control and all things work together for good. So we should always praise the Lord no matter what the situation is. Praise is the only appropriate response, in blessing and in suffering, in noonday light or in darkness. As one popular song of praise goes, 'Blessed be your name', even on a 'road marked with suffering'.

Indeed, in her songs, testimonies and prayers, the church only knows of praise.[2] Billman and Migliore observe, 'Psalms of lament are poorly represented in the worship books of most mainline denominations. With notable exceptions, it would appear that prayer and worship in many Christian congregations fail to make room for the experiences of lament, protest, and remonstration with God.'[3] Ellington notes the emphasis on praise in his study of how testimonies are done in some groups of Pentecostal churches.[4] While formerly they were spontaneous, testimonies have been censored in order to make sure that what is declared in public has the effect of 'building up' the congregation. A 'negative' testimony – one in which the problem has not yet been resolved – would not be a 'good promotion'. When it comes to prayers, these too tend to be limited to praise. This came to me as a matter of personal experience when one of my church members came to me asking for prayer, but told me I should not tell anybody about it. She was about to take an exam which would qualify her for a job. Unfortunately, she did not pass the exam. And when someone from the church came to know about it, she denied that she ever took the exam. Why? Because you do not share something that has not been answered. There is no place for unanswered prayers in the church.

This is the situation that confronts those who approach the subject of lament with a view to preaching it. How do we preach lament in a church dominated by praise? How do we preach lament in such a way that it is not eclipsed

---

[to the biblical lament tradition] the western Church has lost the tradition of lament.' He explains that part of this may be cultural. 'The British temperament in particular is famous for its stoic reserve and endurance in the face of struggle. Time and again I have stood with mourners after taking a funeral and overheard the bereaved being congratulated for "being strong".'

2. W. Brueggemann, *The Message of the Psalms: A Theological Commentary* (Minneapolis: Augsburg, 1984), p. 51.

3. K. D. Billman and D. L. Migliore, *Rachel's Cry: Prayer of Lament and Rebirth of Hope* (Eugene, OR: Wipf & Stock, 1999), p. 13.

4. S. A. Ellington, 'The Costly Loss of Testimony', *Journal of Pentecostal Theology* 16 (2000), pp. 48–59.

by praise? These are the questions that we need to address as we discuss the topic of how we develop sermons on lament.

Contrary to the prevailing attitude in the church with respect to lament, we believe that lament is vital to the life of the church. As the title of this chapter indicates, lament is important, worthy of being preached from the pulpit. Equally, preaching is one of the important ways whereby we can recapture this rich tradition. For preaching, as is widely acknowledged, remains central in most Protestant churches.[5] What gets proclaimed in the pulpit has the status of the important. Indeed, we may say that a major part of the reason for the absence of lament in the church lies in the fact that lament is seldom preached, if it is preached at all.[6]

We seek to remedy this gap by focusing on the subject of preaching the lament psalms. We begin by noting three things about the lament psalms, which are also true of the Psalms in general: they are poetry, theology and prayer.[7] Or, to formulate it more homiletically:

The lament psalms are   **p**oetry
The lament psalms   **p**oint to God (theology)
The lament psalms are   **p**rayer

As a work of poetry, the psalms of lament are concerned primarily with experience. 'Poetry', writes Perrine, 'takes all life as its province. Its primary concern is not with beauty, not with philosophical truth, not with persuasion, but with experience.'[8] Thus the lament psalms are not primarily sermons. Rather, they are depictions of the psalmists' experiences of suffering. In the lament psalms, we are presented with different images of suffering. Through these depictions and images the psalmists convey their view of God, the life of faith and the reality of life. Like poetry in general, the lament psalms 'bring us a

---

5. G. Goldsworthy, *Preaching the Whole Bible as Christian Scripture* (Grand Rapids, MI: Eerdmans; Leicester: Inter-Varsity Press, 2000).

6. There are at present few materials on preaching lament. Most books on the subject deal with preaching the Psalms in general, with minimal treatment on how one can actually preach on lament.

7. T. G. Long, *Preaching and the Literary Forms of the Bible* (Philadelphia: Fortress Press, 1988), p. 44; J. C. McCann and J. C. Howell, *Preaching the Psalms* (Nashville: Abingdon Press, 2001), p. 35.

8. L. Perrine, *Sound and Sense: An Introduction to Poetry*, 4th ed. (New York: Harcourt, 1973), p. 9.

sense and a perception of life'.[9] The task of the preacher is to see the different ways in which these experiences are presented, to feel their texture and shape as it were, to discern what 'perception of life' they are trying to communicate, and to attempt to participate in their experiences.

Specifically, we try to answer the following questions:

1. How are the experiences of the psalmists expressed in the lament psalms?
2. What do these tell us about their view of God and the reality of life?
3. How can we participate in these experiences?

In response to the first question, I would like to propose that one of the ways in which the psalmists present their experiences of suffering is through the movements between lament and praise. In what follows, we try to look closely at these different movements, discern what they are trying to convey, and finally think of how we can participate in them. A comprehensive guide on preparing sermons on lament is impossible to accomplish here. What I intend to do is provide one possible way of developing a sermon on lament by focusing on the movements in the lament psalms. Attempts to relate the lament to Christ and the Christian life will also be made. An outline will be provided at the end to illustrate what a sermon on lament might look like.

The dynamic movements in the lament psalms: the lament as poetry

In approaching the lament psalms as poetry, we need to consider, among other things, the 'movement within the poem'. This, according to Berlin, is one of the ways a reader can make sense of a poem.[10] In the lament psalms in particular, we find the presence of a movement in terms of mood. Berlin observes in Psalm 13, for instance, how in reading the psalm one 'traverses the same emotional path from despair to hope'.[11] Similarly, Alter sees in this psalm what he calls a 'surprising emotional reversal impelled by the motor force of faith'.[12]

---

9. ibid., p. 4.
10. A. Berlin, 'Introduction to Hebrew Poetry', in *NIB* 4 (Nashville: Abingdon Press, 1996), pp. 301–315 (p. 314).
11. ibid.
12. R. Alter, *The Art of Biblical Poetry* (New York: Basic Books, 1985), p. 66.

From lament to praise

This 'emotional reversal', known more popularly among form critics as the 'sudden change of mood', is a characteristic feature of the lament psalms. With very few exceptions, lament psalms contain within them a movement between the elements of lament and praise. Most common among these is the movement from lament to praise. Psalm 13, mentioned above, is a classic example of this movement. This psalm begins with a lament:

> How long, O LORD? Will you forget me forever?
> How long will you hide your face from me?
> How long must I take counsel in my soul
> and have sorrow in my heart all the day?
> How long shall my enemy be exalted over me?
> (vv. 1–2)[13]

But at the end the psalm moves towards expression of trust and vow of praise:

> But I have trusted in your steadfast love;
> my heart shall rejoice in your salvation.
> I will sing to the LORD,
> because he has dealt bountifully with me.
> (vv. 5–6)

This movement, according to McCann and Howell, should be captured in preaching: 'That drama of lament moving to praise is an effective, powerful word for those who dare to pray the Psalm – and the preacher must capture that same transformation of mood.'[14] Theologically, this movement is a climactic event. Brueggemann remarks that the movement from lament to praise 'cuts to the heart of the theological issue for faith'.[15] They testify to the experience of Israel as narrated in their history – that God indeed answers; that he delivers his people from their trouble whenever they cry to him.

And so, to the question 'How do we preach lament in a church dominated

---

13. Unless otherwise indicated, the translations are taken from the ESV.
14. McCann and Howell, *Preaching the Psalms*, p. 75.
15. W. Brueggemann, *The Psalms and the Life of Faith* (Minneapolis: Fortress Press, 1995), p. 72.

by praise?' we respond first by acknowledging that praise remains central in the lament. As the movement in the lament psalms indicates, praise forms an important place in the people's experiences of suffering. In their sufferings, the psalmists begin with lament, but they often end in praise. They declare that the overall direction of the life of faith is from lament to praise. Praise pierces even through the darkest night. Thus, even in a church dominated by praise, we need to continue to affirm the place of praise in the lament.

On the other hand, highlighting only the movement from lament to praise can lead to a distorted view of the lament psalms, and consequently to a limited application of the lament. We can read too much praise into the lament to the point that lament ceases to be lament, but a mere prelude which one has to go through as quickly as possible.[16] McCann and Howell warn us of the tendency to see too much 'optimism' in the lament and to rush towards resolution or praise.[17] Writing from a liturgical perspective, Witvliet observes a similar tendency to rush towards resolution in the use of the lament in liturgy. He acknowledges, 'One problem in liturgical lament is that we arrive too quickly at the vow of praise, the happy ending, glossing over the pithy cries of lament that conceal deep and brooding affections'.[18] Likewise, in his critique of the provision of lament in the *New Patterns for Worship*, Bradbury writes, 'In summary, whilst *Facing Pain* offers a service with some elements of lament, it falls prey to the temptation to introduce themes of hope too early and for this reason runs the risk of diluting the impact of hope and salvation when it breaks in at the end.'[19] He suggests that we give more time to the expression of lament, even delaying the section of 'Finding Hope' towards the very end as the final address.

From a pastoral and practical point of view, a one-sided emphasis on the movement from lament to praise can be detrimental to the life of faith. One may get the impression that a solution to one's problem is always underway. As Stocks cautions us in the application of Psalm 13, 'Considerable care is

16. F. G. Villanueva, *The 'Uncertainty of a Hearing': A Study of the Sudden Change of Mood in the Psalms of Lament* (Leiden: Brill, 2008), p. 251.

17. McCann and Howell, *Preaching the Psalms*, pp. 76–77.

18. J. D. Witvliet, *Worship Seeking Understanding* (Grand Rapids, MI: Baker, 2003), p. 46. Witvliet is making this comment coming from an understanding of the lament shaped by the form-critical view of the lament, which sees only a movement from lament to praise.

19. P. Bradbury, *Sowing in Tears: How to Lament in a Church of Praise* (Cambridge: Grove, 2007), p. 20.

necessary in discerning the suitability. For example, in the case of a person who is struggling with the onset of dementia . . . it would not be helpful to suggest that the condition would improve.'[20]

In my view, the difficulty in the application of lament such as those cited above stems from a limited understanding of the lament psalms. This understanding is dictated by the form-critical view, which only sees lament in terms of the movement from lament to praise. But as I have sought to demonstrate elsewhere, the lament psalm is not limited to the movement from lament to praise.[21]

Alternation between lament and praise

In addition to the movement from lament to praise, one encounters an alternation between the two elements. We find this feature in at least four psalms: Psalms 31, 35, 59 and 71. Here, we briefly discuss Psalm 31.[22] This psalm begins with a lament:

> In you, O LORD, do I take refuge;
> let me never be put to shame;
> in your righteousness deliver me!
> Incline your ear to me;
> rescue me speedily!
> Be a rock of refuge for me,
> a strong fortress to save me!
> (vv. 1–2)

In verses 7–8 we find a movement to praise:

> I will rejoice and be glad in your steadfast love,
> because you have seen my affliction;

---

20. S. P. Stocks, *Using the Psalms for Prayer through Suffering* (Cambridge: Grove, 2007), p. 22.

21. For a more comprehensive discussion of the different movements in the lament psalms, see Villanueva, *The 'Uncertainty of a Hearing'*.

22. Some consider Psalm 31 as composite. We do not have access to the actual history of the composition of the psalm. What I am interested in here is the form as we now have it. In its present form we have alternation between lament and praise. We will argue below that this is a deliberate move to convey a particular perspective on suffering.

you have known the distress of my soul,
and you have not delivered me into the hand of the enemy. . .

This would make a typical lament like Psalm 13. But then the psalm moves on, and in the next verse we find the psalmist back in a situation of lament. Immediately following his testimony of deliverance we hear the psalmist pleading for mercy:

Be gracious to me, O LORD, for I am in distress;
my eye is wasted from grief. . .
(v. 9)

If earlier the psalmist has declared, 'you have seen my affliction' (v. 7), here he is crying out to the Lord, 'for I am in distress' (v. 9). In both verses (7 and 9), the words for affliction and distress come from a similar Hebrew root, *yr*. Moreover, in verse 8, the psalmist has just testified, 'you have not delivered me into the hand of the enemy'. But a few verses later, we hear the psalmist again asking God to 'rescue me from the hand of my enemies and from my persecutors!' (v. 15).

Then, like a pendulum, the psalm moves back again to praise:

Oh, how abundant is your goodness. . .
Blessed be the LORD,
for he has wondrously shown his steadfast love to me. . .
(vv. 19–21)

So we have in Psalm 31 an alternation between lament and praise.

Return to lament after praise
From the previous psalm, we see that although lament does move to praise, the movement is 'not a one-time, irreversible turn', as Brueggemann acknowledges.[23] Lament, even when it has already turned to praise, can revert to

---

23. Brueggemann, *The Psalms and the Life of Faith*, p. 117. Unfortunately, although Brueggemann acknowledges that praise can turn back to lament, in his elaboration of the lament psalms he presents the movement as always from lament to praise. In his book *The Message of the Psalms* he only highlighted the movement from disorientation to reorientation and the reader cannot help but get the impression from his book that lament always moves to praise. See, for example, McCann and Howell's reading of Brueggemann: 'the movement is always to reorientation' (*Preaching the Psalms*, p. 76).

lament and actually end there. Psalm 12 proves this. This psalm begins with a lament:

> Help, LORD, for the godly are no more;
> the faithful have vanished from among men.
> (v. 1 NIV)

Here the psalmist is not simply uttering a pious statement about righteousness and being godly. Rather, he is crying out to God because he has experienced life when the godly are no more. The words used to describe the wicked are pregnant with meaning, ascribing potential for abuse to the wicked. It speaks of 'the tongue that makes great boasts . . . who say, "With our tongue we will prevail, our lips are with us; who is master over us?"' (vv. 3–4). It is possible that the psalmist and his community have experienced abuse at the hands of these wicked people, as the next verse indicates:

> 'Because the poor are plundered, because the needy groan,
> I will now arise,' says the LORD. . .
> (v. 5)

Here we are told that the 'poor are plundered', explaining why the psalmist is crying out for help. At the same time, these words form a part of the divine response to the lament. In response to the lament, God says, 'I will now arise.' This statement is significant. Often the shift from lament to praise is explained in terms of an oracle of salvation, delivered by a cultic prophet to the person who is suffering. Accordingly, the reception of the oracle leads to assurance and praise, which explains the change of mood from lament to praise. In Psalm 12 we have a direct response from the Lord. With such an unprecedented response, the psalmist praises the faithfulness and truthfulness of Yahweh's words (v. 6) and expresses confidence in Yahweh. In verse 7 he declares that Yahweh will 'guard us from this generation forever'. Thus we see a movement from lament to praise at this point.

The psalm could have ended with the declaration of hope in verse 7, but the psalm unexpectedly reverts to the lament at the end. Right after his expression of hope and trust in Yahweh, the psalmist pens these words: 'On every side the wicked prowl, as vileness is exalted among the children of man' (v. 8). And with this note the psalm ends, closing not with the expected vow of praise. The psalm began with the cry, 'Help, LORD, for the godly are no more.' In view of the divine response in the middle of the psalm, the logical and 'more appropriate' ending would have been 'the wicked are no more', or at

least their power has been placed under control. But no, the psalmist admits
that in fact the wicked are still very much active, prowling around like dogs,
free as ever to do as they wish. Tragically, this came about in spite of the fact
that God has already spoken. We are thus left with an element of tension, as
praise returns to lament.

The reverse movement from praise to lament

The return to lament after praise is further reinforced by the reverse movement from praise to lament in Psalm 9/10. This psalm, which appears as two
separate psalms in the English Bible, is actually one psalm. The use of the
acrostic to construct Psalm 9/10 and the absence of a superscription in Psalm
10 points to this. In addition, there are significant repetitions in Psalms 9 and
10 which tie the two together. Most relevant among these is the repetition of
the phrase 'in times of trouble'. This phrase unites the two psalms and at the
same time serves as a literary device in marking the movement in the psalm.
The psalm begins with thanksgiving:

> I will give thanks to the LORD with my whole heart;
> I will recount all of your wonderful deeds.

In verse 9 the psalmist declares:

> The LORD is a stronghold for the oppressed,
> a stronghold in times of trouble.

Here the psalmist expresses confidence in Yahweh, claiming that he is a
'stronghold in times of trouble'. But slowly, as one reads through the psalm,
one notices a change in tone. In verses 19–20 there is a transition to petition.
From a form critical perspective, one would expect at this point an expression
of praise. But instead of praise, we have a lament:

> Why, O LORD, do you stand afar off?
> Why do you hide yourself in times of trouble?
> (10:1)

Here the phrase 'in times of trouble' is repeated, but the tone has changed. The
context is no longer that of thanksgiving, but lament. With the characteristic
cry of the lament – 'why?' – the psalm has turned from praise to lament. What
started out as a psalm of thanksgiving in the first half of the psalm (Psalm
9) becomes a lament in the second half (Psalm 10). Indeed, so sudden and

unexpected is the change that Gunkel thinks the acrostic has to be blamed.[24] The employment of the acrostic in the composition of Psalm 9/10 led to the formulation of the lament in 10:1. This verse falls on the letter *lamed*, thus the use of the word *lmh*.

This shows how the more dominant movement from lament to praise has often dictated scholars' approach to the lament psalms, preventing them from seeing the more dynamic movements between lament and praise. But as demonstrated in the foregoing, the movement between lament and praise is more dynamic and unpredictable than many scholars are prepared to acknowledge. Lament does move to praise, and quite often at that. But it is also capable of moving in the opposite direction from praise to lament, of returning to lament even after a movement to praise, and of alternating between lament and praise.

The need to consider the other movements in the lament

It is these other movements that we need to consider in preaching lament, in addition to the more common movement from lament to praise. We need to preach the 'whole counsel of God' and not just one part, no matter how dominant this may be, as in the case of the movement from lament to praise. Past scholarship on the lament psalms has highlighted only the movement from lament to praise. This has led to a distorted view of the lament and has hampered the application of lament. I have argued that in our reading of the lament psalms for preaching, we pay attention to the variety of movements in the psalms of lament. Broadening our perspective on lament by considering its rich and dynamic movements leads to a much-needed balance in the presentation of lament in preaching. As N. T. Wright remarks:

> The Psalms join together what often look to us like polar opposites as we come into God's presence. They pass swiftly from loving intimacy to thunderstruck awe and back again. They bring together sharp, angry questioning and simple, quiet trust. They range from the gentle and meditative, to the loud and boisterous, to lament and black despair, and on to solemn and holy celebration. There is a wonderful peace in working through from the great cry that opens Psalm 22 . . . to its concluding praise that God has heard and answered the prayer, and then stepping straight into the serene trust and assurance of Psalm 23 . . . There is a wise and healthy balance about

---

24. H. Gunkel, *Die Psalmen*, Handkommentar zum Alten Testament (Göttingen: Vandenhoeck & Ruprecht, 1926), p. 33.

reading one after the other, the tub-thumping triumphalism of Psalm 136 . . . and the shattering desolation of Psalm 137.[25]

What do we make of these movements, especially those containing the element of tension?

It is easy to fall into the temptation of seeing these other movements as mistakes or mere coincidences, best ignored or disregarded. But could it be, as Dornisch remarks in her comments on the element of tension in the book of Job, that these are ways through which the psalmists try to communicate to us their own experiences of ambiguity and complexity?

> Are we not sometimes tempted to a systematization which precludes the play of symbolic meaning on multiple levels? Do we not sometimes let historicism, or the genetic problem, or awareness of internal inconsistencies in the text, interfere with our understanding of the many levels of meaning, the intended symbolic or paradoxical incongruities, and even the resistance to systematization, all of which are precisely ways the author uses to communicate the complexity and ambiguity of the human condition?[26]

Alter explains concerning the function of poetry: 'Poetry, working through a system of complex linkages of sound, image, word, rhythm, syntax, theme, idea, is an instrument for conveying densely patterned meanings, and sometimes contradictory meanings, that are not readily conveyable through other kinds of discourse.'[27] He acknowledges that there is a 'meaning' or message in poetry. Being poetry, this message is not straightforward. In the case of the lament psalms, I have suggested that this message comes to us through the different movements in the lament. In what follows, we try to discern what message or 'word' is communicated through the various movements.

The word in the lament: lament as theology

The movement from lament to praise: God answers and delivers

As noted above, the movement from lament to praise testifies to the God who answers prayer. This movement affirms the common experiences of

25. N. T. Wright, *Simply Christian* (London: SPCK, 2006), pp. 130–131.

26. L. Dornisch, 'The Book of Job and Ricoeur's Hermeneutics', *Semeia* 19 (1981), pp. 3–29 (p. 14).

27. Alter, *The Art of Biblical Poetry*, p. 113.

God's people, who, in their suffering and trouble, have found God to be their deliverer. This movement is important for people who find themselves stuck, wanting to just hide under their pillow and no longer get up. It points the way forward, beyond suffering, towards healing and restoration.

The alternation between lament and praise: restoration is a process

However, the alternation between lament and praise reminds us that the road towards restoration can be long. Restoration involves a process that cannot be rushed.[28] For some the transformation may take weeks, for others months and even years. Maybe for others the solution may not come this side of eternity.

Unfortunately, we do not like process. We like to think that all our problems have already been resolved, all our issues sorted. Especially with a view of the Christian life which one-sidedly emphasizes victory, it is so easy to live a life of denial, to live with the illusion that we are always OK, even perfect. But human life remains very much a process. Indeed, to be human is to be partial, incomplete, undone. We cry for help and get help. Yet the next time around we are back on our knees, pleading for mercy that God deliver us. And it is only from our ability to live with grace in the midst of our imperfections that healing flows. As Calvin declares, 'Creatures of such instability, and liable to be borne away by a thousand different influences, we need to be confirmed again and again.'[29] The life of faith is characterized not only by certainty, but by uncertainty.

The reverse movement from praise to lament: faith is not all about answers

The reverse movement from praise to lament presents a challenge: not everyone makes it towards the movement to praise. It is a brave acknowledgment of the reality that life does not always bring that which we seek. There are times when what comes is a reverse of what we hope for. Worsening condition instead of healing. Bankruptcy instead of recovery. Defeat instead of victory. As Hebrews 11 declares about those whose lives were marked by faith, many have experienced deliverance, but not everyone did. Some 'were sawn in two, they were killed with the sword. They went about in skins of sheep and goats, destitute, afflicted, mistreated' (Heb. 11:37). These are people of faith for whom the following words of the psalmist were not fulfilled: 'I have been young, and now am old, yet I have not seen the righteous forsaken, or his children begging for bread' (Ps. 37:25).

---

28. cf. T. Longman III, 'Lament', in D. B. Sandy and R. L. Giese, Jr (eds.), *Cracking Old Testament Codes* (Nashville: Broadman & Holman Publishers, 1995), p. 213.

29. J. Calvin, *Commentary on the Book of Psalms*, trans. J. Anderson (Edinburgh: Edinburgh Printing Co., 1846), p. 423.

Lathrop relates about scribes in Armenia who wrote in their colophons the following:

> In bitter and grievous times, when many in the land were persecuted, some dwelt among bushes, some fell prey to the wolves, many became victims of famine, fathers disavowed their children. It was a sight to behold, the awesome moaning and lamenting over the dear ones, for the mother wept over her son, the sister over the brother, the bride over the bridegroom; and they received no consolation from any corner, neither from God nor from man.[30]

Those who died in the hotel fire in Manila cried with all their might for salvation and deliverance to come. But none came. Instead of salvation and deliverance there was only destruction, chaos and loss as the expected outcome towards praise did not occur.

How do we respond in situations like these?

The lament psalms containing the reverse movement from praise to lament instruct us that it is all right to mourn, to grieve and to lament over the lack of divine action. As Berlin remarks on the lament in Psalm 137, 'The poet is exquisitely aware that in the wake of the destruction the poetic discourse about Jerusalem (an important earlier form of praise to God) must change from praise to lament.'[31]

The reverse movement from praise to lament represents a view of the life of faith that may cause uneasiness, but it is an important dimension that needs to be presented. We need to be careful that we do not always enforce a theology of deliverance in all situations. In his discussion of the lament in Psalm 22, Ricoeur argues: 'We must not . . . confine ourselves to giving the framework of traditional history, where deliverance in fact answered the people's supplication, as the background of the dynamism that leads from lament to praise. The lament has to be set within the context of an exile where one does not know whether it will repeat the Exodus.'[32]

30. G. W. Lathrop, 'A Rebirth of Images: On the Use of the Bible in Liturgy', *Worship* 58 (1984), pp. 291–304 (p. 300).

31. A. Berlin, 'Psalms and the Literature of Exile: Psalms 137, 44, 69 and 78', in P. D. Miller and P. W. Flint (eds.), *The Book of Psalms: Composition and Reception* (Leiden: Brill, 2005), pp. 65–86 (p. 71).

32. P. Ricoeur, 'Lamentation as Prayer', in A. LaCocque and P. Ricoeur, *Thinking Biblically* (Chicago and London: University of Chicago Press, 1998), pp. 211–232 (p. 223).

Confronted with uncertainties, loss and failure, the reverse movement from praise to lament points to the God who is sovereign, whose rule embraces all of life, including tragic experiences. An important message of the lament is that even these experiences of tragedy are brought to God, even when there are no answers. As one of my students puts it, not all psalms are happy; some are intensely sad. They try to make sense out of suffering and failure. They ask God for help and receive none. This inclusion of such hopeless cries eloquently testifies to God's acceptance of human struggles. These psalms are not the final word on sufferings. They show, however, that wrestling with God has value even when we fail to find the answers.

The return to lament after praise: ambiguity and the element of tension remains even with the divine response

The return to lament after praise tells us that even when we have already received the answer to our prayers and have already experienced deliverance, the element of ambiguity remains. Sometimes the answer becomes another form of a question.[33] The return to lament shows a God who remains inscrutable, mysterious, even with receptions of his revelations. We stand before this God, humbled, aware of our finiteness and limitations in the face of his infinite wisdom and power. What is amazing is that this God does not expect us to know everything, to be infinite. There is room for lament in the form that Psalm 12 takes.

Absence of movement: the message of Psalm 88

One other group of psalms which contains a similar message to those lament psalms containing the other movements are those which contain no movement at all, such as we find in Psalm 88. Although the focus of the present chapter is on the lament psalms containing a movement between lament and praise, this psalm deserves to be mentioned here, though only briefly.[34] Psalm 88 plays an important role in the whole drama of movement between lament and praise. It represents the stage between the movements. In this psalm, time is suspended, all movements stilled, and the attention is drawn towards the lament itself. Indeed, the psalm contains no movement, not even a direct petition or plea. Instead, lament is explored in all its depth from beginning to end. So dark is

---

33. cf. J. Goldingay, 'The Dynamic Cycle of Praise and Prayer', *JSOT* 20 (1981), pp. 85–90 (p. 88).

34. I acknowledge the significance of this psalm for preaching, thus requiring separate and more thorough treatment.

the psalm that it actually ends with the word 'darkness'. Brueggemann argues that such psalms are important, 'precisely because they do not carry with them any articulated resolve of the issue. They leave us lingering in the unresolved, dangling in the depth of the pit without any explicit sign of rescue. That is an important statement to have in the repertoire, precisely because life is like that. Faith does not always resolve life.'[35]

Praying the lament psalm as a way of preaching it: lament as prayer

To preach the lament psalms, we need to pay attention to the various movements between lament and praise and discern what these tell us about God and the life of faith. But to understand the lament psalms more deeply, they need to be experienced. The function of poetry is not simply to 'tell us *about* experience but to allow us imaginatively to *participate* in it'.[36] Or, as Ciardi remarks, for poetry the 'concern is not to arrive at a definition and to close the book, but to arrive at an experience'.[37] Merton applies this to the Psalms: 'To understand the Psalms, we must experience the sentiments they express, in our own hearts.'[38]

One way of experiencing the sentiments of the lament psalms is by listening to the sufferings of others. For as we listen to the sufferings of others, and to our own, our ears are trained so that we are prepared to hear what the lament psalms are saying. But another way of experiencing the lament psalms is by doing what Jesus did — by actually praying the lament psalms. One value of praying the lament psalms is that the sufferings of others are opened up for us.[39] We listen to the sufferings of others in order to be more attuned to the lament psalms. Conversely, as we pray the lament psalms we become more acquainted with the sufferings of others.

Jesus himself prayed the lament psalms. At the cross he quoted Psalm 31:5: 'Into your hands I commit my spirit' (Luke 23:46). As will be remembered, this psalm alternates between lament and praise (see above). He also quoted the

---

35. Brueggemann, *The Message of the Psalms*, p. 78.

36. Perrine, *Sound and Sense*, p. 6.

37. John Ciardi, *How Does a Poem Mean?* (Boston: Houghton Mifflin Company, 1959), p. 666.

38. Thomas Merton, *Praying the Psalms* (Collegeville, Minnesota: Liturgical Press, 1956), p. 13.

39. McCann and Howell, *Preaching the Psalms*, p. 59.

words of Psalm 22:1: 'My God, my God, why have you forsaken me?' (Matt. 27:46). It was suggested that Jesus was actually praying his way through the Psalms during his suffering.[40] Earlier, his disciples asked Jesus to teach them how to pray. He did not give them a lecture on prayer. Instead, he gave them the 'Lord's prayer'.[41] Now, on the cross, Jesus continues to teach them how to pray. By praying the Psalms, and especially the lament psalms, Jesus points the way further into the heart of God where all our sufferings are validated, accepted and embraced. Praying the lament psalms makes us one with Jesus in taking the sufferings and brokenness of our world.

We need not go far to realize the brokenness of our world. In our own community, we find people who are suffering, struggling with so many issues. Unfortunately, the church has often missed out in reaching to the suffering in her midst because lament has been left out. I have been a pastor myself in Manila. What I have noticed was that Sunday after Sunday we were singing songs of victory, most of which are from the West, which do not fit in with our experiences as a suffering people.

This led me to the lament psalms. I started teaching and preaching on the lament psalms whenever appropriate (e.g. Holy Week, funeral services and topical sermons on prayer). I did this for a period of about two years. Then one Sunday morning, after the worship service was finished, just when everybody was starting to go out, a mother came forward and began sharing. This is not the typical 'I have a problem, *but* by God's grace I am now OK' testimony. She shared her struggles. The lady was in serious difficulty and she just poured out her heart. Many of the members who were leaving returned to their seats and listened as this mother shared her laments to the congregation. As the pastor, I just allowed her to pour out her heart. Afterwards, I came forward, placed my hands on her shoulders, and led the congregation to a prayer of lament. The prayer did not end on a positive note. No, I prayed a prayer of lament, similar to the lament psalm that moves from praise to lament. When I opened my eyes, I saw that a number of people in the congregation were also in tears. But I sensed a release, peace flowing in our hearts as a community after we had joined this lady in her lament. It was such a liberating experience as people saw that we do not always have to end on a victorious or positive note. It is OK not to be OK.

---

40. W. L. Holladay, *The Psalms Through Three Thousand Years* (Minneapolis: Fortress Press, 1993), p. 347.

41. J. L. Mays, *Preaching and Teaching the Psalms* (Louisville: Westminster John Knox Press, 2006), p. 3.

Summary and application

In the lament psalms I suggested that we:

1. Pay attention to the particular movement in the lament psalm between lament and praise.
2. Identify what experiences of suffering are depicted in the movement. We are not concerned here with the specific *Sitz im Leben* of the psalm, but with the shape and texture of the experience. The lament psalms, being poetry, allow for multiple applications.
3. Discern what message/s about God, the life of faith and reality in general we can derive from the depictions of sufferings.
4. Participate in the lament psalm by actually praying the words of the psalm, experiencing the movements between lament and praise yourself, and bringing your own experiences and that of others as you identify with the sufferings depicted in the psalm. Specifically, we may ask, 'What particular experiences of suffering in the lives of others or myself are similar to that expressed in the psalm?'

Here we try to apply the principles to Psalm 12, which we discussed earlier. This psalm is a good place to start because it contains verses which provide an opportunity to explain what lament is. The lament psalm is a cry 'from the depths' of suffering, uttered or addressed to God.

1. What is the movement in the lament psalm?
There is a movement in this psalm from lament (vv. 1–4) to expressions of certainty (praise) (vv. 6–7). In the middle of the psalm we find an explicit response from Yahweh, which explains the shift to the element of assurance in verses 6–7. But in spite of the divine response in the middle of the psalm, the psalm returns to lament at the end. Following the words of certainty and assurance is the statement which basically expresses the same concern that the psalmist was expressing at the beginning: 'On every side the wicked prowl. . .'

2. What experiences of suffering are depicted in the movement?
As I have mentioned, it is possible that the psalmist is suffering as a result of the wicked people's oppressive acts (vv. 1–4). But reading the overall movement in the psalm adds another dimension to his suffering: he is suffering in spite of the fact that God supposedly has already answered. Implicit is the question of the presence of wickedness in a world supposedly controlled by God. This leads us to the next question.

3. What message/s about God, the life of faith and reality in general can we derive from these experiences?

The experience of suffering reflected in Psalm 12 teaches us that there are times when the element of tension persists even with the divine response.

4. Experiencing Psalm 12

Pray the words of the psalm. Specifically, we may ask, 'What particular experiences of suffering in the lives of others or our own are similar to that expressed in the psalm?' Here we may cite, as one example, pursuing a degree. We lament our way through our studies and move to praise as we successfully complete the degree. But then the uncertainties of securing a job after the study can be so daunting that we find ourselves again back in the situation of lament.

Sermon outline on Psalm 12: 'Return to Lament'

A.   The movement in the lament: from lament to praise then back to lament
     1. From lament (vv. 1–4)
        a. Cry for help (v. 1)
           • 'Help!' (v. 1)
        b. Arising out of suffering (vv. 1–4)
           Life when there are no more godly people around:
           • Lies (v. 2)
           • Pride (v. 3)
           • Oppression (v. 4; cf. v. 5)
        c. Addressed to God
           • 'Help, O LORD!' (v. 1)
           • 'May the LORD cut off all flattering lips' (v. 3)
     2. To praise (vv. 5–7)
        a. The divine response (v. 5)
        b. Assurance resulting from the divine response (vv. 6–7)
     3. Back to lament (v. 8)
        a. The lament at the beginning: 'The godly are no more' (v. 1 NIV)
        b. The situation at the end: 'On every side the wicked prowl. . .' (v. 8)
B.   The psalmist's experience of suffering
     1. Life when there are no more godly people around (vv. 1–4)
     2. Uncertainty in spite of the divine response (v. 8)

C. The message of the psalm
   1. The life of faith: tension and ambiguity remain
   2. God: divine inscrutability
Conclusion

Bibliography

ALTER, R., *The Art of Biblical Poetry* (New York: Basic Books, 1985).

BERLIN, A., 'Introduction to Hebrew Poetry', in *NIB* 4, pp. 301–315 (Nashville: Abingdon Press, 1996).

BERLIN, A., 'Psalms and the Literature of Exile: Psalms 137, 44, 69 and 78', in P. D. Miller and P. W. Flint (eds.), *The Book of Psalms: Composition and Reception* (Leiden: Brill, 2005), pp. 65–86.

BILLMAN, K. D. and D. L. MIGLIORE, *Rachel's Cry: Prayer of Lament and Rebirth of Hope* (Eugene, OR: Wipf & Stock, 1999).

BRADBURY, P., *Sowing in Tears: How to Lament in a Church of Praise* (Cambridge: Grove, 2007).

BRUEGGEMANN, W., *The Message of the Psalms: A Theological Commentary* (Minneapolis: Augsburg, 1984).

BRUEGGEMANN, W., *The Psalms and the Life of Faith* (Minneapolis: Fortress Press, 1995).

CALVIN, J., *Commentary on the Book of Psalms*, trans. J. Anderson (Edinburgh: Edinburgh Printing Co., 1846).

CIARDI, J., *How Does a Poem Mean?* (Boston: Houghton Mifflin Company, 1959).

DORNISCH, L., 'The Book of Job and Ricoeur's Hermeneutics', *Semeia* 19 (1981), pp. 3–29.

ELLINGTON, S. A., 'The Costly Loss of Testimony', *Journal of Pentecostal Theology* 16 (2000), pp. 48–59.

GOLDINGAY, J., 'The Dynamic Cycle of Praise and Prayer', *JSOT* 20 (1981), pp. 85–90.

GOLDINGAY, J., *Psalms: Vol. 2 (Psalms 42 – 89)* (Grand Rapids: Baker Academic, 2007).

GOLDSWORTHY, G., *Preaching the Whole Bible as Christian Scripture* (Grand Rapids, MI: Eerdmans; Leicester: Inter-Varsity Press, 2000).

GUNKEL, H., *Die Psalmen*, Handkommentar zum Alten Testament (Göttingen: Vandenhoeck & Ruprecht, 1926).

HOLLADAY, W. L., *The Psalms Through Three Thousand Years* (Minneapolis: Fortress Press, 1993).

HOSSFELD, F-L. and E. ZENGER, *Psalms 2* (Minneapolis: Fortress Press, 2005).

LATHROP, G. W., 'A Rebirth of Images: On the Use of the Bible in Liturgy', *Worship* 58 (1984), pp. 291–304.

LONG, T. G., *Preaching and the Literary Forms of the Bible* (Philadelphia: Fortress Press, 1988).

LONGMAN III, T., 'Lament', in D. B. Sandy and R. L. Giese, Jr (eds.), *Cracking Old Testament Codes* (Nashville: Broadman & Holman Publishers, 1995).

MAYS, J. L., *Preaching and Teaching the Psalms* (Louisville: Westminster John Knox Press, 2006).

McCANN, J. C. and J. C. HOWELL, *Preaching the Psalms* (Nashville: Abingdon Press, 2001).

MERTON, T., *Praying the Psalms* (Collegeville, Minnesota: Liturgical Press, 1956).

PERRINE, L., *Sound and Sense: An Introduction to Poetry*, 4th ed. (New York: Harcourt, 1973).

RICOEUR, P., 'Lamentation as Prayer', in A. LaCoque and P. Ricoeur (eds.), *Thinking Biblically* (Chicago and London: University of Chicago Press, 1998), pp. 211–232.

STOCKS, S. P., *Using the Psalms for Prayer Through Suffering* (Cambridge: Grove, 2007).

VILLANUEVA, F. G., *The 'Uncertainty of a Hearing': A Study of the Sudden Change of Mood in the Psalms of Lament* (Leiden: Brill, 2008).

WILLIAMSON, H. G. M. (2003), 'Reading the Lament Psalms Backwards', in B. A. Strawn and N. R. Bowen (eds.), *A God So Near: Essays on Old Testament Theology in Honor of Patrick D. Miller* (Indiana: Eisenbrauns, 2003), pp. 3–15.

WITVLIET, J. D., *Worship Seeking Understanding* (Grand Rapids: Baker, 2003).

WRIGHT, N. T., *Simply Christian* (London: SPCK, 2006).

5. PREACHING PRAISE POETRY

David G. Firth

Introduction – praise poetry and worship

If the use of texts in worship resources is any guide, then the OT's praise poetry, understood specifically as poems which offer praise to God (as opposed to the praise of others such as we find in the Song of Songs), ought to be a pulpit staple. The most obvious examples of such poetry occur in the Psalms, though it occurs at a number of other points and these texts may also provide assistance in preaching psalms of praise. A glance at the Scripture index in several contemporary hymn books (including contemporary collections which are less structured than traditional hymn books) indicates that these are texts which are widely deployed. To take a representative example, the index in *Baptist Praise and Worship*[1] lists seventy-one direct references to the Psalms as opposed to only forty for the rest of the OT. The only biblical book to approach this is Luke's Gospel with sixty-five references, followed by Matthew with forty-five. However, Advent, Christmas and Easter account for the bulk of these, while the majority of references to Mark and John are also weighted towards Easter. Roughly half of all biblical references are to

---

1. Alec Gilmore, et al. (eds.), *Baptist Praise and Worship* (Oxford: Oxford University Press, on behalf of the Psalms and Hymns Trust, 1991), p. 1064.

either Psalms or one of the Gospels, although the clustering of Gospel references means that references to the Psalter are more widely distributed, so congregations are likely to encounter them across the year. Congregations will not necessarily recognize every biblical reference they encounter, but it does suggest that those composing songs for worship are particularly conscious of the Psalms.

It might be objected that even though most praise poetry is found in Psalms, most psalms are not what we now call praise. One need not be captive to the search for ideal forms that dominated much of the twentieth century, but it still provides a reasonable model for describing the contents of the various psalms. By most analyses, about half of all psalms can be classified as complaints. Allowing for the other types identified by critics, praise is not therefore the dominant voice. We need to offset this with the observation that the Hebrew title of Psalms (*Tehellim*) means 'praises', so the category of praise is made somewhat wider, but it remains the case that more psalms are focused on complaint than on praise. However, we should note that the individual complaints normally end with a vow of praise, with Psalms 88 and 143 the notable exceptions, and that even in the midst of complaint, psalmists sometimes make an observation expressing the praise of God (e.g. Ps. 35:9–10).

Even allowing for this, the contemporary preponderance of praise poetry is remarkable. Only two of these seventy-one references to the Psalms are not taken either from a praise psalm or from the few verses within complaint psalms which anticipate the giving of praise. The two references to other passages (Pss 55:1–2; 61:1) are both addresses to God at the beginning of prayers. Of these hymns, only Seddon's 'Listen to My Prayer, Lord' actually takes up the content of the complaint (from Ps. 61) in the balance of the song. To the extent that this is representative, it strongly suggests that praise poetry (especially from the Psalms) is constitutive of contemporary worship, and that the distribution of such songs across the church calendar means these texts will be encountered on a regular basis.[2] Churches which employ the various lectionaries will encounter more psalms. But, to take the *Revised Common Lectionary* as an example, although many psalms are employed, they are often abridged so that the note of praise is more prominent than it might be if the

---

2. John D. Witvliet, *The Biblical Psalms in Christian Worship: A Brief Introduction and Guide to Resources* (Grand Rapids: Eerdmans, 2007), pp. 116–120, notes that more than 3,500 songs based on Psalms have been registered with CCLI, the licensing source for many churches, and that these form the core of musical worship in many seeker-sensitive and charismatic churches.

Psalter were simply read through. In short, praise poetry is a well-represented element of contemporary Christian worship. We might therefore expect praise poetry to be a staple of contemporary preaching. Our prayer, whether liturgically formalized or in the freer expression of contemporary song, draws on such praise and inevitably shapes belief. Yet, although one may suspect that such practices in worship do shape much contemporary belief, it would not seem that praise psalms constitute a significant portion of texts employed in preaching.[3] It falls beyond the scope of this paper to explore the reasons for this, but the position argued here is that a proper understanding of how praise poetry functions within the OT as a whole will open up possibilities for proclamation.

The canon, praise and proclamation

It may not be possible to explain why pastors do not often preach praise poetry, but it may be that the exegetical models typically taught have worked against this. In particular, attention to the dominant critical approach has rightly highlighted that most psalms, and all the praise psalms, are human words addressed to God. In preaching we seek to bring God's word to his people, but we are therefore confronted with a dilemma. If preaching, and here we specifically mean expository preaching, is making clear God's word, then do we not subvert the fundamental purpose for which these psalms were written? Taking seriously the function of the psalms as human words to God, and that we are able to employ them so widely in other parts of worship, Gowan therefore suggests that 'the integrity of the psalmists' words addressed to God in praise or lamentation ought to be preserved and that ordinarily they ought not to be considered as texts to be expounded to a congregation'.[4] The problem, how the psalms as human words to God became God's word to us, is thus resolved in the negative. Attention to their origin shows that they were always human words, and critics like Gowan could not therefore treat them in any other way. Since most introductions to the Psalms continue to be structured along this model, it is not surprising that those called to preach lack the tools to preach Psalms with confidence.

---

3. Similarly, J. Clinton McCann and James C. Howell, *Preaching the Psalms* (Nashville: Abingdon, 2001), p. 15.

4. Donald E. Gowan, *Reclaiming the Old Testament for the Christian Pulpit* (Edinburgh: T. & T. Clark, 1980), p. 146.

However, the developing interest in the function of the canon provides an opportunity for preachers. The Psalms are a point where Brevard Childs's insistence on the importance of attention to the canon has been particularly significant,[5] and this insight has been helpfully developed by a number of scholars since then.[6] Fundamentally, although there are a range of approaches which call themselves 'canonical', they are united by their emphasis upon the intentional formation of the Psalter and the conclusion that it has been shaped with an instructional purpose. Hence, the various praise poems we possess within the Psalter are not there simply because they reflect someone's words to God. They are recorded because they also instruct those who read the Psalter in some way about the life of faith, and in particular about the nature of the God whom we praise. Many have also argued that this shaping of the book includes the placement of the various psalms in relationship to one another, but this remains a controversial area in Psalms research, and since significant exegetical resources that follow this approach have not yet emerged to assist pastors, it is excluded from this discussion. A similar perspective can be developed concerning the other praise poems that are scattered across the OT (e.g. Exod. 15:1–18, 21; 1 Sam. 2:1–10; 2 Sam. 22). Although they are presented as the words of the character concerned, they are presented precisely because they contribute in some way to the message of the book. The canonical process has rendered these poems as God's word to us, albeit a word where we need to take seriously their origin as human words to God, but therefore as texts needing to be preached.

Praise as instruction

Preaching praise poetry will thus take seriously both the fact that these are texts offered to God and that through the canonical process they are also God's word to us. Hence, we cannot ignore the critical insights developed through the twentieth century precisely because this has explored one side of this equation. As we shall see, this means that we cannot treat praise as an all-encompassing category, but rather as a label for several different groups

---

5. Brevard S. Childs, *Introduction to the Old Testament as Scripture* (London: SCM Press, 1979), pp. 504–525.

6. See David G. Firth, 'The Teaching of the Psalms', in Philip S. Johnston and David G. Firth (eds.), *Interpreting the Psalms: Issues and Approaches* (Leicester: Apollos, 2005), pp. 159–161.

of poems which reflect different life settings. However, in considering these insights we also need to consider the insights of those who have studied the canonical process and understand that the insights that came from recognizing the standard forms employed with the Psalter are now more a guide to the instructional function of the various poems in the finished text than a definitive guide to their origins.[7] That is, where the various classifications were typically used as a tool for reconstructing the life setting in which a given poem originated, we can now see this insight as offering instruction for those who read these texts, who see in them a reflection of their own experience. Given that the compilers of Scripture had access to a wider range of poems than we now possess, we can assume that these were chosen because they offered prayers that were appropriate for others to adopt and that therefore instruct others on how to pray to and, more specifically, praise God.[8] To take an example from the complaint poems, critics have recognized that several psalms probably arose in the context of those who were accused of various acts and who sought their vindication from God.[9] A canonical approach takes this seriously, but also notes that these are now offered as both an exemplary resource for prayer for all who suffer something similar and also as instruction through practice of how one is to pray in such circumstances. Indeed, it is because these poems have been transmitted without rubrics as to their use that the possibility of their wider application is opened up. Preachers who note this can take seriously both these poem's origins and also the way they continue to instruct. Awareness of the poetic forms available thus permits the analysis of their abiding function, and it is this that guides us in proclamation.

It might be noted that praise poetry is seldom intentionally didactic, meaning preachers might be tempted to read something into the text in order to have something to preach. This is especially the case if we imagine that preaching always requires three points which develop a central theme. In such a model, the sermon is essentially an argument for a proposition. It is possible to preach some psalms in this way (especially the so-called 'wisdom psalms'

---

7. On the idea of psalm type as a guide to function, see David G. Firth, *Surrendering Retribution in the Psalms: Responses to Violence in the Individual Complaints* (Milton Keynes: Paternoster, 2005), p. 143.

8. The processes by which this might happen are outlined in David G. Firth, *Hear, O Lord: A Spirituality of the Psalms* (Calver: Cliff College Publishing, 2005), pp. 123–129.

9. Psalms 7 and 17 are representative examples.

like Pss 1, 37), but for most we need to develop a more indirect model of instruction that follows the pattern of the poems themselves. In effect, this means taking into account both the poem's origin and its function within the canon. As preachers, we need to let our congregations hear these poems as words of praise offered by individuals or the community to God, but also to appreciate that their inclusion in the canon means that they offer an indirect form of instruction, either through thematic modelling on different aspects of praise or through the intratextual dialogue they create with other poems, a feature especially important in preaching psalms.[10] As preachers we therefore need to let these poems work in an indirect way, though at the same time we need to guide our congregations on how they might begin to make their own connections from these poems.

One additional element needs to be introduced at this point, because we have so far treated 'praise' as a general category. But taking seriously the insights of criticism means we must recognize that 'praise' covers several rather different types of poetry. To stay for the moment with Gunkel's classifications, there is an important distinction between hymns which offer fairly generalized praise of God and thanksgivings which respond to a point where God has acted for his people. This division was helpfully analysed by Westermann, who distinguished between descriptive and declarative praise.[11] Where descriptive praise tends to look at Yahweh's general nature as Creator, Redeemer and so on (thus matching Gunkel's hymns), declarative praise recounts a narrative of how Yahweh has wrought deliverance for a worshipper who now gives thanks (thus matching Gunkel's thanksgiving). Westermann's key insight is that declarative praise forms the link between praise and lament (or complaint) in that these psalms offer thanks for deliverance from situations which largely conform to those brought in petition in the complaint psalms. As we shall note, this is an important element to note within the intratextual dialogue created within Psalms.

This has been taken further by Walter Brueggemann, who has argued that the whole of the Psalter can be organized into the pattern of orientation, disorientation and reorientation.[12] Where Westermann demonstrated the

---

10. On these elements, see Firth, 'The Teaching of the Psalms', pp. 171–174.

11. Claus Westermann, *Praise and Lament in the Psalms* (Atlanta: John Knox Press, 1981), pp. 30–33; *The Psalms: Structure, Content and Message* (Minneapolis: Augsburg, 1980), pp. 25–27.

12. Walter Brueggemann, *The Message of the Psalms: A Theological Commentary* (Minneapolis: Augsburg, 1984), pp. 18–23.

possibility of a dialogue within the Psalter between the complaints and his declarative praise, Brueggemann goes further since his proposal allows that the complaints (disorientation in Brueggemann's scheme) may themselves engage in a dialogue with (among others) the psalms of descriptive praise. Westermann's descriptive praise largely matches Brueggemann's orientation, since these psalms set in place for us a pattern through which we are to view the world, a pattern in which the power and presence of God is affirmed. Likewise, Brueggemann's new orientation is largely Westermann's declarative praise, since these poems express the poet's wonder in the discovery of how Yahweh has been at work. The orientation is affirmed, but it cannot be held without some critical awareness.

Brueggemann is aware that the structure he suggests can be employed in a simplistic manner, and is careful to suggest that there is a constant movement between these states, but for our purposes the interesting point is the way this opens up the dialogue within the Psalter. But there is an important limitation to Brueggemann's analysis, and that is that it excludes any eschatological element. Yet if we are to take seriously the theme of the reign of God as something central to the Psalter,[13] then it is essential to recognize that the closed loop Brueggemann's proposal could presume needs to be expanded to allow for prayer and praise that moves beyond the point of new orientation. It can be argued that this comes out of his decision to exclude the royal psalms and Songs of Zion from his analysis because they did not seem helpful to his programme,[14] and yet it is these psalms which point beyond the cycle he suggests. In the case of the royal psalms, this is largely a function of their canonical function in a book which no longer has a king in Jerusalem as a point of reference, so that prayer and praise concerning the king inevitably takes on an eschatological, and specifically messianic, focus.[15] We thus need to allow for the possibility of hope beyond orientation,[16] for praise which anticipates what God will do beyond our own experience. It

13. James L. Mays, *The Lord Reigns: A Theological Handbook to the Psalms* (Louisville: Westminster John Knox Press, 1994), pp. 12–22.

14. Brueggemann, *The Message of the Psalms*, p. 10.

15. On the royal psalms, see Jamie A. Grant, 'The Psalms and the King', in Johnston and Firth (eds.), *Interpreting the Psalms*, pp. 101–118. Grant demonstrates that these psalms are much more than messianic, since there is also a process of democratization, but the messianic element is central to the function of these poems to point beyond themselves.

16. See Firth, *Hear, O Lord*, pp. 101–122.

is at this point that an explicitly Christian reading of these poems becomes possible, since the eschatological hope of the Psalter finds its focus in Jesus, although at the same time it is still rooted in the way these poems relate to other psalms.

As we have noted, praise poetry is not restricted to the Psalms, and some narrative contexts help us to see how this process might function outside the Psalter. A good example can be seen in the Song of Hannah (1 Sam. 2:1–10). As has been noted, Hannah's situation with her family reflects the world found in the complaint psalms.[17] Hannah suffers from a loving but condescending husband and from a second wife who is happy to vex her because Yahweh had closed Hannah's womb and she had children (1 Sam. 1:6). The complaint psalms can note the vexatious behaviour of adversaries (e.g. Pss 6:8; 10:14), although of course adversaries are problematic in a range of ways, but the point to note is that Hannah's experience is typical of this situation. Indeed, Psalm 10:14 occurs in a context where the psalmist petitions Yahweh to act against the vexatious and is perhaps representative of the type of prayer Hannah might have uttered in the sanctuary at Shiloh. Certainly, Hannah prays out of her deep distress (1 Sam. 1:10), something not helped by Eli's inability to distinguish between passionate prayer and drunkenness (1 Sam. 1:13). Hannah's experience is one of disorder, of complaint. But at the same time it is clear that she prays precisely because she accepts the fundamental instruction offered by texts which conform to Westermann's descriptive praise. Psalm 97, for example, not only offers descriptive praise to Yahweh, it insists that he preserves the life of his saints (Ps. 97:10), which is what Hannah seeks through children. That is, the possibility of Hannah's complaint arises precisely because the justice of Yahweh that texts such as this celebrate did not appear to be manifest in her experience. In Brueggemann's terms, her prayer is one of disorientation, and this can only arise where the basic orientation appears not to function. A number of psalms are thus prepared to see God as the problem (e.g. Pss 44, 88) and so complain against him, even as they also see God as the solution to the current difficulty, and Hannah's prayer is typical of these texts.

Hannah's situation, however, does not remain one of childlessness. The story celebrates that Yahweh remembered her and so she conceived and gave birth to Samuel (1 Sam. 1:19–20). Hannah's Song (1 Sam. 2:1–10) is thus set at the point where, in fulfilment of her vow, she has delivered Samuel to the

---

17. A. H. van Zyl, '1 Sam. 1:2 – 2:11 – A Life World of Lament and Affliction', *JNSL* 12 (1984), pp. 151–161.

sanctuary where he is to grow up, but also at the point where she has come to see Yahweh acting in a new way. The prayer of praise she offers arises from a new discovery of how Yahweh acts in her life, one which can affirm the goodness of his action even if it is tinged with the sorrow of having delivered her son to the sanctuary. Hannah's Song fulfils several functions within the books of Samuel,[18] but one of those is to reflect on Hannah's experience as one who has discovered how Yahweh has been at work, especially in the motif of the reversal of fortunes where the powerful are brought down and the weak raised up. The Song generates a dialogue with the preceding narrative which itself generates a dialogue with a range of other biblical texts. But Hannah's Song also includes an eschatological edge, both because the reversal of fortunes motif it develops is never fully worked out in present experience and also because the Song raises the question of a king (1 Sam. 2:10), even though no king is yet present. The identity of that king within Samuel is ultimately David, but since this directs us to the promise to David in 2 Samuel 7:1–17, it also points beyond David to a messianic hope. It is no surprise, therefore, that Mary's Magnificat (Luke 1:46–55) draws so heavily on Hannah's Song as it recognizes both the fulfilment of Hannah's Song in her own experience and that of David while also anticipating something greater. The narrative frame thus encourages us to read this praise poem from a number of perspectives, each of which contributes something different and could legitimately be preached to a contemporary congregation.

Hannah's story in many ways matches the sort of textual dialogue we have suggested functions in the Psalms, as well as pointing to the possibilities that such a dialogue opens up for preachers to approach her thanksgiving song from a range of different angles. We could legitimately preach it as a thanksgiving song on its own, as a thanksgiving which reflects back on Hannah's experience, as a thanksgiving which anticipates the main themes of the books of Samuel, or as a thanksgiving with eschatological (and ultimately Christological) themes. All are valid approaches to the proclamation of this praise song and each engages with the surrounding narrative in different ways, although preachers would probably be unwise to attempt them all at once. Although comparatively few psalms offer so many options, such a narrative is implied by many praise psalms, opening up ways in which they too may be preached. Awareness of how these texts interact with one another can also address Brueggemann's concern that sometimes the summons to praise overcomes content so that praise is offered without reason, effectively making praise an ideology of its

---

18. See David G. Firth, *1 & 2 Samuel* (Nottingham: Apollos, 2009), pp. 59–63.

own.[19] It is true that some poems (such as Ps. 150) offer only the summons to praise, not a reasoned basis for praise in its own right that a congregation can adopt, but the summons is not praise, and in the particular case of Psalm 150 it is a summons that comes out of reflection on the whole of the Psalter. The content of the praise summoned there is that which the rest of the book has outlined, praise that reflects on a God whose value can both be described and declared. Indeed, by ending with a summons to praise, the Psalter directs us once again to reflect on the poems that preceded it. Again, it is the interplay between understanding poetic form and canonical function that allows us to see how the poem instructs and thus forms the basis for our preaching. Since the relationships for praise poems outside the Psalter are determined by their own specific textual relationships, we will focus on Psalms for the balance of this chapter.

Thematic modelling

We have suggested that praise poetry tends to offer instruction through either thematic modelling or intratextual dialogue, although in practice most psalms can be approached through both. Thematic modelling occurs where various psalms can be shown to offer a consistent response to a situation, so that even if these individual texts did not have this intention at the compositional level it emerges through the consistent emphasis within the Psalter. It is a form of teaching which emerges through exposure to the book as a whole so that its cadences become the pattern for our own prayer and praise. Such a model of instruction also implies that the editorial process that arranged the book of Psalms was able to exclude poems which for some reason did not conform to these patterns.

As a model for preaching, thematic modelling is particularly well suited to descriptive praise. The reason for this is that these psalms offer praise which is intended to shape our fundamental attitudes to God. We need to know that Yahweh is Creator, Redeemer and Sustainer, a just God who can be depended upon to intervene for his people even though specific instances will usually be lacking in these particular psalms. As a people we are shaped by how these poems offer praise that is instructive through its repetition of themes which become the pattern that we follow. Preachers attentive to thematic modelling

---

19. Walter Brueggemann, *Israel's Praise: Doxology against Idolatry* (Philadelphia: Fortress Press, 1988), pp. 89–122.

might consider treating some of these poems on their own, but it would also be legitimate to bring together several psalms that offer insight into a particular theme.

For example, several psalms offer praise to Yahweh as Creator. Examples of this include Psalms 8, 19, 104 and 148, although creation themes occur more widely than this, indicating that themes developed by the Psalter are related to one another. But if we take these psalms as our examples, we can note that the theme of creation is employed for a very specific purpose, a purpose which also relates to the complaint psalms. Creation is not a doctrine that is discussed in terms of the identity of the creator deity. Most people in the ancient world were happy that their gods created the world, and Israel is consistent with this. But even though it might be tempting to treat creation as an opportunity for polemic with other faiths, this is a relatively limited theme in Psalms. It does occur in Psalm 115:4–8, but although this psalm draws on creation themes (115:16), the polemic against the idols of the nations is primarily in terms of redemption. Only Yahweh, not the gods of the nations, can save. Rather than as polemic, the Psalter presents creation as a theme which evokes praise. But it is, crucially, praise which itself instructs about how to view our world and how it leads us back to God.

Hence, although each of these psalms might be treated on their own, preachers could work through them in a series, because although they are bound by their common theme (that the nature of creation leads to praise), each emphasizes something distinct about that praise. Psalm 8 appears largely to be a meditation on Genesis 1, a reflection on the extraordinary responsibility of what it means to be human within this world so that our common humanity directs us back to the praise of God. Psalm 19, by contrast, focuses on creation as a source of revelation declaring God's glory, although in doing so it places this alongside the more specific revelation of Yahweh through the Torah, so that although creation evokes praise, when taken with the Torah it leads to a reassessment of the importance of us humans being shaped by the knowledge of God. Psalm 104, while also seeing creation as a basis for praise, does so by noting how Yahweh continues to act within creation for the whole of creation. Like Psalm 19, this is applied to those who offer such praise so that each is invited to ensure that their meditations are pleasing to God (104:34), even though it views creation from a very different perspective from Psalm 19. It is thus notable that while each of these psalms praises God for creation, each focuses on a different aspect of creation, but always applies this to the question of human identity before God. Finally, Psalm 148 also praises God, although it would be more true to say that it is largely a summons to praise that is focused on creation, addressing the question of which parts of creation should praise God. Because it is largely summons, it is much more difficult to preach this psalm on its own, although it does offer some limited bases for this praise. The notable element of this psalm is that it is not only the attractive elements of creation that are summoned to give praise. In verses 7–8 we see fire, hail, snow, mist, storms and even the great sea creatures praising God. From the perspective of a subsistence society, these are hardly the elements of creation that we might think should evoke praise, but they do. Psalm 148 thus addresses the theme in a way that critiques the approach to creation that celebrates only mountain tops and lakes, forests and stunning beaches. The harsh landscape of the desert or the terrors of the scorpion also have their part to play in evoking praise. Attention to how the theme is developed points to the way the Psalter instructs. It can thus allow preachers to develop the focus on any individual praise psalm more closely, or to develop the theme overall in a more topical way.

Intratextual dialogue

Where thematic modelling is an approach that is particularly well suited to descriptive praise, intratextual dialogue is more appropriate to declarative praise. The reason for this lies in the fact that declarative praise is linked to the complaint psalms, although, as Brueggemann's model shows, these are in turn linked back to the psalms of descriptive praise. In essence, declarative praise presumes that the psalmist has passed through an experience typical of those we find in the complaint psalms, much as we saw laid out in Hannah's experience in Samuel. In declarative praise, the psalmists are able to testify that the reasons for trusting God that are so central to descriptive praise have been vindicated, although not in any simplistic way. That is, the central affirmations of God's goodness and care are shown to be true, but not in a way that excludes pain and suffering on the part of the psalmists. The psalmists thus give thanks for moments where God's goodness has been found to be true in the midst of pain, so that the teaching model employed invites readers to consider the themes developed in relationship to other poems which approach the relevant themes from different perspectives. This is true both of individual and communal thanksgiving. It is important to stress that the Psalter does not believe that every situation of distress is fully resolved, so that an eschatological element remains.

We can take Psalm 32 as an example of declarative praise. In it, the psalmist begins by pointing to the joy that is found in the discovery of forgiveness by God. As is typical of such psalms, the psalmist employs personal testimony as the mode of instruction with the psalmist variously speaking directly to God and at other times admonishing the community. The result of this is that the testimony itself emerges as instruction that is applied to the life of those who read it. In Psalm 32, this becomes apparent in verse 6, where the psalmist admonishes the community to offer prayer in the certain hope of God hearing, then again in verses 8 and 11 which warn the community against resisting this instruction and also to rejoice in Yahweh themselves. Other psalms are less directive – Psalm 73, for example, is cast almost entirely as a testimony given to God, although the comment about those who are far from God in verse 27 functions both as an assured point of faith offered to God and at the same time as a warning to those who hear this testimony. However, Psalm 32's mixture of testimony and admonition is far more typical. That the testimony to God's goodness is applied means that preachers already have a direct line of application they can develop.

Nevertheless, one can explore the message of Psalm 32 in a richer way by exploring the dialogue it creates with other psalms. An obvious example of this is that the psalm's opening is evocative of Psalm 1. We cannot know that Psalm 32 was deliberately composed to address Psalm 1, but within the current form of the Psalter we can now interpret this psalmist's understanding of blessing through Psalm 1 since they both open with a benediction. But where Psalm 1 does not consider the possibility of the righteous going off the path of righteousness, Psalm 32 testifies to the possibility of forgiveness for those who do, provided they have acknowledged their sin. The dialogue with Psalm 1 thus opens up possibilities for the preacher to explore the nature of the blessed life.

Another dialogue can be developed with other psalms dealing with the possibility of forgiveness. Here, Psalms 103 and 51 would be relevant. Psalm 103 has noted that Yahweh 'forgives all your iniquity' (103:3, ESV), removing our transgressions as far as 'the east is from the west' (103:12). This, of course, is declarative praise. It affirms what Yahweh does, but gives no specific examples, and neither does it say anything about how forgiveness is to be obtained. It offers something about Yahweh's character which is a basis for praise, but without telling us how any of this is accessed. Psalm 51, by contrast, is the clearest example of individual penitential prayer in the Psalter. Here, the psalmist petitions Yahweh for forgiveness, not on the basis of sacrifices (a further dialogue here might consider the place of sacrifices through texts like Ps. 40:6–8), but on the basis of his grace. Combined with a range of words describing Yahweh's mercy, the psalmist also employs the principal words for sin (Ps. 51:1–2), a combination repeated only in Psalm 32:1–2. Moreover, where Psalm 51:13–15 promises that if restored the poet will teach transgressors to return to Yahweh, so Psalm 32:6–11 does exactly this.

Attention to this dialogue can provide preachers with a richer understanding of forgiveness, highlighting why it is important that the psalmist's testimony is already applied in Psalm 32. God can be praised as one who forgives, but, as becomes clear, forgiveness is an act of divine mercy and the measure of the experience of true forgiveness is a passion to declare its possibility to others. This dialogue also leads to a richer understanding of Psalm 51, because it affirms that Yahweh does indeed forgive, while taken together these two psalms affirm that the claims of Psalm 103 can be grounded in actual experience, showing how forgiveness might be both affected and experienced. Although preachers could reasonably explore this intratextual dialogue on its own, such a dialogue also opens the way to point to the forgiveness that is available in Jesus, a connection that arises quite naturally from this. By exploring this dialogue within the Psalter, preachers can also encourage congregations to see that praise is itself reflective, and that by considering praise in light of other circumstances we might learn not only from the act of praise, but also from its content. At the same time, through reflecting on the nature of this dialogue, we can also create natural links to the gospel which open the way for a specifically Christian understanding of praise.

Attention to such dialogues might suggest that issues are always resolved within the Psalter, but, as we have noted, there remains an eschatological edge to the Psalter as a whole and to its praise in particular. Staying only with the issue of forgiveness, we can note that Psalm 85 accepts that Yahweh has forgiven his people (vv. 1–3), but it also acknowledges that forgiveness in one circumstance does not mean that God's people cannot place themselves once more under his judgment for sin, so that forgiveness and restoration are once again sought (vv. 4–7). Thus, when this psalm offers praise for Yahweh's righteousness (vv. 8–13), it does so from the perspective of knowing that forgiveness can be received, but also that more is needed. There is not yet any sense of forgiveness as something that is complete. A psalm like this leaves open the eschatological need of the people, looking forward to the time when God will act decisively for his people. Such a prayer again leads to reflection on the forgiveness God offers in Christ, although if we take seriously the 'now but not yet' dimension of the kingdom of God, we will recognize that such a hope is both found in Christ now and will be found in Christ in the future. We need to avoid making facile connections to Christ, but also to acknowledge that the eschatological edge found in the Psalter also points us to him.

Conclusion

Although the evidence suggests that poems of praise are more often used as an element of sung worship rather than as the content of the sermon, these poems actually provide texts for preaching that enable the congregation both to join the experience of praise and also to learn from it. In doing so, preachers need to allow the less direct teaching model of such poems to operate. Praise does not teach in a set of points that can be subsumed under a central heading. Rather, praise instructs because it invites us to make this praise our own. In doing so, we need to hear the psalm on its own terms (and thus draw on the dominant critical insights of the last century) and also as part of a wider body of literature (and thus draw on the insights of those interested in canonical form). This might be through consideration of its narrative context, although in the case of particular psalms it will be through their relationship to the rest of the Psalter. Preachers still need to note the different models of instruction offered, but if they do they will discover a rich fare to place before their congregations.

Sermon outline on Psalm 99

Introduction

Psalm 99 is a poem of descriptive praise, extolling the reign of God. In doing so, it focuses on the paradox of God's holiness. This paradox is that God is utterly removed from us and yet utterly present with us, and it is this that summons our worship. It is a text best approached through thematic modelling, especially through a study of the theme of the reign of God developed in Psalms 93, 94 and 97.

1. *A summons to worship* (Ps. 99:1–3): Yahweh's holiness is not abstract, but is experienced because he is King, not only in Zion but over all peoples, summoning all to praise. Christians can note how this is developed through the theme of the kingdom of God, both through a comparison with the other psalms mentioned, but also through Jesus' proclamation of the kingdom.

2. *A worker of justice* (Ps. 99:4–5): Yahweh's holiness is applied through justice. This is not hypothetical, but something Israel has actually experienced. The holy God works to bring justice in the world, and this too summons praise.

3. *An interacting God* (Ps. 99:6–9): Yahweh's holiness leads him to interact with his people, seen in the examples of Moses, Aaron and Samuel (probably because each was associated with the ark). More than that, the holy God is also a forgiving God. The one who is unutterably holy interacts with his people to forgive, and this too summons worship.

Conclusion

The holiness of God is a summons to worship, because this holy God continues to work among all peoples to establish justice and to bring forgiveness. No clearer example of this is available than the cross.

Sermon outline on Psalm 66

Introduction

Psalm 66 is a poem of declarative praise, a response to the works of God. Where Psalm 46 had summoned all to come and see the works of God without referring to the possibility of suffering, Psalm 66 makes a similar invitation from the perspective of those who have suffered. It is a text best approached through intratextual dialogue, for which Psalms 7 and 46 are particularly helpful.

1. *An invitation to praise and see* (Ps. 66:1–7): All are summoned to praise God because of what he has done, although the basis for this praise is rooted more in the great saving acts of the past (vv. 6–7). Christians can extend this to include the cross and resurrection.
2. *Reasons for blessing God* (Ps. 66:8–12): The psalm now provides reason why all should bless God, moving from the great salvation story of the opening verses to more specific circumstances here. Thus God's actions are not restricted to the past, but are part of the continuing life of believers.
3. *A vow of worship* (Ps. 66:13–20): Just as Psalm 51 had vowed to instruct sinners, so this psalmist promises both to come into the sanctuary and fulfil vows and also to instruct sinners. Thus we move from what God has done for the nation to what he has done for an individual, placing the individual's testimony within the great salvation story. And this story also instructs those who hear it. In this case, the forgiveness referred to probably alludes to those psalms prayed by those accused of crimes (e.g. Ps. 7), but it thus shows that God's care reaches all.

Conclusion

Thus the whole world can bless God as one who brings salvation for all, who continues to work for all, and whose care reaches to all. Blessed be God!

Suggested further reading

McCann, J. Clinton and James C. Howell, *Preaching the Psalms* (Nashville: Abingdon Press, 2001).

Mays, James L., *Preaching and Teaching the Psalms* (Louisville: Westminster John Knox, 2006).

Wallace, Howard Neil, *Words to God, Words from God: The Psalms in the Prayer and Preaching of the Church* (Aldershot: Ashgate, 2005).

6. PREACHING WISDOM

Tremper Longman III

Wisdom literature is a neglected portion of the OT at least as far as biblical theology is concerned. The three books that compose the wisdom literature of the OT – Proverbs, Job and Ecclesiastes – have a tangential relationship with the redemptive history and such important theological concepts as covenant, law and cult, raising the question of how they fit into the rest of the canon.

On the other hand, the relevance of these three books is immediately apparent not just for their ancient context, but for modern congregations as well. Proverbs imparts wisdom for living life well. Ecclesiastes grapples with the perennial question of the meaning or purpose of life. Job struggles with the question of justice. Why do righteous people suffer and evil people prosper?

Even so, preaching from these books is not an easy task. Each book raises its own distinct questions. Does Proverbs promise too much when it seems to say that the wise person will thrive while the fool will languish? Is the book devoid of theology, only imparting practical advice? Is life's 'meaninglessness' the final word in Ecclesiastes? Is the best it has to offer *carpe diem*? What is the relationship between the positive admonition to fear God, obey the commandments and expect the coming judgment (12:13–14) and the rest of the book that comes up so empty in terms of a positive assessment of life and even of God? How might one preach Job with all its competing voices clamouring to give an opinion on Job's predicament? Does Job really say anything helpful about suffering?[1]

Finally, for those who take Jesus' words in Luke 24:25–27, 44–48 as indicating that the whole OT (the Law of Moses, Prophets and Psalms [as the first book of the Writings]) anticipates his coming, how do Proverbs, Ecclesiastes and Job connect to the gospel?

The following essay considers these questions by examining the three books one by one.

Preaching from the book of Proverbs

Proverbs presents unique challenges to the preacher, some that are in keeping with wisdom literature in general and others that are unique to this particular book.

Understanding the structure and genres of Proverbs

The macro-structure of the book of Proverbs has two parts. Discourses or speeches, typically of a father to his son (i.e. 1:8–19) and occasionally by Woman Wisdom to all the young men, compose the first nine chapters. These speeches, perhaps seventeen in number, typically have a call to listen before presenting advice and encouraging obedience by the description of benefits as well as negative consequences for neglecting the advice.

The second part of the book contains proverbs *per se*. Proverbs are short, pithy admonitions, observations or prohibitions. They are typically two lines, but can be longer. Indeed, on occasion there are much longer passages, most notably the poem concerning the virtuous woman (31:10–22).

For the purposes of this study, it is most important to note the macro-structure of the book (discourses [1 – 9] and proverbs [10 – 31]), because it will bear on our understanding of the theology of the book, which is critical for its proper preaching.

Understanding the addressee

In order to understand the proper application of a text, the preacher must be aware of the original audience. Most biblical authors have a contemporary audience in mind. In the case of Proverbs, we take note of the frequent address of a father to his son, particularly in chapters 1 – 9.

---

1. D. B. Burrell, *Deconstructing Theodicy: Why Job Has Nothing to Say to the Puzzle of Suffering* (Grand Rapids: Brazos Press, 2008).

Above, we mentioned the typical dynamic of the discourses in the first nine chapters. Most are speeches of a father to his son or sons (see 1:8–19). Others (1:20–33; ch. 8; 9:1–6, 13–18) contain the words of Woman Wisdom (or Folly) to all the men near her. The addressees of the discourses are clearly male. The proverbs in the second part of the book do not name the addressee explicitly. However, often the content discloses that again a young male is explicitly in mind. The warnings, encouragements and observations are shaped towards men, as the following examples indicate:

> The one who finds a wife finds a good thing,
> and he obtains favor from Yahweh.
> (18:22)

> The constant dripping on a day of heavy rain
> is similar to a contentious wife.
> (27:15)[2]

At first blush, we might conclude that Proverbs is only meant for a young male audience, which of course would make it difficult to preach. Indeed, some feminist scholars find Proverbs a very difficult book to appreciate in spite of the fact that it uses a female figure to represent God's wisdom.[3] Before coming to the conclusion that the book was only meant for men in its original setting, we must examine the preface to the book. Proverbs 1:2–7 serves as a preface, which introduces the audience. As we might expect, we do find there references to the 'simple' and the 'young', but no explicit gender marker. Even more remarkable, the preface instructs the reader that even the 'wise' can benefit from the teaching of the book (1:5). So even though a young male ('my son') is the addressee of the book, the preface broadens the audience to include, in my estimation, the entire covenant community. While, for instance, large portions of Proverbs warn about predator women (see particularly chs. 5 – 7), the preacher then must be careful not to restrict the teaching of the book to males only. Indeed, in a modern context, it is arguably more urgent to warn women about predator males than men about predator women (as is done in Prov. 5 – 7).

---

2. Translations from Proverbs are taken from T. Longman III, *Proverbs*, BCOTWP (Grand Rapids: Baker, 2006).
3. C. R. Fontaine, *Smooth Words: Women, Proverbs and Performance in Biblical Wisdom* (Sheffield Academic Press, 2002).

The reader and the preacher need to be sensitive about the application of a proverb like 27:15 cited above. Proverbs does not believe that the cause of problems in a household is only restricted to contentious women. There are plenty of contentious men as well, and women need to be equally warned about them.

Of course, Proverbs is really no different from any other biblical book. The interpreter/preacher must be aware of the original audience as he or she thinks through how a text might be appropriately applied to a new and different audience.

Practical advice from the book of Proverbs

Proverbs is best known for its good practical advice. The preface of the book states that its purpose is 'to teach people wisdom and discipline' (1:2 NLT).

What is wisdom? We begin by acknowledging that wisdom is a skill of living. A wise person knows how to say the right thing at the right time and do the right act at an opportune moment. Timing is everything when it comes to skilful living. Even something as seemingly positive as a warm greeting can have a negative effect if uttered at the wrong time:

A loud and cheerful greeting early in the morning
will be taken as a curse!
(27:14 NLT)

The principle of saying the right thing at the right time (15:23) extends to every statement we make.

If timing is everything, then just memorizing proverbs is not good enough. Indeed, proverbs in the hand of a fool are useless or even dangerous (26:7, 9). Since proverbs are not necessarily true in all situations, the wise person needs to cultivate the ability to read circumstances and other people. It will only be then that the sage knows whether, say, to answer or not answer 'a fool according to his folly' (see Prov. 26:4–5 NIV).

The preacher can help his congregation by taking the role of the father (without condescension), addressing his son and explaining the rich practical instruction that the book of Proverbs offers. Proverbial wisdom is much like what is today called 'emotional intelligence'.[4] Studies of emotional intelligence

---

4. See the classic work by D. Goleman, *Emotional Intelligence: Why It Can Matter More Than IQ*, 2nd ed. (New York: Bantam, 2006).

show that one's Emotional Quotient correlates much higher with success in life than one's Intelligence Quotient (IQ) in terms of the ability to get and keep a job and to have rich relationships. Proverbs imparts skills to navigate pitfalls of life and maximize success.

Preaching topically from the book of Proverbs

As we observed above, Proverbs has two main parts. Each of the seventeen discourses of the first part[5] could be the subject of a sermon. Preaching from the second part of the book presents a unique problem in that the individual proverbs seem randomly ordered. Consider the first three proverbs:

> A wise son makes a father glad,
> and a foolish son is the sorrow of his mother.
> The treasures of the wicked do not profit,
> but righteousness extricates from death.
> Yahweh will not let the righteous starve,
> but he will push away the desire of the wicked.
> (10:1–3)

There is no theme that binds these three proverbs. Further, proverbs on the same subject may be encountered throughout the collection. For instance, the theme of the fourth proverb in 10:4, laziness, is also the subject of 6:6–11; 10:5, 26; 12:11, 24, 27; 13:4, etc.

How then should one preach from the second part of Proverbs? My view is that the most successful preaching from the book is topical. All the proverbs on a particular subject should be gathered together and studied so the preacher can impart the wisdom of the whole book on a particular subject like laziness.[6]

However, some scholars believe that the proverbs' random organization is only apparent. If one reads closely, a deep structure emerges that reveals units within which individual proverbs should be interpreted. One of the pioneers of this type of study is Knut Heim,[7] who believes that units are formed by

---

5. See discussion in Longman, *Proverbs*, pp. 36–39.

6. Two commentaries provide thematic essays on subjects within Proverbs: D. Kidner, *Proverbs*, TOTC (Leicester: Inter-Varsity Press; Downers Grove: InterVarsity Press, 1964); and Longman, *Proverbs*.

7. K. M. Heim, *Like Grapes of Gold Set in Silver: An Interpretation of Proverbial Clusters in Proverbs 10:1 – 22:16* (Berlin: Walter de Gruyter, 2001).

phonological, semantic, syntactic and thematic repetition. While many contemporary commentaries agree with Heim that there are coherent units in Proverbs 10 and following,[8] they do not agree as to exactly what that deep structure looks like. The whole endeavour comes across more like the imposition of a structure than a discovery of one. In any case, preachers should consider this issue, since commentators differ among themselves concerning this and their approach to the subject does affect their interpretation.

What is the theology of Proverbs?

Although Proverbs does impart practical advice to its readers, it would be a mistake to say that its teaching ends there. As a matter of fact, wisdom does not even start there:

> The fear of the LORD is the beginning of knowledge.
> (1:7a NRSV)

The wisdom that Proverbs teaches is thoroughly theological. The foundation or start of wisdom is a proper attitude towards God, that attitude being 'fear'. Perhaps the word 'awe' fits the context best, although 'fear' when properly understood fits the context as well. The reason why fear is the beginning of wisdom/knowledge is because it demonstrates at a gut level that a person knows they are not the centre of the universe, but rather are dependent on God. With such an attitude they will turn to God for advice rather than being 'wise in their own eyes/estimation' (Prov. 3:7; 21:2; 26:5, 12, 16; 28:11).

The book of Proverbs makes this point through the development of the figure of Woman Wisdom. Indeed, we will see that the way Woman Wisdom is presented in the book of Proverbs transforms the very concept of wisdom into a theological idea.

Embracing Woman Wisdom

As noted above, Proverbs 1 – 9 are discourses and 10 – 31 contain the proverbs *per se*. Often readers isolate these two parts, not recognizing that the discourses are a hermeneutical preamble to the proverbs.

The major metaphor of Proverbs 1 – 9 is the path. There are two paths, the straight path that leads to life and the crooked one that leads to death. Eventually everyone's path passes a high point where they hear a feminine

---

8. Recently, B. K. Waltke, *The Book of Proverbs 1 – 15*, NICOT (Grand Rapids: Eerdmans, 2004); and *The Book of Proverbs 16 – 31*, NICOT (Grand Rapids: Eerdmans, 2005).

voice calling from the 'pinnacle of the heights of the city' (9:3). A woman issues an invitation to all the men going by: "'Whoever is simpleminded – turn aside here,'" she says to those who lack heart. "Come, eat my food, and drink the wine I mixed. Abandon simplemindedness and live. March on the path of understanding'" (9:4–6). The woman is identified as Wisdom. Before a response is possible, however, the men receive a second invitation. A woman called Folly, also living on the 'heights of the city', calls out, "'Whoever is simpleminded – turn aside here,'" she says to those who lack heart. "Stolen water is sweet; food eaten in secret is pleasant'" (9:16–17). The men, with whom the readers of Proverbs must identify, are faced with a decision. With whom will they dine?

Who are these women? While Folly appears here for the first time, the reader is acquainted with Wisdom from her speeches in 1:20–33 and 8:1–36. From these earlier speeches, we learn that she is, as her name suggests, the very epitome of wisdom. She is righteous in all her dealings and truthful in speech. She acts out in the open, as opposed to Folly who has secret motivations. Most intriguing is her association with creation (8:22–31). She witnessed, if not participated in, the creation process as the firstborn ('Yahweh begot me at the beginning of his path,' 8:22) and 'craftsman'[9] (8:30) beside God. Since Wisdom was involved in creation, she knows how it works, thus those who know her will navigate life well.

But who is she? The location of her house on the 'pinnacle of the heights of the city' (8:3) reveals that she represents Yahweh's wisdom and so Yahweh himself. In ancient Israel, the temple occupied the high point of the city. Note too that Folly's house is also on the 'heights of the city'. She thus represents the 'wisdom' that is really folly offered by false gods. Accordingly, the choice between Wisdom and Folly is a deeply theological one and this transforms 'wisdom' and 'folly' beyond the category of practical advice.

The reader is to carry this theological understanding of wisdom and folly over to the proverbs of chapters 10 and following.

For example, Proverbs 10:1 observes, 'A wise son makes a father glad, and a foolish son is the sorrow of his mother.' In the light of the decision between Woman Wisdom and Woman Folly, we should understand this proverb to claim that children who bring joy to their parents are acting like proper worshippers of Yahweh, while those who bring grief are acting like idolaters.

Ministers fall short, then, when they preach the proverbs as just so much

---

9. For alternative translations and arguments for 'craftsman', see Longman, *Proverbs*, p. 207.

good advice. The choice between Wisdom and Folly is a choice between the true God and idols. We may say more in the light of the NT. The NT describes Jesus as the epitome of God's wisdom (Luke 2:40–52; Mark 1:21–22; 6:2; 1 Cor. 1:18–31; Col. 2:3). Even more to the point, the NT associates Jesus with Woman Wisdom (Matt. 11:18–19; Col. 1:15–17; John 1, esp. vv. 1, 10). Thus the Christian preacher understands that the decision to follow Jesus is a decision to live with wisdom. Living by any other principle (particularly being 'wise in our own eyes') is folly.

The limits of wisdom: preaching from Ecclesiastes and Job

The emphasis in Proverbs is on the acquisition of wisdom. The father urges his son to 'embrace' wisdom (4:8). The path of wisdom is the way to life and the path of folly is the way to death.

Ecclesiastes and Job warn against over-reading the benefits of wisdom. Ecclesiastes 7:15–18, for instance, states:

> Both I have observed in my meaningless life. There is a righteous person perishing in his righteousness, and there is a wicked person living long in his evil. Do not be too righteous and do not be overly wise. Why ruin yourself? Do not be too wicked and do not be a fool. Why die when it is not your time? It is good that you hold on to this and also do not release your hand from that. The one who fears God will follow them both.[10]

Job is a man who is the epitome of the wise man of Proverbs. He was 'innocent and virtuous, fearing God and turning away from evil' (1:1).[11] Rather than prospering, Job suffered greatly. What is the message of these books to a modern congregation? How do Job and Ecclesiastes relate to the message of the book of Proverbs?

Preaching Ecclesiastes

At first glance, Ecclesiastes appears to send a strange message. 'Meaningless, meaningless, all is meaningless' – the word 'meaningless' (*hebel*) reverberates

---

10. Translations from Ecclesiastes are taken from T. Longman III, *Ecclesiastes* (Grand Rapids: Eerdmans, 1998).

11. Translations from Job are from my forthcoming Job commentary.

throughout the book. The book virtually begins (1:2) and ends (12:8) on that note. A closer look at the book, however, demonstrates that 'meaninglessness' is not its final message.

Two voices

Readers of Ecclesiastes often miss the subtle but clear presence of two voices in the book. The main speaker of the book is Qohelet. Qohelet is a Hebrew transliteration of the name that is rendered 'the Teacher' in most modern translations, but traditionally it is translated 'the Preacher'. The Hebrew actually means 'one who assembles a group' or 'Assembler', and the difference between the modern and traditional translation of the name has to do with the assumed nature of the audience assembled. For now, we should observe that Qohelet speaks in the first person in 1:12 – 12:7.

In the prologue (1:1–11) and the epilogue (12:8–14), though, there is a second voice that is speaking about Qohelet. He is speaking to his son about Qohelet (12:12).[12] Since he speaks in the frame of the book, Fox coined the term 'frame narrator' to refer to this unnamed wise man, although we will also refer to him as the second wise man or second sage.[13]

The important interpretative point of this observation that will be critical for proper preaching of the book is that we must distinguish the message of Qohelet from the message of the frame narrator. The message of the book is to be associated with the latter, not with Qohelet. We will observe a similar phenomenon with Job, where there are many voices, but only one normative voice (Yahweh's).

The message of Qohelet (1:12 – 12:7)

Life is meaningless

Qohelet's fundamental point is: 'Life is hard and then you die.' He diligently looked for purpose in life, considering work (2:18–23; 4:4–6), pleasure (2:1–11), wealth (5:10 – 6:9), power (4:13–16) and even wisdom (2:12–17). Each time he concluded that life was meaningless.

Throughout his reflections, he gives three reasons for this sorry state of affairs.

Death: Life is meaningless because we die. Although he speaks of death

---

12. Interestingly, the second voice emerges also briefly in 7:27, to show his presence as the one who is narrating Qohelet's autobiography to the son.

13. M. V. Fox, 'Frame Narrative and Composition in the Book of Qohelet', *HUCA* 48 (1977), pp. 83–106.

often, 12:1–7 is his most forceful and final statement. In this passage, Qohelet likens our bodies to a house and its inhabitants. The house is falling apart and the people inside are languishing (12:3). Our bodies, like the house and its inhabitants, fall apart with age. The infirmities of the people in the house may point specifically to trembling hands, bending backs, as well as loss of teeth and eyesight.[14] In any case, it all ends with death (12:7).

Injustice: Qohelet was also upset with the lack of justice in the world. He expected good people to be rewarded and bad people to be punished, but his observations of life did not bear the principle out. In 9:11, he sadly concludes, 'The race is not to the swift, the battle not to the mighty, nor is food for the wise, nor wealth to the clever, nor favor to the intelligent, but time and chance happen to them all.'

Time and chance: The end of 9:11 leads to the final reason why Qohelet found life meaningless. God had ordered the universe so there was 'a season and a time for every activity under heaven' (3:1, see vv. 2–8). He is aware of this because God 'also places eternity in their (human) hearts'. However, this knowledge brings him frustration, not joy (see 3:9–10, 11b). The wise need to know the proper time for their actions and speech, but God has not let them in on it (3:11b).

Carpe diem

Since life is meaningless, Qohelet encourages a *carpe diem* attitude. Grab whatever enjoyment one can out of life. In 2:24, he proclaims that 'there is nothing better for people than to eat and drink and enjoy their toil'. He repeats this idea on five other occasions (besides 2:24–26, see 3:12–14, 22; 5:18–20; 8:15; 9:7–10). If there is no ultimate purpose in life, then the best strategy for living is to try to numb the pain by momentary pleasures that distract one from the harsh realities of life, since such people 'do not remember much about the days of their lives for God keeps them busy with the pleasure of their hearts' (5:20).

The message of the frame narrator

The frame narrator's words are found at the beginning (1:1–11) and at the end of the book (12:8–14). The prologue simply sets the mood for Qohelet's words that follow. What is significant for our understanding of the frame narrator's message is the epilogue. Here he evaluates Qohelet's message for his son.

---

14. See Longman, *Ecclesiastes*, pp. 269–271.

He begins by summarizing Qohelet's bottom line, 'meaningless, meaning-less' (12:8). He then continues by complimenting Qohelet as a competent sage. He tells his son that Qohelet 'was a wise man. He also taught the people knowledge. He heard, investigated, and put in good order many proverbs' (12:9). He even goes so far as to say, 'Qohelet sought to find words of delight, and he wrote honest words of truth.'[15] Such teachings are painful (like goads and firmly implanted nails, 12:11) and the son need not dwell long on such teachings (12:12).

And, indeed, as we consider Qohelet's words and insights, we can agree that his message is a true one when understood within the parameters he himself sets. His observations are based on what he sees (a motific word in the book) and what he experiences. Although the language is anachronistic for Qohelet, we would say that he is looking at life in a fallen world.

However, the frame narrator does not leave his son 'under the sun'. He has had enough exposure to that type of thinking ('End of the matter. All has been heard', 12:13a). He concludes by giving a charge to his son, and of course to all subsequent readers who now occupy the place of the son as recipients of the lesson of the father (the frame narrator):

> Fear God and keep his commandments, for this is the whole duty of humanity. For God will bring every deed into judgment, including every hidden thing whether good or evil. (12:13b–14)

Although brief, this statement carries a powerful message. In it, the frame narrator admonishes his son to have a proper relationship with God (to fear God) and maintain that relationship by obeying his commandments and living in the light of the coming judgment. Even further, the father gives his son the resources for an 'above the sun' perspective that allows him to know more than he can see and experience by alluding to the wisdom literature ('fear God'), the Torah ('obey the commandments') and prophets (the coming judgment).

Implications for preaching Ecclesiastes

The frame narrator is teaching his son about the meaning or purpose of life. He uses Qohelet as a foil to show his son that as long as he tries to find meaning in this world, he will fail. In a way, the book of Ecclesiastes functions as an idol

---

15. I have changed my translation and understanding of this verse since publishing my commentary: see Longman, *Ecclesiastes*, p. 278.

buster. If one makes money, power, status, pleasure, work or any created thing the most important thing in their life, they will be deeply disappointed.

Most mortals fail to learn this lesson. Even if, say, money has not brought them the satisfaction that they had hoped for, it is always possible to think that a bit more money might. It is for this reason that I believe the author of the book chose to associate Qohelet with Solomon. Solomon had abundant money, pleasure, wisdom, but he ended his life miserably. And if Solomon could not find meaning in these things, then 'what can anyone who comes after the king do but that which has already been done?' (2:12b). There is not enough money for people who were created to live in Eden but who must live in this fallen world.

The frame narrator tells his son to place God first (12:13–14). Jerome heard this message and used Ecclesiastes to advocate the contempt of the world and encouragement towards a withdrawal from the world. But Ecclesiastes never advocates withdrawal from the world, but putting it in its right priority. In other words, put God first, and work, pleasure, wealth, wisdom, etc. can find their proper secondary place in our lives.

The message of the book directs the modern preacher in its proper application. People, including Christians, today find themselves pursuing ultimate meaning in the same areas that Qohelet explored. Preaching on Ecclesiastes provides a good occasion to remind people that God must come first or else life will disappoint.[16]

No sermon, however, is complete without consideration of a passage's broader canonical context. How should the Christian read Ecclesiastes in the light of the coming of Christ?

Paul may allude to Ecclesiastes in Romans 8:

> Yet what we suffer now is nothing compared to the glory he will reveal to us later. For all creation is waiting eagerly for that future day when God will reveal who his children really are. Against its will, all creation was subjected to God's curse. (Rom. 8:18–20a NLT)

The Greek word translated 'God's curse' is *mataiotēs*, the word used in the Greek OT to translate 'meaningless' in Ecclesiastes (*hebel*). When Paul speaks of God subjecting creation to *mataiotēs*, he is thinking of the fall, but, as mentioned above, Qohelet reflects 'under the sun' realities. Paul, however, does not

---

16. See D. Allender and T. Longman III, *Breaking the Idols of Your Heart: How to Navigate the Temptations of Life* (Downers Grove: InterVarsity Press, 2007).

stop with Qohelet. He does not remain mired in 'under the sun' thinking. He continues: 'But with eager hope, the creation looks forward to the day when it will join God's children in glorious freedom from death and decay' (Rom. 8:20b–21 NLT). The message of the NT is that it is Jesus Christ himself who subjects himself to the fallen world and particularly to death in order to free us from death (Gal. 3:13; Phil. 2:5–11). Jesus experienced the effects of the fallen world (*hebel*) on the cross, abandoned by God, in a way that Qohelet could not even imagine. He removed the victory of death (1 Cor. 15:50–57), so that life can be meaningful.

Conclusion

From the above description of Ecclesiastes, it follows that the preacher must pay close attention to the book-length context of any particular passage. Qohelet's message is not the ultimate message of the book and should not be isolated and preached as God's word to the congregation. Qohelet is a confused wise man, who is used by the frame narrator as a foil to teach his son important lessons about life and his relationship with God. What he says is true, but only within the limited parameters that he sets ('under the sun'). It does not follow that everything Qohelet says is wrong, but the reader cannot assume that it is correct unless it is taught elsewhere in Scripture.

Second, the book of Ecclesiastes is hard to preach in an extended series. That does not mean there is only a single sermon from the book. As an idol buster, the book allows the preacher prophetically to critique workaholism, the love of money, illicit pleasure, blind ambition and much more. But a weekly series on the book could get tedious, since the critique would lead the preacher to move from Qohelet to the frame narrator's critique to Jesus Christ as the answer to Qohelet's depressing conclusions about life. Preaching from Ecclesiastes once a year would be a wonderful discipline and helpful to congregations.

Preaching from Job

When it comes to sermons on Job, preachers will encounter many of the same issues and challenges as we met with Ecclesiastes. Ecclesiastes had two voices; Job presents multiple voices. The frame narrator's message was the message of Ecclesiastes. Yahweh's speeches in Job 38:1 – 42:6 provide the message of the book (in interaction with Job, the three friends and Elihu). Any passage from Ecclesiastes has to be preached in the context of the whole book, and the same is true for Job.

The author[17] of Job communicates his message through plot and characterization. In order to describe that message, we will begin by an interpretative summary of the different parts of the book that carry its plot.

The plot of Job

Prologue

The book begins by introducing the reader to all the main characters except one. Elihu makes an abrupt and surprising entry into the plot in 32:1. The first to be introduced is Job himself, a man 'innocent and virtuous, fearing God and turning away from evil' (1:1). In other words, he is the epitome of the wise person in Proverbs. God himself will affirm the narrator's assessment (1:8; 2:3) and even the Accuser agrees, although the Accuser argues that his righteousness is self-interested. The Accuser's charge becomes the basis of Job's suffering. Will Job remain righteous even if all the personal benefits of righteousness (wealth, large and happy family, health) are removed?

The answer comes quickly after the first test where the Accuser removes his wealth and his family. Job remains steadfast in his loyalty to Yahweh (1:23). In the second test, the Accuser attacks Job's health. Even so, Job is resolute (2:10).

The prologue ends with the arrival of the three friends – Eliphaz, Bildad and Zophar – in anticipation of the next section of the book.

The debate

When Eliphaz, Bildad and Zophar are referred to as a group, they are usually called Job's 'friends', the quotation marks casting suspicion on whether or not they really were his friends. The prologue, though, informs the reader that they sat in empathetic silence with Job for seven days, and it is Job who breaks the silence with his lament in chapter 3.

The lament is like a lament in the Psalms, but not really. In the Psalms, the lamenter, like Job, lays bare his suffering soul. Unlike the psalms, though, Job does not address his complaints to God. He rather complains about God, similar to the grumblers in the book of Numbers (see, for instance, ch. 11). Furthermore, the laments of the psalms often articulate confidence or even praise of God. Even the dark Psalm 88 refers to God as the 'God of my

---

17. In this chapter I am interested in the message of the present, canonical form of the book regardless of whether it was written by a single individual or by a process of growth over time.

salvation' and the mere fact that he is still praying to God shows a glimmer of hope, not found in Job's lament. Even though Job articulates a desire to talk to God, it is a desire to set God straight (a theme that climaxes in 31:35–37).

The three friends cannot stand by and listen to what they perceive as near blasphemy, so they begin hammering Job with their questions and accusations. Job does not take their charges without protest and counter-arguments. Three cycles of interchange are given in chapters 4 – 27. Eliphaz, Bildad and Zophar take their turns in order with Job responding individually to each one.

The three friends are united in their approach. Although it might be possible to identify Zophar as the most vicious of Job's attackers, his argument is the same as the other two: 'If you sin, then you suffer. Therefore, if you suffer, then you are a sinner. Job suffers greatly, so he must be a great sinner.' What is the solution to Job's predicament? He must repent.

Job too has a perspective on his situation. Interestingly, he shares the same basic belief in proper retribution as the three friends. They are correct in stating how the world should work. He, however, is convinced of his righteousness (and we the readers know he is correct in this). Accordingly, he believes that the problem has to do with God. He is unjust. Given this diagnosis, Job believes that the only recourse is to confront God and thus he wants an audience with the Almighty.[18]

In this debate, the three friends and Job all consider themselves to be sages. Thus they reflect on Job's circumstances and offer their guidance. An important and interesting part of the debate is their claims to wisdom and their ridicule of the wisdom of others. Of the many examples, we will cite only two. Zophar, for instance, is indirectly referring to Job when he says 'an empty-headed person [i.e. Job] will get understanding when a wild donkey gives birth to a human!' (11:12). Job responds in kind as illustrated by his sarcastic statement to the friends, 'you are the people, and wisdom will die with you!' (12:1).

This dimension of the debates reveals the most important question that the book of Job addresses: 'Who is wise?'

With Job's assertion of his own wisdom and his attacks on the justice of God in the body of the debate, chapter 28 takes the reader by surprise. In this powerful and beautiful poem, Job clearly asserts the wisdom of God. Wisdom

---

18. Although at times he believes such an audience would be unhelpful, since God would just overwhelm him with his power (9:21–35).

is inaccessible to human effort. Only God is wise, so the proper attitude is to fear God, the beginning of wisdom (28:28). One might almost expect the book to end here, and indeed this chapter anticipates the conclusion of the book. But Job continues in the next three chapters, reverting to his complaints and challenges to God. His moment of theological clarity in chapter 28 gives way to the pain of his suffering as he bemoans his present situation, protests his innocence and once again asserts his desire to take God to court (31:14b–35).

Elihu

Job will get his wish. He will have an encounter with God, but before that happens we hear from a speaker hitherto not introduced Elihu.

Elihu has been a bystander listening to the debate between Job and his three friends. The latter have run out of arguments and energy, but now Elihu takes over. He presents himself as a person with a new perspective on the matter. He is unhappy with the three friends for not persuading Job and with Job because he is maintaining his innocence. Elihu is not an elder, so he grounds his authority not in his age, but rather in 'his spirit', that is the 'breath of the Almighty' that is in him (32:8). However, when one looks at his position closely, it appears that he is simply repeating arguments already presented by the three friends. Granted that he puts more emphasis on the disciplinary nature of suffering (33:19–28), but the friends had noted this as well (e.g., 5:17–27). For the most part, Elihu hammers Job with the argument from retributive justice (34:10–30). Despite the fact that Elihu's final words (ch. 37) anticipate God's following speech, he does not rightly diagnose Job's predicament, so he is ignored not only by the human participants in the drama, but also by God. No one responds to Elihu.

Yahweh's speeches and Job's response (38:1 – 42:6)

The climactic moment of the book begins in chapter 38 when God speaks to Job out of a whirlwind. He is obviously displeased with Job and begins to pepper him with questions and assertions that demonstrate that he, not Job, is all-powerful and all-wise. Job responds appropriately by ceasing his complaints (40:4–5) and repenting in dust and ashes (42:6).

Epilogue (42:7–17)

After Job's repentance, God informs Eliphaz as representative of the three friends that they have not spoken 'correctly about me' (42:7) as Job has. To avoid judgment, they must ask Job to intercede for them with prayer and sacrifice. God's statement raises a problem. God was obviously upset with Job in the speeches and Job himself acknowledges that he questioned God 'with ignorance' (42:2). Thus it is not immediately obvious in what way Job spoke correctly about God. Upon reflection, though, it seems best to say that Job never 'cursed God and died' (2:9). Rather than fleeing from God, he pursued him to find an answer. It is also possible that Job's 'right' speech included the fact that he repented that he had questioned God's wisdom.

In the epilogue, God also restores his fortunes. Indeed, his wealth is doubled while his sons (seven) and daughters (three) are restored to their original number. This restoration also presents an issue that needs to be addressed. If one reads carelessly (or with mischief), one might conclude that the book undermines its own message. After all, the three friends said that Job had sinned and if he repented he would be restored. But a close reading reveals that Job never repented of sin that led to his suffering. The story has the consistent message that Job was an innocent sufferer. Job repented rather of a growing impatience with God.

Important considerations in preaching Job

The above summary of the structure, plot and message of the book allows us to make some comments about preaching this fascinating and unique book.

The many voices of the book

There are many voices in the book speaking at cross purposes, but God's speeches provide the normative perspective of the book; all the other speeches need to be evaluated in the light of God's speech. Consequently, any particular passages must be preached in the light of God's speeches and the epilogue. A passage from Eliphaz taken out of context is not God's word to modern readers and constitutes the worse kind of prooftexting.

The main theme of Job

We often turn to Job when we want to preach about suffering. But we must remember that it is not really about suffering. Its main theme is wisdom and its source. The book is a wisdom debate. The suffering of Job becomes an occasion to address the issue of wisdom. The human participants all fail to provide the necessary wisdom, but in the end God asserts the fact that he alone is wise.

Even so, indirectly, Job does speak to the issue of suffering. Most importantly, it disabuses the reader of the mistaken and dangerous idea that all suffering is the result of sin. All the human participants of the book held this view. From the very start of the story, though, the reader knows that Job's suffering is not connected to sin. This is not to say that sin does not lead to suffering in some instances, but it is not the exclusive reason why a person might suffer. The book of Job continues to be important, since the idea of an absolute and mechanical connection between sin and suffering continues until today. We often judge ourselves ('What did I do to deserve this?') and others ('What did they do to deserve this?') based on this false principle. By not giving Job or his friends an answer to the question of why Job suffered, the book tells us that suffering is often a mystery and the only appropriate response is to trust God who is all-wise and all-powerful.

Preaching Job from a New Testament perspective
Looking at Job from a NT perspective suggests many possibilities by which Christian preachers can legitimately present the gospel in a sermon on the book. I will suggest only four.

First, as I argued above, the book is about wisdom and asserts the wisdom of God. As we saw above in our study of Proverbs, the NT presents Jesus as the embodiment of God's wisdom.

Second, Jesus, like Job, is an innocent sufferer. This observation highlights the contrast between the two. Jesus suffered voluntarily, while Job was compelled to suffer for reasons beyond his knowledge. Additionally, Jesus' suffering was redemptive, while Job's was not. The story of Job's suffering is for the purpose of teaching us about wisdom and suffering, so it serves a didactic and not a redemptive purpose. But in that contrast, the preacher can naturally introduce the redemptive suffering of Jesus. It is instructive to us that it was the regular practice of the early church to read Job in the week before Easter.

Third, we should point to a series of texts within Job that have been used in a special way to point to Jesus. These texts speak of an 'umpire' between God and Job (9:32–35), a 'witness in heaven' who might arbitrate for Job, and finally his confident assertion that 'my redeemer lives' (19:25). A full exposition of these complex texts is not possible here.[19] However, the traditional treatment of these texts as messianic prophecies is not sustainable. Even so, in the light of the NT, we recognize that Job's desires are indeed fulfilled in Jesus Christ, who is God himself.

Finally, the NT deepens our understanding of how God is involved in our suffering. God addresses our pain by entering into it. He sent his Son to suffer and die on the cross. The final word to suffering is the resurrection.

---

19. See my forthcoming Job commentary.

Sermon outline on Ecclesiastes 12:1–7

The horror of death

Death is horrible. It often comes with great pain and always results in separation from loved ones. The Teacher felt deeply the sting of death.

1. Death ends life. The Preacher presents a powerful metaphor of growing old and dying. He likens our bodies to a house and its inhabitants that languish. We get weaker and lose many of our faculties and then are gone and buried. Life is precious, but when it comes to an end it is destroyed ('the silver thread is snapped', v. 6).

2. According to the Teacher, death renders all of life – every status, achievement, purpose – meaningless. Take wisdom, for example (2:12–17). In this life wisdom has a relative advantage over folly because it helps us navigate life. But death comes to both the wise and the fool and therefore in the long run even wisdom is meaningless. The Teacher's best advice is to grab whatever enjoyment you can out of life to forget the harsh realities of death (*carpe diem*).

3. The second wise man tells his son that the Teacher's words are true. It is true that life is difficult and then you die. That is, his conclusion is true 'under the sun'. So in 12:13–14, he tells his son to adopt an 'above the sun' perspective. In spite of what the Teacher said, it is important for his son to have a proper relationship with God ('fear God'), to maintain that relationship by keeping the commandments, and to live in the light of the coming judgment.

4. The good news is that Jesus has come to free us from the sting of death. Yes, God has subjected creation to frustration ('meaninglessness'), but to redeem it. This redemption comes through the work of his Son, who dies on the cross so that we might live. He has defeated death and thus life can be meaningful. Death is no longer the end of the story.

Further reading

ALLENDER, D. and T. LONGMAN III, *Breaking the Idols of Your Heart: How to Navigate the Temptations of Life* (Downers Grove: InterVarsity Press, 2007).

GOLEMAN, D., *Emotional Intelligence: Why It Can Matter More Than IQ*, 2nd ed. (New York: Bantam, 2006).

LONGMAN III, T., *Ecclesiastes* (Grand Rapids: Eerdmans, 1998).

LONGMAN III, T., *How to Read Proverbs* (Leicester: Inter-Varsity Press; Downers Grove: InterVarsity Press, 2002).

LONGMAN III, T., *Proverbs*, BCOTWP (Grand Rapids: Baker, 2006).

LONGMAN III, T. and P. ENNS (eds.), *Dictionary of the Old Testament: Wisdom, Poetry, and Writings* (Downers Grove: InterVarsity Press, 2008).

WITHERINGTON, B., *Jesus the Sage: The Pilgrimage of Wisdom* (Minneapolis: Fortress, 1994).

WALTKE, B. K., *The Book of Proverbs 1 – 15*, NICOT (Grand Rapids: Eerdmans, 2004).

WALTKE, B. K., *The Book of Proverbs 16 – 31*, NICOT (Grand Rapids: Eerdmans, 2005).

7. PREACHING THE SONG OF SOLOMON

Grenville J. R. Kent

'The Bible is full of sex. Haven't you noticed?'

'The Bible?'

'The Song of Solomon, for example.'

'Ah, ah, no, now that is the passionate declaration of love from a devout man to God.'

'No, it's about sex . . . You read it again, Reverend.'

(Rev. Goodfellow [Rowan Atkinson] and Grace, *Keeping Mum*, 2006)

The minister in the dark comedy film *Keeping Mum* is a good man, but overwork has made him boring in the pulpit and in life. His sexually neglected wife is on the brink of an affair. His children are under-fathered: his son invisible, his daughter seeking male attention by sleeping around. While watching his wife prepare for bed, he reads the Song of Solomon again and new understanding dawns. Without spoiling the ending, I can say the ancient text helps transform him and his marriage, children and ministry (though not his mother-in-law).

Is the Song of Solomon transformative for Christians today? When did you last hear it preached or taught? I regularly ask my first-year students, some 80% of whom come from various Christian denominations, and only about 10% can recall any teaching ever from the Song. When I ask what church taught them about sex, they say, 'Ummm, no premarital sex.' That is a good start, but is it a biblical theology?

In fairness to preachers, speaking about sex is difficult in Western culture. Sex is everywhere, selling products and almost reduced to a product itself, the holy grail of materialism, the meaning of life for hedonists. Meanwhile, Christianity has the image of being anti-sex and hypocritical. We must sadly admit that countless cases of sexual abuse by priests have cost churches millions in damages and, worse, have damaged many people's faith in God, trust in relationships and ability to enjoy sex. The credibility of Christianity and clergy on the topic of sexuality could be at an all-time low, so that sometimes our best start is a heartfelt apology for times when churches have not followed Jesus, who had the highest concern for child protection (Matt. 18:6). Today most secular messages about sex, whether from universities or popular media, promote a naturalistic worldview which accepts only evolutionary origins of human life and sees in sex nothing deeper than selfish genes rewarding reproductive behaviour. Thus ultimate morality is impossible.

Secular thinkers also pour scorn on Christian attempts to reason about sexual ethics, labelling them unhealthy and authoritarian. The church's centuries of asceticism and traditional low view of sex, caused by Platonic baggage about the body, have left a deep impression, so that today even our broadest moral and spiritual thinking can so easily be heard as medieval. Publicly expressing a biblical worldview on sex is a countercultural act that requires balanced research, strategic thought and a dash of courage.

Preaching about sex is challenging enough in churches. Global denominations are developing fault-lines over questions of sexual ethics, including the same-sex debate. At times knee-jerk moral outrage and culture-warring have replaced pastoral care and being a friend to sinners; at times fashionable views seem to be rewriting biblical commandments. Is any congregation without a tragic and complicated divorce situation? And pornography is an ever-present temptation to Christians: Rick Warren's 2002 survey of 1,351 clergy, as reported on pastors.com, found that 54% admitted viewing pornography in the past year, and 30% in the last month. With so many sensitive issues in play, the preacher's easiest path may be to talk about something else.

Yet silence is not faithful teaching. Christians probably receive more messages about sex from secular media each day than they do from spiritually and psychologically aware sources each year. Can preachers be content to allow biblical wisdom to have so little share of voice, or for important questions to be discussed everywhere but church? Many Christians wait for a word from God. They need to be gospelled, not guilted. Those of us whom the Spirit has made overseers to feed the church of God (purchased with his own blood) need encouragement not to be timid in making known all the counsel of God (Acts 20:27–28; cf. Mal. 2:7).

There is also an apologetical urgency in offering biblical teaching about sex. Sex can point beyond itself to the numinous and the divine, suggesting intuitively that we are not just mammals but souls. Yancey observes that sex could start 'a powerful rumor of transcendence that could point to the creator . . . who invested in it far more meaning than most people could imagine'. And yet church prudishness can mute that natural revelation. 'We have desacralized it . . . by suppression and denial . . . Sexual power lives on, but few see in that power a pointer to the One who designed it.'[1] Somehow God's brand name has been removed from one of his most popular products.

A European campus evangelist recently observed to me that, for students considering Christianity, questions about Christian sexual ethics are as important as whether Christ's resurrection was historically true. I was surprised to hear that from such a convincing resurrection apologist, but he argued that young people want to know that Christianity is true in a modernist sense, but also that it is life-enhancing – that it 'works'. When Christian sexual ethics are being critically examined by seekers, the underlying question may go to the character of God: is he a cosmic killjoy or an all-wise friend in whose presence is fullness of joy and pleasure for evermore? Does his *torah* enlighten eyes and revive spirits and give joy to hearts, or make body and spirit drab and dowdy? These are fair theological questions which deserve both experiential and intellectual answers, and to which the Song of Solomon is very relevant.

Yet the Song is almost silenced. Churches following a lectionary will hear one passage, compared with two for Ecclesiastes and seven for Proverbs, and then a relatively 'safe' (rather than explicit) passage about a romantic getaway in spring (2:8–13). And many churches have never heard the Song. Preachers may not feel trained in its exposition. A dozen seminary teachers globally have acknowledged in conversation that a student could get through their entire course without one lecture about the Song. Many sources on preaching do not mention it,[2] even in chapters on wisdom literature or poetry. Ironically, in

---

1. Philip Yancey, *Designer Sex* (Downers Grove: InterVarsity Press, 2003), pp. 8–9.

2. Exceptions include Walter C. Kaiser, Jr, *Preaching and Teaching from the Old Testament: A Guide for the Church* (Grand Rapids: Baker, 2003), pp. 94–99; Terry G. Carter, J. Scott Duvall and J. Daniel Hays, *Preaching God's Word: A Hands-On Approach to Preparing, Developing, and Delivering the Sermon* (Grand Rapids: Zondervan, 2005), pp. 277–278; Elizabeth Achtermeier, *Preaching Hard Texts of the Old Testament* (Peabody: Hendrickson, 1998), pp. 116–120; Graeme Goldsworthy, *Preaching the*

the past when the Song was usually read as an allegory for the love between God and the pious soul, it was more often taught and preached. Yet in the nineteenth century, when scholarship largely shifted to a literal reading, both academics and preachers practically stopped using the Song. Yet it is still in the Bible.

> Those of us who believe that the whole canon is relevant to modern Church and society would conclude then that the battle is only half won if, when the text's true nature is recognized, it is then not used.[3]

This gagging of Scripture has the danger of leaving 'aspects of reality untouched by God's Word for God's people, which means that romantic love . . . must be learned from something other than God's Word'.[4]

How not to read the Song

1. Allegorize it

The Song has often been read as an allegory, a symbolic story whose details primarily represent other realities. The Targums interpreted it as symbolizing Israel's history. Christians have used a similar method to read themselves into it. Bernard of Clairvaux wrote eighty-six sermons applying it to mystical love between the soul and Christ, and did not preach past the first two chapters in his lifetime. These interpreters seemed to expect that canonical Scripture would mention God, and sensed that it had to do with divine love for people. Chave imagines the process:

> First, there was a love song . . . composed perhaps in a courtly circle but sung by ordinary people . . . of human, sensual, sexual love. Then someone saw the potential of this song as a simile for God's love for humans . . . Then a dose of 'piety' was introduced. It no longer felt quite right to say that God was like the lover in the Song. Defending 'the otherness of God' was part of it, but a growing distaste for

---

Whole Bible as Christian Scripture (Leicester: Inter-Varsity Press, 2000), p. 191; William P. Tuck, 'Preaching from Daniel, Ruth, Esther and the Song of Songs', Biblical Preaching (1983), pp. 151–168 (pp. 165–167).

3. Tremper Longman III, Song of Songs (Grand Rapids: Eerdmans, 2001), p. 62.

4. Zack Eswine, Preaching to a Post-Everything World: Crafting Biblical Sermons that Connect with Our Culture (Grand Rapids: Baker, 2008), pp. 32–33.

the material world and the human body was the stronger motive. The Song became viewed as an allegory; not a simile but a coded message.[5]

Today the allegorical method is generally questioned as very subjective, and built on the interpreter's imagination rather than on the text itself. Garrett demonstrates this by sketching the history of the interpretation of one detail in the Song – breasts.[6] For Hippolytus of Rome (d. 235) they symbolized the OT and NT which Christians suck for spiritual milk (cf. 1 Pet. 2:2). For one thirteenth-century rabbi, they symbolized the king and the high priest, or Moses and Aaron. Roman Catholic interpretations included Mary's breasts which fed Jesus, or the words she received from her divine bridegroom. A seventeenth-century preacher reasoned that breasts are beautiful and provide food and affection to children, and so they must represent the believer's ability to nurture and disciple others, and also the warmth and kindness of Christ, whom believers have taken into their bosoms. An American preacher suggested Christ looked at believers as a man looked at his wife's beautiful breasts – but then seemed troubled by that thought. Others saw them as Christian pastors feeding the saints, or as the two ordinances of Protestant worship, and a range of other things which sound devotional but suggest questions after a moment's thought. The existence of so many differing interpretations reveals the major problem of the allegorical method – its subjectivity and dependence on the interpreter rather than the text. Commentators have read in their existing theology, performing spontaneous word associations until the text itself is secondary to what they bring to it. This can hardly be preached with biblical authority.

Genuine allegories – those clearly intended by the writer – usually announce themselves by details that clearly do not work literally and often give a clear, if brief, statement of their message. For example, Jotham's political parable is obviously not literal – trees do not talk – and it finally delivers its own punchline with a propositional statement (Judg. 9:7–20). Similarly, Ezekiel's sustained and disturbing sexual allegory is introduced by a clear statement of its message and target: 'confront Jerusalem with her detestable practices' (16:1–3 NIV). It

---

5. Peter Chave, 'Towards a Not Too Rosy Picture of the Song of Songs', *Feminist Theology* 18 (May 1998), pp. 41–53 (p. 41).

6. Duane Garrett, 'Song of Songs', in Duane Garrett and Paul R. House, *Song of Songs/Lamentations* (Nashville: Thomas Nelson Publishers, 2004), pp. 59–76. For a different view on literal and/or allegorical reading, see Iain Provan, *Ecclesiastes/Song of Songs* (Grand Rapids: Zondervan, 2001), pp. 237–248.

masterfully makes each detail count in describing Israel's history of apostasy, but the political meaning is primary, and some details are impossible for any literal woman: she could hardly be the sister of cities like Sodom (v. 46; see also vv. 24, 27, 31). By contrast, the Song is (usually) understandable at a literal level. It works as a love poem, and contains nothing that would demand other levels of interpretation. It offers no clear indication that its literal meaning is not enough. So breasts mean breasts.

Some have claimed that without the allegorical method the Song may never have been included in the Bible because it would have seemed too sexual and secular. This claim rather underestimates the perceptiveness of those who recognized inspiration, and does not explain why they would bother to allegorize a disturbing book rather than ignore it if it did not already have canonical authority. Recent study has also questioned whether there is sufficient historical evidence for this claim.

Having said this, the Song clearly functions as a metaphor or simile for God's love for people, as I will explain briefly below.

2. Overdramatize it

Some read the Song as a drama and try to find a sustained narrative behind it, yet to do this, they import stage directions, character backstories and narrative details that are not in the text. While the text contains narrative flashes and inferences, a preacher must be careful that any attempt to novelize or imagine a narrative beyond the text is declared to the audience as speculation. A fictional context can too easily push the text in other directions and replace biblical authority with human imagination.

How to read the Song

How can Christians read the Song as Scripture? Finding an interpretative method or hermeneutic is difficult and controversial. Here are some suggestions.

1. Read it as wisdom

The Song's wisdom credentials are not obvious, because it is a hybrid genre (wisdom/love poetry) and also because it is not overtly preachy or didactic but teaches subtly. For example, instead of moralizing heavily against adultery, it depicts a wife (and by metonymy a marriage) as a beautiful garden with its own spring of living water, full of spiciness and satisfaction, and private within protective walls (4:12–15). Those who miss the subtlety of this poetry can read a similar proverbial statement with three of the same images, but which directly tells the reader what to do (Prov. 5:15–22). By contrast, the Song promotes rather than moralizes. It is wisdom in easy style. Scholars debate whether the Song is wisdom in a strict form-critical sense, yet many recognize its value in conveying wise ideas and include it at least loosely with Israel's wisdom tradition.

Let us consider a few wisdom themes which can be preached.

(a) One key idea is to link sex with emotional intimacy. After an explicit depiction that is Edenic in its shamelessness about her beloved's naked body, the woman proudly says, 'This is my lover, this is my friend' (5:16 NIV). What more subtle way to show that sex at its best involves emotional, mental, physical and spiritual desire for connection and closeness? Lover and friend in one – this is still news for many.

(b) The Song states that wealth cannot buy love (8:6–7). The lines unfavourably comparing Solomon's best vineyard to 'my own' private vineyard (8:11–13) also obliquely make this point. The Solomon figure may be shorthand for quantity rather than quality of relationships, and for wealth, or could be the male character self-deprecating by saying his wealth is nothing compared to his love. Either way, this point is often forgotten in a materialistic society.

(c) This wisdom does not hide from the dark side of sexual experience in a fallen world. In two matching passages, the woman expresses her fear of loss and abandonment (3:1–4) and of abusive treatment by watchmen who beat her and remove some of her clothing (5:2–8). Both passages are perhaps best understood as dream sequences, since one mentions sleeping with one's heart awake and the other describes seeking the lover at night in bed. They express the vulnerability and abuse – whether real and remembered, or imagined and feared – of the female character. These are not often read at weddings. Preachers seeking a simple 'sex is good' message will avoid them, yet they function dramatically as a dark background which contrasts with the sparkling beauty of loving sex in the Song, and thematically by depicting the dangerous and damaging potential of sex and the vulnerability particularly of women.

These passages can speak powerfully to people who have suffered from the sexual selfishness of others. A university student said (and allowed me to quote her) that her uncle had sexually abused her as a child and other men had sensed and exploited this vulnerability. She instantly connected emotionally with these darker passages, and said they acknowledged her pain and validated her experience, but also gave her hope that the female character who had experienced these things could go on to have a loving and sexually fulfilling relationship. Her reading is exegetically defensible: poetry, with all its potential for multivalence, can speak deeply and personally to the emotions.

One thinks today of sexual harassment and assault, of abuse, of people-smuggling for prostitution linked with drugs, of female pawns of the porn industry, of the tendency of pornography to addict and relationally stunt its users and put pressure on their partners, of children in sex tourism destinations and of countless issues that damage people. These need fearless prophetic comment.

(d) The Song is often read as portraying gender equality. Its strong female lead has some of the best and wisest lines, speaking first and last and more than the male. She often initiates lovemaking: this may not be clear in versions which label him Lover (active) and her Beloved (passive), but by my reckoning she invites him twelve times (1:2, 4; 2:10; 4:16; 7:11, 12; 8:2–4, 5b, 14; including four imagined or dreamed of: 1:13; 2:3; 3:4, 11) compared to his four (2:4; 4:6; 5:2 failed; 7:8 remembered or wished for; not 5:1 because it follows her invitation in 4:16).

Power is shared. Even though the curse in Eden predicted the woman desiring a husband who rules over her (Gen. 3:16), here the curse seems undone as the woman enthuses that her husband's desire is for her (7:10), and ruling over her is not mentioned (even though some understand the male as a king). And she is not the passive object of the male gaze, but also gazes at his body and equally appreciates physical beauty as part of the person (7:1–5; cf. 5:10–16). For much feminist scholarship, the Song 'reclaims human sexuality and celebrates female sexuality', while 'embodying gender balance and mutuality'.[7] This is useful preaching material to move towards Christian equality (cf. Gal. 3:28) and defend the Bible from the charge of sexism.

(e) Part of the Song's wisdom is its practical understanding of what a person is. The woman speaks of 'the one my soul loves' (3:1–4 NRSV).

---

7. Renita J. Weems, 'The Song of Songs: Introduction, Commentary, and Reflections', in *NIB* V (Nashville: Abingdon Press, 1997), pp. 366, 364. Cf. J. Cheryl Exum, 'Ten Things Every Feminist Should Know about the Song of Songs', in Athalya Brenner and Carol R. Fontaine, *Song of Songs: A Feminist Companion to the Bible* (Sheffield: Sheffield Academic Press, 2000), who has argued that the song promotes soft-head romanticism that stops women thinking hard for themselves, presents a man's point of view of his ideal woman rather than letting a real woman speak, controls feminine sexuality and exhibits the female body.

This is not the disembodied soul of dualism or the bloodless Platonic relationship, but the *nepeš* or whole person, being, self or life. So the ideal love presented in the Song involves all that comprises a person, and includes the God-created senses in giving and receiving love – hearing a sexy voice, smelling a spicy scent, tasting a fruit-flavoured kiss or the lover's body, looking with desire at wife or husband and enjoying touch of the most intimate kind.

This connects with a biblical theology of the body and of creation, and portrays a God who is interested in our bodies – creating them 'very good',[8] redeeming them after the fall, healing them, meeting their needs, inhabiting them as his temple, teaching us to use them in holiness and honour (1 Thess. 4:4), preserving our whole spirit and soul and body blameless until his coming (1 Thess. 5:23), ultimately resurrecting and re-creating them (Phil. 3:21). This is embodied spirituality. Amazingly, God even took a human body as the Logos *became* flesh.

One practical implication of this is that a relationship can never be 'just physical', because a person is not the merely physical being constructed by secularism. Sexual intimacy by nature involves heart and soul. This suggests that sex that ignores spirit is likely to be unsatisfying and potentially hurtful.

2. Find God's subtle presence

It is challenging to do theology when the Song has no obvious mentions of God. History suggests a reason for this. Fertility religions, so common in OT times, taught that nature's ongoing productiveness depended on male and female gods having sex: archaeologists have found songs which describe orgiastic deities. Worshipping them often meant participants watched or participated in so-called sacred sex. A shrine prostitute was called a *qĕdēšâ*, from the word for holy, and was distinguished from an ordinary prostitute or *zōnâ*. Israel was constantly tempted by fertility cults as practised by shapely Gentile neighbours (e.g. Num. 25). So if Yahweh had appeared directly in the Song, the culture may well have misunderstood him as condoning fertility religion or

---

8. 'The Song can be read as an extended commentary on the "very good" spoken over creation.' Elizabeth Huwiler, 'The Song of Songs', in Roland E. Murphy and E. Huwiler, *NIBC: Proverbs, Ecclesiastes, Song of Songs* (Peabody: Hendrickson Publishers, 1999), p. 242. See also Barry G. Webb, *Five Festal Garments: Christian Reflections on The Song of Songs, Ruth, Lamentations, Ecclesiastes, Esther* (Leicester: Apollos; Downer's Grove: InterVarsity Press, 2000).

even as just another fertility god. The Song clearly separates worship and sex. It is 'a non-mythological, non-cultic, non-idolatrous, outright, open celebration of God-given sexual love'.[9]

Yet there are hints of God. The man, in a man's toe-to-head appreciation of his wife, enthuses:

> The curves of your thighs are like jewels,
> the work of a master craftsman.
> (7:1, my translation)

That creates quite a mental picture which may not automatically lead the thoughts to theology, yet who else could be the *'amman* (master craftsman or artist)? The unforgettable curves of a desirable body are thanks to God. What an attractive way to state the doctrine of creation!

In the final chapter, the woman's hymn to love says love is *šalhebetyāh*, or literally a 'flame of Yah' (8:6). The 'Yah' added on the end is the first syllable of the divine name Yahweh. It can probably also be used to suggest importance or large size rather than the deity ('almighty' rather than 'the Almighty'), yet here it seems to refer to God as the source of love: 'If the blaze of love, ardent love such as between a man and a woman, is indeed the flame of Yahweh, then this human love is explicitly described as originating in God, a spark off the Holy Flame.'[10]

The same poem also has the line, 'Many waters cannot quench love' (8:7 NIV). Alter, reading with Genesis as background, sees waters here as 'the primordial waters that God divided and hedged in to create the world', hence the reference is to 'love on a cosmic scale' overcoming the forces of chaos and disorder.[11] This would place human love in the setting of God's own redemptive love shaping the world. This is the love that is stronger than death (8:6).

These are the merest hints at God's presence, avoiding any misinterpretation of Yahweh in sexualized terms, yet preaching them can highlight God's

---

9. John G. Snaith, *The Song of Songs* (Grand Rapids: Eerdmans, 1993), p. 5. For a summary of research on fertility religions in the Ancient Near East, see Richard M. Davidson, *Flame of Yahweh: Sexuality in the Old Testament* (Peabody: Hendricksons, 2007), pp. 83–132.

10. Davidson, *Flame of Yahweh*, p. 630.

11. Robert Alter, 'Afterword', in Ariel Bloch and Chana Bloch, *The Song of Songs: A New Translation with an Introduction and Commentary* (Berkeley: University of California Press, 1995), p. 131.

name subtly watermarked onto his gift of sex. Presumably God could have designed us to reproduce using windblown pollen, and so the fact that sex is pleasurable and companionable can offer clues to his character and his purposes for us. Love and sex are 'very good', and the gift reflects the Giver. If humans are made relational in the image of a God who *is* love, then the Song gives preachers the chance to mention God's love for us, as later ultimately revealed in the self-giving love of Christ: greater love has no-one than this.

3. Read of redemption

In the context of the canonical story of paradise lost, the Song claims paradise can be found. After Trible,[12] one can see links as follows:

Genesis	Song of Songs
The lovers are locked out of the garden.	The lovers are back in a garden.
The garden begins 'very good', with trees 'pleasing to the eye and good for food', but eating from the forbidden tree causes the curse of 'thorns and thistles' (2:9; 3:18 NIV).	Weeds are around (2:2), but the girl is a perfect garden, and love happens in a private paradise of scented, tasty, exotic plants.
The lovers are tempted, partly by their senses (3:6), to take fruit from the forbidden tree.	The couple enjoy their senses. The woman says the man is the best tree in the forest (2:3): playful temptation.
The curse involves increased birth pains.	Motherhood is mentioned positively (1:6; 3:4, 11; 6:9; 8:1, 2, 5), although procreation is not the stated aim.
Work becomes sweat-faced hard labour.	Work can be onerous (1:6) or a delight together (1:7).
Curse: 'Your desire (*těšûqâ*) will be for your husband, and he will rule over you' (3:16 NIV). The word *těšûqâ* is also used of personified sin (4:7).	The woman enthuses, 'I belong to my lover, and his *těšûqâ* is for me' (7:10 NIV). In an egalitarian reversal, the curse is turned to blessing.
Curse: death (3:20–24).	Love is stronger than death (8:6).

12. Phyllis Trible, 'Love's Lyrics Redeemed', in *God and the Rhetoric of Sexuality* (Philadelphia: Fortress Press, 1978).

Similarly, Davidson organizes his analysis of all the sexual passages of the OT in this way:

I   'Sexuality in Eden: The Divine Design'.
II   'Sexuality outside the Garden', where the fall affects everything but humanity receives God's grace, revelation and laws.
III 'Return to Eden': the Song of Songs.[13]

So the Song, when read in the Bible's grand narrative, becomes another chapter in the story of fall and redemption. Garrett writes:

> The message is that the mutual pleasures of love are good and possible even in this fallen world. The Song is testimony to the grace of God and a rejection of *both* asceticism and debauchery.[14]

4. Read it as a metaphor
There are many ways in which human love relationships reflect God's love, and provide useful comparisons with it. The motif of marriage with God and its matching opposite, adultery against God, are often used throughout Scripture (e.g. Exod. 34:15–16; Lev. 17:7; perhaps Num. 25:1; Isa. 54:6–7; Ezek. 16, 23; Hos. 1.2, Mal. 2.14, Eph. 5.21–33, Rev. 19:6–8). This metaphor is sustained across Scripture and the Song can be usefully read as part of it, and yet the key is not to strain the text in trying to make every detail descriptive of human love for God. It is better, in my opinion, to let the Song be what it is – a human love poem – and then make broad comparisons with the human relationship with God.

5. Read in its original culture

> Your nose is like the tower of Lebanon,
> looking towards Damascus.
> (7:4 NIV)

> Your teeth are like a flock of sheep just shorn,
> coming up from the washing.
> (4:2 NIV; cf. 6:6)

---

13. Davidson, *Flame of Yahweh*, section titles, pp. vii–xiv.
14. Duane A. Garrett, *Proverbs, Ecclesiastes, Song of Songs* (Nashville: Broadman, 1993), p. 378.

If your spouse is offended by your comparing their nose to Warwick Castle or any other military installation, or their teeth to farm animals, do not try to blame the Bible. Blame your inadequate exegetical method, which should read a text in its original culture. Audiences today find these images funny, and there is value in pointing out their cultural distance from this ancient text so that they do not judge it by the standards of contemporary poetry. Yet these cultural comparisons should beware of simplistic assumptions about ancient culture (e.g. 'women had no value'). Historical accuracy promotes faithful exegesis.

6. Live with difficult questions

The Song is a challenging text. Some of its vocabulary is unknown and recon-structed by educated guesses. Some words appear for the only time in the Bible. (Both of these suggest an author with a wide vocabulary.)

The speakers are not indicated except by gendered grammar and context, and there are lines where the speaker's identity is debatable.

It is difficult to choose a passage to preach when the structure of the work is often debated: Keel sees 42 poems, Murphy 9, Longman 23, Goulder 14, the MT paragraph markers suggest 19 sections, Pope refuses to divide it, others suggest the poems are not connected and the Song of many songs is a very loose anthology. Shea and Garrett see chiasms which agree on the central section (4:16 – 5:1) though not all details. One should make up one's own mind by poring over the text.

This is further complicated because the Song seems not to be a linear nar-rative, but a collection of poetic memories, of unforgettable love in a timeless, eternal present. Its structure is non-sequential. This is relevant to the question of why sex is described well before the wedding is depicted in 3:11. Some see unmarried sex in the Song, but arguments based on a sequential narrative are not convincing.

The role of Solomon (1:5; 3:9, 11; 8:11, 12) is debated. Is he the male character or only alluded to as a literary image? Was the historical Solomon its author (or co-author, if a woman's voice or hand shaped the text), or should we understand the attribution (1:1) as suggesting it was wisdom associated with his court? Modernist scholarship tended to rule Solomon out, largely on linguistic grounds, but newer linguistic theories challenge this.[15]

These are interesting and important questions and will influence one's

---

15. For a summary, see Garrett and House, *Song of Songs/Lamentations*, pp. 16–22. On interpretative questions more generally, one excellent summary is Greg W. Parsons, 'Guidelines for Understanding and Utilizing the Song of Songs', *Bibliotheca Sacra*

interpretation but, rather than argue here for my views, let me acknowledge that however one answers them, the text can be usefully exposited. Even if a preacher needs to go gently about some questions, major themes are clear. Some audiences will find the smaller questions and debates interesting, while others like the fruits of scholarship to be cut up for them on a plate. These questions are little foxes that need not eat our grapes. (Oops, I just allegorized Song 2:15.)

Simply put, the best method of reading the Song is to analyse how its poetic devices and symbols work and what they mean, and to look for life applications of this wisdom. Fortunately, excellent commentaries are now available, some of which I have footnoted.

Preaching the Song: practical suggestions

1. Be age-appropriate

One Jewish tradition said a man should not read the Song until he was thirty years old. More recently, the average male accessed pornography at eleven, and today pressures can arrive even younger due to media and peer group in an increasingly sex-saturated culture. Seven-year-olds may be introduced to pornographic websites and even coerced into sexual behaviours by their school peers. One survey of girls aged six to mid-teens found that one in four had sex before the age of fourteen. By contrast, the girls most confident in their choice to abstain were 'actively involved in youth groups attached to local churches, or had a strong group of close girlfriends, who were clear about what they would and would not do at parties'.[16] Sensing this, many involved parents, whether Christians themselves or socially connected with church, welcome Christian values and want teaching to happen quite young as long as they are in control. Advertising the topic in advance and offering a crèche or children's event, or

---

156 (October–December 1999), pp. 399–422. For a practical treatment, see Bryan Wilkerson, 'The Joy of Preaching Sex', *Leadership* (Winter 2006), pp. 44–49.

16. Maggie Hamilton, *What's Happening To Our Girls? Too Much, Too Soon* (London: Penguin, 2008), pp. 52–53, 161. See also Catherine Itzin (ed.), *Pornography: Women, Violence and Civil Liberties* (Oxford University Press, 1992); Diane E. Levin and Jean Kilbourne, *So Sexy So Soon: The New Sexualized Childhood and What Parents Can Do To Protect Their Kids* (New York: Ballantyne Books, 2008). From a Christian perspective, Eva Marie Everson and Jessica Everson, *Sex, Lies and the Media: What Your Kids Know and Aren't Telling You* (Eastbourne: Kingsway Communications, 2005).

even just screening a Bible cartoon, allows parents to listen themselves, and to decide whether their children are ready for the material.

2. Be positive

If people expect guilt and unreasonable restrictions, surprise them with grace and God's flair. There are texts that rebuke sexual sin, but this one gives preachers the chance to portray an ideal so good that people will not be content to settle for less, and yet so real and possible and 'near' (Deut. 30:14) as to give hope to the bruised and the cynical. Offer people a positive alternative to compulsive lusts and the hollow feelings they leave behind. We have all heard the dark jokes about marriage, but the Song paints a brighter picture. Celebrate marriage as God's gift, but also encourage the single Christian – who may feel like an odd sock left in the drawer – that sex is not everything, that love in many forms can still happen to them and that a single Saviour knows how they feel.

3. Deal with guilt

One pastor described his first attempt to preach on sex after several years in a church. He knew many young people were sexually active and cohabiting before marriage, and worried how they might respond. He was surprised to find that they thanked him for 'talking straight' and some requested pastoral counselling. Yet many Baby Boomer parents made huffy comments to him at the door and about him in the car park. The pastor made a point of visiting them, and heard stories about old guilts – affairs, abortions, marriages begun with pregnancy. Some married people felt their relationship was sexually cold and emotionally stuck, and had almost given up hope. So he began addressing these issues pastorally. He concluded that he should have tackled the topic earlier, and that next time he would emphasize even more the forgiveness and healing Jesus offers sexual sinners, while also calling for high standards and gospel transformation.

As a visiting speaker, I was once verbally attacked at a church door by a lay leader. I said, 'I'm sorry you feel like that. My aim was to present Scripture, and I'd welcome your suggestions on how to do better.' He offered no suggestions, but loudly and angrily complained that the topic should be mentioned at all in God's house. It was six years until I was invited back to that church, and then I was sad to hear that he was living alone. His wife had discovered him showing hardcore pornographic films to their pre-teen children. Fearing he was grooming them for abuse, she had taken them away. The case had been in the newspapers. If preaching offends someone, it may of course be that my character flaws are getting in the way of God's message, but the Spirit of truth may be reproving sin (John 16:8) and people ignore him at their peril. The gospel Jesus preached called for repentance (Mark 1:15).

Yet preachers must major in the gospel of grace of the Saviour who took my sins to the cross, and in God's love for faulty people, or else we only push people deeper into self-reproach and hopelessness, or build false hopes like surface moralism and legalism. A poem about God's redemption of love and sex is a good chance to speak about the divine, self-giving love behind the cross.

4. Dialogue with the listeners' culture

If preaching is bridge-building, then preachers could usefully do double exegesis: of text and of culture. Why not compare and contrast a passage of the Song with the themes of a popular song or influential TV sitcom? (To avoid misperceptions, you may want to explain that this is not your usual media diet!) Affirm what you can, recognizing that God is not left without witness in any culture, and then critique and challenge. Respect the culture while letting Scripture begin to transform the culture.

5. Welcome questions

It can be useful to offer a question time after the message – either live or anonymous in writing via the collection plate or SMS text. That may sound terrifying, but there is no shame in admitting we need to do more research and get back to people, or even just kindly acknowledging a difficult question and the personal experience behind it. Questions can help an audience feel heard and also give a preacher valuable insights about the listeners. If you know a psychologist or medical doctor with a strong Christian worldview on this topic, they may team up with you.

6. Preach not just rules but a broad, God-honouring theology of sex

Show how God's invention of sex reveals his love and creativity, and a wish for human joy. Taking the doctrine of creation seriously means sex is a good gift from a good Creator.

7. In word choice, be frank but tasteful – as the Song is

This will require pastoral sensitivity and tact.

8. Take gradual steps

Do not feel pressure to do it all in one message, but cover aspects as part of a balanced sermonic diet.

Perhaps invite a visiting specialist for the first presentation, or to do heavy lifting for you on a specific issue. They are outside local political processes, and people often feel free to open up to someone they will not have to see every week.

9. Do not self-disclose

Targeting oneself in preaching can generally be a useful way of avoiding 'talking down' to an audience, but not on this topic. If you face a congregation week after week, a confessional sermon about your past sins or present struggles may drown out anything else you say and develop a life of its own. Leave breathless confessions to the celebrities.

Church and society need biblical teaching which reveals God as the Source of all that is good and the Redeemer of love and sex and everything else, and which calls people in a fast-changing culture to experience God's grace, love him back, and live by the timeless logic and beauty of his commandments.

Sermon outline on Song of Solomon 4:12 – 5:1: 'I Dig Your Garden'

I do an expository series in four to eight parts working through the text. Here is one section, with an introduction which assumes the audience is unfamiliar with the Song.

Introduction: What is this doing in the Bible?

(a) Read the passage.
(b) Introduce Song of Solomon and its themes.
(c) Describe why it is not often preached.
(d) Briefly mention authorship theories, and the problem of connecting monogamy and Solomon.

1. The male character enthuses (4:12–15)

(a) A garden with a private spring was the height of luxury, called *pardēs*, whence our word 'paradise'. Such gardens were associated with wealthy Solomon (Eccl. 2:4–6; 1 Kgs 4:33).
(b) Here the garden is the woman.
(c) 'Sister' (cf. 5:1) is not literal. It is an expression, like 'baby' in a pop song. Describe the cultural distance.

(d) Spice: this was a 'hot' commodity in the Solomonic age, with high value (1 Kgs 10:2). Some terms in this list have Indian origins exotic to the hearers. And it is spicy in that garden. Who says monogamy must be boring? That is a sexual revolution myth.

(e) A well of flowing or literally 'living' water suggests refreshment, a deep source, spirituality?

(f) Walls as boundaries of monogamy. Briefly explain the parallels with Proverbs 5:15–21, which also teaches hot monogamy. The walls suggest morality and boundaries as protecting the private enjoyment.

(g) Rabbi Shmueli Boteach, in *The Jewish Guide to Adultery*, shows how to keep having affairs – with your spouse![17]

2. The female character invites (4:16)

(a) Come in!

(b) Invitation to intimacy on all levels. The best sex involves everything a person is: mind, emotions, spirit, body.

(c) She is 'her' garden: a free, strong, self-possessed woman.

3. The male character (5:1a)

(a) Delights in her. Sensual pleasures like scent and taste, like sexual delight, are here celebrated by the Bible in their proper place.

(b) She is also 'his' garden (cf. 4:16 above). They own each other (cf. 2:16).

4. The chorus approves (5:1b)

Reflection

(a) In biblical context, a garden can also suggest Eden.

(b) We are not living there now. The fall has damaged sexuality: give examples.

(c) Yet love and sex are still gifts from the Creator, and a good marriage is like sneaking back into paradise.

(d) Similarly, in the overall story of the Bible, the gospel restores believers to a superb garden, a new Eden with 'no more curse' (Rev. 22:3).

---

17. Rabbi Shmueli Boteach, *The Jewish Guide to Adultery* (London: Hodder & Stoughton, 1999).

Conclusion

(a) What practical wisdom does this offer? Hot monogamy as God's ideal.
    Application: How can you make choices contributing to that? If you
    are married? If you are single?

(b) What does this say about God? Creator. Giver of good gifts. Redeemer,
    calling us back to Eden and to completeness in the gospel.

    The fact that God kindly gives us advice infers that he knows we are
    fallen and broken in some ways and need his grace, and he is happy
    to forgive us, understand us and help us. If he made us relational, this
    suggests that he wants a relationship with us.

    Application: Co-operate with his plans in Christ for you, because he
    wants your happiness.

Recommended further reading

RICHARD M. DAVIDSON, *Flame of Yahweh: Sexuality in the Old Testament* (Peabody:
    Hendricksons, 2007).
DENNIS P. HOLLINGER, *The Meaning of Sex: Christian Ethics and the Moral Life* (Grand
    Rapids: Baker Academic, 2009).
JUDITH K. BALSWICK and JACK O. BALSWICK, *Authentic Human Sexuality: An Integrated
    Christian Approach* (Downers Grove: InterVarsity Press, 1999).

8. PREACHING FROM ISAIAH

H. G. M. Williamson

In order to avoid any misunderstanding, two limitations to the following chapter should be made clear at the start. First, although I preach regularly, I have no academic expertise in homiletics; whether my own practice or my comments in this chapter coincide with what is deemed to be best theory must be for others to judge. I shall not relate my comments to such discussions in any way.

Second, I believe that there are many matters of presentation in preaching which are of great importance in making a sermon an arresting and effective means of communication. These, however, are not peculiar to preaching from Isaiah, and I therefore take them for granted here. This should not be taken to mean that they are not of significance in sermon preparation.

General orientation

The book of Isaiah is long and has many sections which are quite distinct from one another, even though they are criss-crossed with allusions and even citations. What is more, there is universal agreement (quite apart from the question of authorship) that they relate to different historical situations which are separated by at least 200 years. More narrowly, there is clearly a gap between the oral proclamation of the prophet and the written form of his words which we have.

Given that sermons should be based on the text, it is clear that our primary focus in sermon preparation should be on the literature we have rather than our best guesses at the historical circumstances which gave rise to it. These particular words and deeds of the prophet rather than others were deemed sufficiently valuable to warrant recording, and this too implies an element of gap between event and record. Our task, then, is to try to do justice to the book by unearthing and proclaiming that message in a contemporary manner. The inevitable distance between history and textual record should encourage us; as preachers we are not asked to be research students in ancient history, but careful readers of the material we have – something that is more readily within our grasp.

At the same time, this all means that both the original proclamation (when there was such) and the whole process leading to the formation of the book we have now was grounded in an appreciation of its relevance, whether in judgment or encouragement. It was not written to serve as a work of systematic theology, still less as some sort of almanac concerning far-off future days with no links to the present. In what follows, therefore, we shall be trying to consider ways whereby the inscripturated word of the past can be meaningfully incorporated into a proclamation for today. We do not see it as valuable to pursue lines of thought which find here all manner of coded messages relating to other fields of thought or belief. I am aware that many people come to the Bible with all sorts of bizarre notions about what they are going to find, not least from the prophets, but I have to content myself in the present context by asserting that these have no genuine relation with the real scriptures as we have received them and that they cannot, therefore, detain us further now.

Problems of date and authorship

One of the best-known results of scholarship in regard to the OT is the hypothesis that the book of Isaiah was written by more than one author over an extended period of time, and many of the commentaries that preachers will use take this more or less for granted. This can raise problems both for the preacher and for the congregation.

So far as preachers are concerned, they may or may not share this point of view, and indeed many will admit that they do not feel competent to make a judgment on the matter. This, however, has always seemed to me to be considered a larger problem than it need be. On the one hand, scholarly opinion about authorship of the book is now far more complicated than it used to be. Many who are not specialists may have it in mind that the common opinion is that there were three Isaiahs – the eighth-century BCE prophet who was responsible for Isaiah 1 – 39 in Jerusalem, a prophet at the end of the exilic period who wrote Isaiah 40 – 55 in Babylon ('Deutero-Isaiah'), and a third prophet who wrote the last eleven chapters of the book sometime after the return to Jerusalem from exile ('Trito-Isaiah').

In fact, no scholar takes that simple view, and the variations in opinion are legion. Chapters 1 – 39 encompass material from all periods, for instance, although quite which bits belong where is disputed. Again, many are now beginning to hypothesize that the second main section of the book is also less unified than used to be thought, and this is even more so with the third. Hence, when consulting a commentary in order to have some sense of historical setting for the passage under consideration, secure results may be hard to come by.

On the other hand, however, the preacher may be resistant to such notions, and so be put off from benefiting from the study aids, or at best may feel a sense of despair at the uncertainties. My own approach, and consequent advice, when preparing to preach is not to focus so narrowly on authorship, but rather to ask what setting the passage evidently addresses. Sometimes this question cannot be answered, in which case one need say nothing about it; other forms of contextualization for the sermon will have to be used. Congregations are quickly switched off by rants against scholarly views about the Bible which have no relevance to the proclamation of the passage in hand. At the same time, there is little disagreement between scholars of all shades of opinion, including conservative evangelicals, that whoever wrote chapters 40 – 55, for instance, was not addressing an eighth-century BCE audience in Jerusalem, but rather the concerns of a later community in a very different setting. The imaginatively sensitive evocation of the despair of the exilic community who thought that God had forgotten or abandoned them (e.g. 40:27) is one that resonates still with individuals and groups in all manner of twenty-first-century situations too, so that the application to them of the message of comfort (40:1), encouragement (e.g. 43:1–7) and persuasion to recover faith in God's power, concern and ability to move again in unexpected ways (e.g. 40:12–31) is readily available. Equally, the harsh judgment of those in positions of influence or authority in the much earlier kingdom of Judah who manipulate their position to personal advantage (e.g. 1:21–26; 3:13–15; 5:1–7) can still bring its challenge to those in positions of privilege and responsibility today.

Consideration of the audience addressed by the passage will thus bring the text to life for the preacher in preparation and this, it may be hoped, will transfer to the sermon as well! How much of this background preparation should be brought into the sermon itself, however? My own practice here is to say that much depends on the circumstances of the particular sermon. If I am invited as a guest preacher to deliver a single sermon from Isaiah to a congregation that I do not know at all, I avoid directly addressing such issues altogether. Without being in the least dishonest, it is perfectly possible to discuss the passage in its likely setting without any implication that it was written by an author or at a date which one does not in fact consider likely. A few in the congregation may appreciate what is going on, but most will not and will not suffer from it. After all, a sermon is not a lecture. But in the case of undertaking (as I have done) a series on Isaiah 40 – 55 in my own church, where I hope there is a good pastoral and personal rapport, I have briefly stated my views in the first sermon of the series and been pleased to find that it caused not a murmur. One or two were sufficiently interested to want to talk further about it, which is always an encouragement to a preacher. The majority, I suspect, knew me well enough to accept that 'Hugh has some funny ideas, but he is all right really', and others may have been too polite to express disagreement. I felt it was right to be open about my opinions (even if only briefly), and if there was disagreement it did not surface or appear to be damaging. And I have never known any congregation that agreed about everything. The opportunity for debate is to be welcomed.

Approaches to preaching from Isaiah

There has been a dramatic change in scholarly analysis of the book of Isaiah in recent years, and the consequences of this may not always have reached the commentaries upon which preachers currently rely. Nevertheless, these developments should be a help and encouragement to preachers, provided they are willing to invest the necessary time in sermon preparation to benefit from them.

Although there is no going back on the variety of material within the book, there has recently developed a far greater appreciation of the many ways in which the different sections of the book hold together. Many of the standard textbooks and commentaries still treat the three main sections of the book, outlined above, as though they were to all intents and purposes different books. They are analysed and interpreted in isolation from one another.

This is no longer generally thought to be appropriate. While the understanding of the mechanics of how it came about vary from one scholar to another, there is nevertheless a much greater acknowledgment by all that the parts are more closely related to each other than was previously realized. At the simplest level, this may be seen from the many ways that various themes are

taken up and handled differently in the different sections of the book, this no
doubt reflecting the changing circumstances that are being addressed. I could
here give a long list of such themes, and indeed monographs are now regularly
appearing that take one or another of these as the basis for a full analysis.

It has long been known, for instance, that the distinctive title of God as the
'Holy One of Israel' comes about twenty-five times in Isaiah and only very
rarely elsewhere. (To be more precise, it should be specified that it comes only
twice in chapters 56 – 66, and then by way of citation, and that it does not
appear at all in such late sections as chapters 24 – 27.) In the first part of the
book, in passages which sound most like the judgment sayings of the original
prophet, God as the Holy One seems threatening to his people in their rebellion against him. In the second half of the book, however, the same title is
used frequently to describe the God of encouragement, comfort and deliverance, and this too seems occasionally to be reflected by way of an echo in the
earlier chapters as well. The title was probably drawn (if its use twice in the
Psalms may be believed) from the worship of the Jerusalem temple, where in
the days of the monarchy the people will have believed that it spoke of how
God guaranteed their political freedom and victory. As with other such elements, Isaiah turns this on its head, however, and indicates that this same God
can equally threaten his own people if they do not follow and serve him in a
qualitatively different manner from the surrounding nations. He is like many
preachers who use a familiar line of a hymn to overturn easygoing assumptions about the congregation's situation. But in the second half of the book
that judgment is pictured as past, and the prophet seeks to turn his people's
attention forward to the creatively new work that God is about to do. And
as part of that the familiar title, which has come to be seen as threatening,
is turned again to announce that the free and sovereign Lord is able to work
as vigorously and surprisingly in grace as he had in judgment. This therefore
opens the reader up to a new appreciation of the rich character of God who
is not bound by institution or routine, but is free to respond to his people's
situations in ways that constantly take us unawares – and ultimately, so far as
this book proclaims, in grace.

Now, I shall mention some other such themes shortly, but having introduced just one so far I wish to emphasize the point that awareness of such
possibilities should be borne carefully in mind when working on a given
passage for exposition. The more detailed commentaries will raise awareness
of some of these topics, but at this stage of research others may need to be dug
out with the help of a concordance. While of course, as emphasized above, a
given passage will need to be interpreted in the light of the circumstances it
addresses (insofar as this is recoverable), equally it needs to be opened up in

the light of the wider book as a whole, which time and again demonstrates by its repeated use of such themes that no one passage is sufficient on its own to do justice to the complete subject for a proper exposition.

The devastating critique of the misuse of the cult (formal public religion!) in 1:10–17, for instance, should not be separated from the very different but closely related considerations of the same theme in 43:22–28 and 58 (i.e. from the second and third sections of the book) in order to gain the right sense of balance of similar underlying notions being reapplied in different historical and social circumstances.

Again, nobody should read the closing verses of the first chapter without taking into account the use of very comparable language in 65:1–5, 66:17 and 24. If the opening chapter of the book is thus paralleled at its close, it makes us think (along with other considerations) that perhaps chapter 1 is best interpreted as some sort of introduction to the whole – a laying out of the message of judgment (1:2–9), of the possibility of full forgiveness (1:10–20) and of the need for individual response to that message (1:21–31) which in large measure reflects the overall shape of the three main sections of the book as a whole. Preaching on one part thus invites exposition in the light of the wider whole.

Another major theme which runs throughout the book derives from the extremely difficult 'hardening saying' in 6:9–10. It may well be that this was originally written up in the context of the Syro-Ephraimite crisis which dominates the next two or three chapters (see especially the echo of 'this people' in 6:9, 10; 8:6, 11, 12), but in the course of time its application was seen to be wider and more long-lasting, as several later allusions make clear (starting as early as 1:2–3). Beyond the judgment, however, we find that this negative notion is reversed and turned positively. It is surprising, once one has this in mind, how often allusions in chapters 40 – 55 appear to show that eyes and ears that once were closed have now been opened or the like. And in even further development, the saying which was clearly originally given in a metaphorical or 'spiritual' sense is turned in a more literal direction so that physical blindness and deafness too will find healing (e.g. 35:5–6). Both negative and positive uses of this theme are referred to more than once in the NT as well, both in relation to the parables and to Jesus's healing ministry, so we find again that there is rich material here for a preacher to reflect on and apply as appropriate.

Space precludes attention here to all such themes (even if I were aware of them all!). One will be treated more fully in the next section by way of example, and the messianic theme in particular after that, but it may suffice to list here at least a selection of the other possibilities that would be worth exploring if any were to surface in the passage chosen for a sermon: glory, darkness and light, the Spirit, the raised banner or ensign, the vineyard (and indeed other metaphors drawn from the botanical world), former and new things (or equivalents). Again, a concordance or a more advanced commentary will quickly lead the preacher to the appropriate passages for consideration. Other topics may not be so pervasive as these and yet have at least one other clear reference within the book, such as 28:1–4 (especially v. 4) and 40:6–8.

In all this, experience suggests that in fact there are very few extended passages in the book of Isaiah which do not have parallels, citations or allusions elsewhere in the book. This needs to be taken carefully into account in sermon preparation if the message delivered is to be fair to the book we have (let alone the Bible more widely). Any single passage in Isaiah can easily be made into an excuse for a one-sided presentation which can result in serious distortion. Of course it may be appropriate to emphasize one aspect of the material in particular in any given circumstance, but it would be a mistake either to suggest that the harsh words of judgment are left without a corresponding message of deliverance or equally that the salvation offered is cheap, since contextually it so clearly follows severe judgment. This wider frame of reference may also help to explain the seemingly awkward sudden shifts from judgment to promise even within a single paragraph in the first half of the book. While a Christian preacher will naturally introduce the fuller understanding of these matters which comes from the NT, it makes for homiletically good practice mainly to remain within an exposition of a passage that is rooted in its nearer context, rather than appearing to pull theological rabbits out of NT hats. And as I have suggested here, Isaiah allows every possibility for that if it is taken seriously as a book.

Thematic considerations

It may help to discuss one prominent theme in a little more detail by way of specific example.

In common with some other parts of the OT, as well as elsewhere in the Ancient Near East, the first half of the book of Isaiah stresses the need for 'justice and righteousness' in various spheres of life. In fact, there are some dozen occurrences of this word pair. This is not language we commonly use today, so that it needs some unpacking.

By observing uses in context, including topics with which these values are contrasted, we soon learn that this goes far beyond just the administration of the criminal legal system (although that is included). It speaks rather of the need for probity, including compassion, in all walks of social and political life; one scholar has even gone so far as to gloss it with the phrase 'social justice'.

This may have taken very different forms in antiquity than it does today, but the general area is one of obviously continuing need at various levels of local, national and international life.

According to Isaiah's presentation, these qualities used to be characteristic of Zion in what he portrays as the golden era of Davidic rule, even though things have declined seriously since (1:21–23). He concludes his famous parable of the vineyard by asserting that God still looks for these qualities in the present time, but instead he finds only their opposite – bloodshed and the cry of oppression (5:7, with the clever use of word-play). However, he is confident that they will once again characterize the restored Zion of the future as pictorially God as builder of the new city declares that 'I will make justice the line and righteousness the plummet' (28:17 NRSV). Their importance is underlined still further by the fact that they should be the concern of the ideal king (32:1) and indeed will be of the royal child whose birth is announced in 9:6–7. Many other passages could be cited where these words either occur together or on their own in this first part of the book to demonstrate how central a concern this was to Isaiah and how the perversion of justice and righteousness was a significant cause of the judgment that he anticipated.

When we turn to the next part of the book, however, we find a remarkable contrast. To be sure, there are some elements of continuity (e.g. in 42:1–4, although the two words 'justice' and 'righteousness' do not appear in tandem at any point in Isaiah 40 – 55), but more commonly we find 'righteousness' singled out and used in a very different way. It appears several times in parallel with the word for 'salvation', so that, whereas in 1 – 39 it was something that people in positions of responsibility had to do or perform, now it becomes part of the gracious deliverance and provision by God. There are those, indeed, who would understandably translate it as 'victory', 'deliverance' or the like in these chapters; examples include 41:10; 45:8; 46:13; 51:5, 6, 8, among others.

Finally, and remarkably, we find that these two apparently contrasting uses are brought into relationship in the twofold use of the word at the very start of the third section of the book, 56:1 (NRSV):

Maintain justice, and do what is right,
   for soon my salvation will come,
   and my deliverance be revealed.

Here the parallel form familiar from chapters 1 – 39 reappears in the first line as an urgent imperative, whereas in the following lines 'righteousness' (the rendering of the NRSV, cited above, is 'deliverance') is used in parallel with 'salvation', as in chapters 40 – 55, as indicative of God's imminent deliverance and as motivation to obey the command of the first line. This theologically rich intertwining of the two preceding sections of the book is then taken up and developed in various ways in the concluding chapters.

These remarks are only the sketchiest outline of a topic of central importance to the book. In preaching, however, the striking balance introduced in 56:1 needs to be kept in mind. In one pastoral situation it may be considered necessary to exhort the congregation to practise justice and righteousness, so that attention will legitimately be concentrated on one or more of the relevant passages in the first half of the book. It would be a mistake, however, to leave the congregation there, with the onus on their responsibilities and no hint that there is a rich source of encouragement from reflection on God's correspondingly salvific righteousness. Conversely, the need may be for a dispirited congregation to be comforted by the good news of God's deliverance as joyfully proclaimed in so much of the second part of the book, but here too it would be unbalanced to concentrate exclusively on that (even though it may well be the major point of the sermon) without any indication that God looks for a response in gratitude in the way that we treat others, especially those who are in more difficult circumstances than we are.

This same theme is also helpful, I believe, in consideration of the specifically messianic prophecies in Isaiah, to which I turn next.

Messianic prophecy

Isaiah has several classical messianic prophecies which feature regularly in most church lectionaries and they are among the passages on which preachers are most likely to concentrate. They raise many exegetical problems of their own, however, so that a few words of guidance here may be helpful. Included prominently among these passages are 7:14; 9:1–7; 11:1–9; 42:1–4; 49:1–6; 52:13 – 53:12; 61:1–4.

There are two main dangers in preaching from these passages which I should hope might be avoided, but sadly are all too often practised. In the first place, they are often applied so directly to Jesus that they are treated in wilful disregard of their present immediate context in Isaiah. The bits that fit the NT tend to be pulled out with no attempt to relate them to other things that are equally prominent in the passage under consideration. Second, there is a tendency to stress so emphatically that Jesus has fulfilled these prophecies that they are emptied of any other content, including matters which I believe should be among the most prominent challenges of Isaiah to the church in the present day. What approach, then, can do justice to these passages as messianic while avoiding these two particular dangers?

In my opinion, the first point to notice is that the emphasis falls more on the task that the figure is to perform than on the identity of the figure in question. In 9:6–7, for instance, the whole drive of the prophecy is that the child has been given in order to establish and uphold the kingdom 'with justice and with righteousness', so that this fits closely with the theme we surveyed briefly in the previous section. We can well imagine that such hopes would have attended the birth of any royal child in ancient Judah; surely this new prospective king (whether Hezekiah or another) will improve the social circumstances of the kingdom over the present state of affairs. The focus in chapter 11 turns out upon inspection to be not so very different. It is also immediately in line with the proverbial saying of 32:1: 'A king should reign in the interests of righteousness and princes rule for the furtherance of justice' (my translation).

When we turn to the second half of the book, we find that the political conditions have changed completely and, as indicated in the sermon outline on 42:1–4 at the end of this chapter, the royal hopes of the first half of the book are turned now to the community of God's people in relation to the nations. The essential task remains, however: three times it is stressed that this new 'servant king', clearly identified in context as Israel/Jacob (see the similar language, including the designation as servant, used of Israel in 41:8–13 as in 42:1–4 of the unnamed servant), will 'bring forth justice to the nations'. And although in the third section of the book the situation has changed yet again, and the people are beginning to wonder why all the great promises do not seem to have been realized in the spectacular fashion that they perhaps had hoped, nevertheless the figure in 61:1–3 recapitulates many of the characteristics of the earlier messianic passages and emphasizes again that he will come to proclaim deliverance for the oppressed, which was such an integral element of justice as envisaged in this book.

This brief sketch suggests to me that it is not going to be a helpful approach in preaching simply to say, 'Here is the text in Isaiah and it predicts Jesus, full stop.' Rather, these are passages that indicate God's purpose for a broken nation and a distressed world. That nation and that world move through all sorts of different circumstances, but the vision remains constant. When Jesus came, he lived in a situation which again was not directly envisaged in Isaiah, namely that of living as an artisan under foreign oppressive occupation. We believe that in that very situation he demonstrated to perfection what it means to inaugurate justice under the constrained political circumstances within which had to operate. His concern for the outcast, his care for the suffering and his love for the unloved are all part of that work, and supremely, of course, his journey to the cross and death there on our behalf fulfilled the work of reconciliation between humanity and God in a way which even surpasses what had previously been envisaged.

This does not, however, exhaust those prophecies. We should not preach their fulfilment in Christ in such a way that we do not realize that as individuals and as the community of the church we too are called to translate those divine values into the modern world, which remains in need of justice, righteousness and peace at all levels, from international relations right the way down to those at the bottom of the social heap in our own neighbourhoods. To hear these passages read at Advent or in Holy Week is not to encourage a smug feeling that all that has been taken care of by Christ, but rather that, as imitators of him, we are challenged to implement these same costly and tiring values in our own changed circumstances.

Theology

Before providing a sermon outline that may serve to illustrate several of the points made above, it might be helpful to add a few comments about the distinctive characterization of God in Isaiah. This is not out of line, of course, with what is found elsewhere in Scripture, but there are one or two distinctive emphases in the book which again it may be worth noting in general as background to preparation for preaching from any one specific passage.

Few would doubt that Isaiah's call or commissioning (it is not quite clear which it is) as recorded in chapter 6 was a foundational experience for the prophet just as its recorded version in writing has become for the development of the book as a whole. Its vocabulary and themes are constantly cited or alluded to elsewhere, and of course its influence on later theology and liturgy is pervasive.

It starts with a vision of God in all his royal majesty (he is called a king in v. 5), and in the first verse the words 'high and lifted up' appear. Grammatically it is, in fact, not quite clear whether these words apply directly here to God or whether rather they qualify the throne on which he is sitting. Either way, however, there can be no doubt, as we shall see shortly, that they came in the course of time to be understood as referring to God.

From this opening statement, a number of other characteristic phrases and words may be seen to take their natural place. The distinctive title 'The Holy One of Israel', already mentioned above, fits in well at this point, for instance, as does the use of the holiness word group more generally in relation to God. 'Glory' is another favourite term in the book, and it takes its place alongside 'holy' as early as 6:3 in the praise of the seraphim which has been adopted into most forms of Christian liturgy as what is technically known as the Trisagion. From there the language ripples out in several different directions. Another characteristic title for God is 'the Lord of hosts' (again, starting from 6:5), the 'hosts' in this context being almost certainly the heavenly armies of the divine king. This too adds to the impression of all-powerful and completely dominating divine power.

Appreciation of this exalted majesty of God was undoubtedly a dominating consideration for Isaiah in his theological worldview. He has a strong sense of hierarchy and a consequent appreciation that it is important for each part of the created order to know its place. At the simplest level, therefore, anything else which claims a 'high and lifted up' position is doomed to destruction because it manifests hubris by comparison with the only truly exalted one who is God himself. Thus the several occurrences of these words with relation to trees, mountains, towers and the like in Isaiah 2:12–17 are sufficient to explain without further justification why the Lord of hosts has a day against them, 'against all that is proud and lofty, against all that is lifted up and high' (NRSV).

The same principle then explains his theology in relation to the Assyrians, for instance. So long as they act in judgment even against Judah, they are regarded as his ministers – 'the rod of my anger, the staff of my fury! Against a godless nation I send him' (10:5–6 RSV). But as soon as they exceed their God-given brief and start to act in arrogant independence (10:7–14), their own fate is sealed (10:15–19), for this again is a clear example of hubris. This is a pattern which we find repeated elsewhere as well.

This theology translates downwards, we may also note in passing, into Isaiah's understanding of the proper ordering of society. There are aspects of this which we today might well find politically incorrect, although it should be remembered in partial mitigation that he has an equally strong sense that those higher up the pile have correspondingly larger responsibilities of care for those lower down, as we have already seen. Nevertheless, it is helpful to appreciate the theology on which some of these more challenging passages, such as chapter 3, are based.

If this brief, but I hope not wholly misleading, characterization of God in the first part of the book is correct, then it is of more than passing interest to see how it is handled later on, not least because of the ways we have already noted that one part of the book is frequently balanced in important ways by another. The most striking way into this is the use of the same vocabulary in reference to God (and where, indeed, 'high and lifted up' has actually become a divine title) in 57:15 (NRSV):

> For thus says the high and lofty one
> who inhabits eternity, whose name is Holy:
> I dwell in the high and holy place,
> and also with those who are contrite and humble in spirit,
> to revive the spirit of the humble,
> and to revive the heart of the contrite.

The majesty of God as recapitulated from the first part of the book is here shown not to make him necessarily remote, as we might otherwise suppose. Rather, when his majesty encounters people of a suitably contrasting disposition he is said to dwell with them quite as much as in the high and holy place. The same sentiment exactly is echoed in 66:1–2, which concludes, 'But this is the man to whom I will look, he that is humble and contrite in spirit, and trembles at my word' (RSV).

This balancing between the parts of the book, which we have found repeatedly in the course of our survey, could be developed further in this regard, of course, but it serves as a reminder once again of the need to consider each individual part of the book in the light of the whole. On this occasion, there is just one further dimension that should be added here, for this same language recurs at the start of the fourth of the so-called servant songs, at 52:13 (RSV): 'Behold, my servant shall prosper, he shall be exalted and lifted up, and shall be very high.' This is a remarkable statement of how the servant (whose identity need not be further considered at this point) will share the status and designation that previously we had thought was reserved exclusively for God. It comes in the introduction to a passage of extended reflection on rejection and suffering and anticipates (as is not unusual in Hebrew narrative) the outcome of the sequence of events which is to follow (cf. 53:12, which brings us back to the same point as this opening). Of the many insights which this affords, let it suffice here to state the obvious, namely that when God finds an attitude of acceptance of the will of God for one's life in the service of others, no matter what the cost, then he is prepared against all expectation to share the highest honours with his servants. It is a pattern which we see most fully realized in the exaltation of Christ, whose very sufferings on the cross are described as his glory in the fourth gospel.

Sermon outline on Isaiah 42:1–4

As a general rule, I find congregations appreciate having a series of clearly indicated points as a way of following the argument. Despite occasional wry comments, I still think that some device such as alliteration is helpful for clarity (provided it is justified by the material). In this case, I have used the three references to 'bringing forth/establishing justice' as the basis. In the interests of brevity, the following outline sometimes uses moderately technical language. Needless to say, this would need to be differently expressed in an actual sermon.

Introduction

This will vary according to local circumstances, of course. One way in is to start with the common experience of pride in a job well done or in some new purchase: 'Look at that!' Here, we see God's pride in his servant. Contrast the 'behold' in 41:24 and 29 concerning idols.

1. His presentation (v. 1)

- Both in form and content this first verse uses royal language, and the combination of all the terms used can refer only to a king. How much of the detail to justify this statement can be presented in a sermon will depend upon the nature of the congregation, time available and so on. The evidence is set out fully in my *Variations on a Theme*, pages 130–136 (full details given below).
- The basis of what this part of Isaiah says about kingship is found in 55:3, where it is clear that the role of human kingship is passed from the Davidic family to the community being addressed. In line with this, we find that at 41:8–13 similar wording is used of the servant Israel/Jacob as in our passage of the unnamed servant.
- The role of this 'royal' servant Israel is to 'bring forth justice to the nations'. This has been understood in an astonishing variety of ways in the past, but in fact it should be straightforward. One of the major tasks of the kings in Israel (as seen, for instance, in the first part of the book) was to administer justice in the nation. This was not just the criminal law, but also the upholding of the rights of all citizens, including especially the poor and dispossessed, who needed a champion to safeguard their interests (social justice). Now, that same role is being transferred to the new community of Israel in relation to the nations. It was needed then – and still is very much in our modern world. This can be illustrated from current affairs, third-world issues, human rights or however seems contextually most appropriate.

2. His patience (vv. 2–3)

- The first verse might lead us to expect that this great task would be carried out by some major programme of public activity. The present description shows that will not be so. There will be no noise or fanfare that would attract attention to the servant. Some of the language here even reflects the preparations for war in Joshua and Judges – but that way too is eschewed.
- The bruised reeds and dimly burning wicks of today's society need help, not publicity. Need or tragedy is sometimes engineered and manipulated by journalists or the media for their own ends; they have a vested interest in there being 'sob stories'. The servant, by contrast, works better and more effectively incognito, with attention fully focused on the needy.
- This passage was cited in Matthew 12:18–21 of Jesus withdrawing from confrontation on occasions (cf. vv. 15–16). This was seen supremely at the cross. The church has too often been attracted by the language of 'power', etc., but that is not the way of the servant.
- This should not be confused with weakness, however:

3. His perseverance (v. 4)

- Note how the start of verse 4 contrasts with verse 3. In other words, the servant needs great personal strength that he can then bring alongside the needy in the administration of justice.
- But how long is 'until'? This ties up with the identity of the servant. Some apply it directly to Jesus, in which case this can be applied devotionally to his work on the cross as effecting the decisive breakthrough in bringing (positive) 'justice' to all people.
- This does not exhaust the prophecy, however. It spoke initially of how God's purposes should be applied in the new circumstances of Israel as no longer a sovereign kingdom but now a witness and servant to the nations. New circumstances, new identities, but God's work continues unchanged.
- By extension, this applies also, then, to the community of God's people today in a world that is still crying out for justice. The circumstances may have changed again (as indeed they had in the case of Jesus), but the task remains. In his ministry and death, Jesus 'fulfilled' this task to perfection, but as imitators of Christ we inherit the task 'until' it is realized now.

Concluding challenge

Our need as communities as well as individuals for that same inner strength that comes from the Spirit of God alone and our task to bring it alongside the crushed and despondent, not for our glory, but to demonstrate that God has decided positively in their favour.

Key bibliographical resources

Of the very many commentaries that are available, the most useful for preachers is John Goldingay, *Isaiah*, NIBC (Peabody: Hendricksons, 2001).

On the second half of the book, I have also derived enormous help from the classic of C. Westermann, *Isaiah 40 – 66*, Old Testament Library (London: SCM, 1969).

For a survey of recent study of Isaiah, see David G. Firth and H. G. M. Williamson (eds.), *Interpreting Isaiah: Issues and Approaches* (Nottingham: Apollos; Downers Grove: InterVarsity Press, 2009).

For an illustration of a thematic study, see my *Variations on a Theme: King, Messiah and Servant in the Book of Isaiah* (Carlisle: Paternoster, 1998).

9. PREACHING EZEKIEL

Daniel I. Block

The problem with preaching Ezekiel

My assignment in this chapter is both enviable and unenviable. It is enviable because when we preach from Ezekiel we preach from one of the most fascinating books in the entire canon. It is unenviable because textbooks on preaching from the OT – whether by homileticians or OT scholars – offer no help in preaching Ezekiel. They abound with references to Genesis, Joshua, the Psalms, Isaiah, Amos and Hosea, but they rarely mention Ezekiel. Could it be that Christians have heeded the counsel of Jewish rabbis who forbade Jews under thirty from reading the beginning and ending of the book? If so, we have extended the prohibition to the whole book, perhaps assuming that there would always be people under thirty in our congregations.

It has not always been this way. Origen (AD 185–254) composed at least fourteen homilies on Ezekiel, which were translated into Latin by Jerome. Gregory the Great (AD 540–604) preached twenty-two homilies on Ezekiel 1 – 3 and 40 between 593 and 594, expressing delight in clarifying obscure texts. By his time the interpretation of the four living creatures in the opening vision as the four evangelists was well established, but he proposed that the four creatures represent all preachers of the word. From the medieval period, Andrew of St Victor's overriding concern in reading Ezekiel's vision was not only to recapture the picture so he could draw it like he drew the temple, but also to know what it meant for the people for whom Ezekiel recorded it. Of the Reformers, Calvin's expositions of Ezekiel are significant because they represent his last written work. Racked by pain, his emaciated body gave out at the end of chapter 20. Nevertheless, his commentary reflects the vigour of his mind and his high view of all Scripture.[1] Modern American evangelical interest in the book tends to revolve around Ezekiel's eschatological vision, particularly the participation of Gog and Magog in the final battles, and the role of the temple and its cult in the millennium. In my native dispensationalist world, Ezekiel was mentioned exclusively in the contexts of prophecy ('end time') conferences, which now seem to have been quite oblivious to the exilic prophet's lofty theology or the practical nature of his message.

So the daunting task before us is to rehabilitate this prophet and to redis-cover the vitality of the book that bears his name. This challenge is much greater today than it was, say, forty years ago. Because of (rightful) increasing sensitivity to issues of gender in recent decades, many are repulsed by the image of God presented in the book, especially in chapters 16 and 23. If in the past Christians *would not* read or preach the book of Ezekiel because they were perplexed by the prophet's visions or the forms of his oracles, today some *cannot* preach it because the book and the God portrayed in it seem irredeemably problematic. According to some interpreters he is devoid of any grace at all. How can pastors today declare its message with authority, vitality and clarity? I propose to answer the question with a series of propositions that together might yield a strategy for thinking about preaching Ezekiel.

Proposition 1: In order to preach from Ezekiel with authority and clarity, we need to understand the prophet – his character (*ethos*), passion (*pathos*) and argumentation (*logos*).

All we know about Ezekiel we learn from the book that bears his name. Ezekiel's own name ('May God strengthen/toughen') may express the opti-mism of his parents at the time he was born, although it also provides a com-mentary on his life. The third-person commentary on the superscription (1:3) identifies Ezekiel as the son of Buzi. He was called into priestly ministry in his thirtieth year, on 31 July 593 BC, which means his birth in 623 BC coincided with the mid-point of Josiah's reign (640–609 BC), shortly before the discovery

---

1. John Calvin, *Commentaries on the First Twenty Chapters of the Book of the Prophet Ezekiel*, 2 vols., trans. T. Myers (Grand Rapids: Eerdmans, 1948).

of the Torah in the temple (2 Kgs 22:3). Despite Josiah's efforts at reform, his untimely death in 609 BC dashed the prospects for a comprehensive political and spiritual renaissance to the ground. Within the next eleven years three kings would succeed him. Everyone would be judged by the Deuteronomist as 'doing evil in the sight of Yahweh', for revitalizing the old apostate ways of Manasseh. In the meantime, the land of Judah, which had been a vassal of Egypt, fell under the control of Nebuchadnezzar. Fed up with Jehoiachin's treasonous behaviour, finally, in 597 BC, Nebuchadnezzar's armies marched into Jerusalem and seized direct control. Nebuchadnezzar deported the royal family and thousands of the nation's foremost citizens (2 Kgs 24:15–16) – including Ezekiel.

Ezekiel's professional office is specified in 1:3. Although some interpret 'the priest' as a reference to Buzi, the epithet actually applies to Ezekiel himself. This is critical for understanding the prophet's role. It is true that chapters 1 – 3 describe Ezekiel's call to prophetic ministry, and he obviously functioned as a prophet. However, the timing of the opening vision and call in his thirtieth year (1:1), when priests were inducted into office (Num. 4:30), and the pervasively priestly stamp in the book, suggests that we should view Ezekiel as a prophetic priest, rather than as a priestly prophet.[2] This book portrays Ezekiel serving the exiles, who had no access to temple and altar service, as pastor and prophetic priest. Although he appears to have resisted the call at first,[3] Ezekiel served Yahweh and his people faithfully for more than two decades (cf. 29:17).

Apart from his professional role, we know Ezekiel for his eccentric behaviour. While prophets were known often to act and speak erratically for rhetorical purposes, in Ezekiel we find a unique concentration of bizarre features: muteness, lying bound and naked, digging holes in the walls of houses, emotional paralysis in the face of his wife's death, images of strange creatures, hearing voices and the sounds of water, his withdrawal symptoms, fascination with faeces (4:12–15)[4] and blood,[5] pornographic imagery, an imaginative

---

2. Ezekiel's priestly background is reflected in his thorough familiarity with the temple layout, his access to the temple (chs. 8 – 11; 40 – 46), his understanding of orthodox and pagan cult forms, his mastery of the spiritual heritage of Israel, specifically levitical/priestly issues, and his concern for a rebuilt temple.

3. See Daniel I. Block, *Ezekiel Chapters 1 – 24*, NICOT (Grand Rapids: Eerdmans, 1997), pp. 11–12.

4. Also his references to idols as *gillûlîm*, 'dung pellets'.

5. The word *dām*, 'blood, bloodshed', occurs fifty-five times.

understanding of Israel's past, etc. Some attribute these features to a pathology arising from early abuse and an Oedipus complex, but this misconstrues the profundity of his message and the sensitivity of his personality. His prophetic experiences, symbolic actions and oracular pronouncements derived from encounters with God that affected his entire being. What other prophets spoke of, Ezekiel suffered. As one totally possessed by the spirit of Yahweh, called, equipped and gripped by the hand of God, Ezekiel was a *mōpēt*, 'a sign, a portent' (12:6, 11; 24:24, 27), carrying in his body the oracles he proclaimed and redefining the adage, 'The medium was the message.' To preach Ezekiel faithfully, we will need to understand the man.

Proposition 2: In order to preach from Ezekiel with authority and clarity, we need to understand his audience.

The purpose of prophetic preaching is to transform the audience's thinking about historical and theological realities, particularly their own spiritual condition, and to bring about change in disposition and action. In Ezekiel's case we identify two audiences – the hypothetical audience and the real rhetorical audience. Many of Ezekiel's oracles are formally addressed to outsiders, hypothetical target audiences often introduced with the hostile orientation formula, 'set your face toward', and a stronger variant, 'fix your face toward' (4:3). These idioms reflect the common gesture of turning towards the person one is addressing. Although the oracles following the formula tend to be cast in the second person of direct address, it is unlikely that the purported addressee ever heard or read the pronouncements.[6] Ezekiel's (and God's) real audience is his fellow exiles; it is their minds and actions he seeks to change. But we never see him preaching in public or to the exiles as a whole. For the first eight years of his ministry he is locked up in his house (3:22–27), which means that if people want to hear him they must come to him. And they do. On three occasions we read of the people's representatives, the elders, sitting before him waiting for a word from Yahweh (8:1; 14:1; 20:1–3), although 33:30–33 suggests that ordinary people would come to his house for entertainment as well.

The book paints a picture of a hardened audience, characterized as 'a rebellious house' (2:5–8; 3:9, 26–27; 12:2–4, 9, 25; 24:3) with obstinate face (2:4),

---

6. See especially the oracles against foreign nations (25:2; 28:21; 29:2; 38:2) and insentient entities (6:2; 20:45–48 [Heb. 21:1–4]; 35:2).

stubborn heart/mind (2:4), stubborn of forehead (3:7, 8), obstinate of heart/ mind (3:7) and resistant to messages from God (3:5–11). Indeed, Yahweh tells Ezekiel that if he intended him to see fruit for his labours, he would send him to a foreign nation where people would listen to him. The book offers no hint of any softening during Ezekiel's life, nor any indication that the fulfilment of Ezekiel's announcements of judgment on Jerusalem (33:21–22) had any effect on the audience. Their hardness plays a significant role in determining the content and shape of his proclamation.

The people's rebellious actions, particularly idolatry (14:1–11), provide the most obvious sign of their hardened condition. But their disposition towards Yahweh was actually ambivalent. On the one hand, they were embittered and cynical towards him, for having betrayed them and letting Nebuchadnezzar's armies enter Jerusalem and drag them off into exile. On the other hand, they continued to bank on Yahweh's covenant commitments to them. Until the news came that Jerusalem had fallen, they staked their security on Yahweh's eternal covenant promises – his grant of the land of Canaan to Abraham and his descendants as an eternal possession; his irrevocable covenant with Israel at Sinai; his promise to David and his descendants of eternal title to the throne of Israel; and his election of Jerusalem/Zion as his eternal residence. But their sense of security in Yahweh was delusional: they forgot that enjoyment of covenant blessings is contingent upon grateful and wholehearted obedience to the covenant Lord. Until 586 BC, Ezekiel's rhetorical aim was to destroy this false sense of security by demolishing the pillars on which it was based. However, once the city had fallen his goal was to rebuild the structure, for these were in fact eternal promises.

Proposition 3: In order to preach from Ezekiel with authority and clarity, we need to understand the nature and structure of the book.

The book displays several features that set it apart from other prophetic books. First, if we can get past the first chapter, we discover this book to be the most intentionally structured of prophetic books. It consists of forty-eight chapters, divided evenly into two major sections, oracles of woe for Judah and Jerusalem (chs. 1 – 24) and oracles of weal for Judah and Jerusalem (chs. 25 – 48; see Fig. 1).

Within these sections there is further evidence of deliberate planning. The form and structure of the collection of oracles against foreign nations are obviously governed by the number seven. Seven nations/states are addressed: Ammon (25:1–7), Moab (25:8–11), Edom (25:12–14), Philistia (25:15–17), Tyre

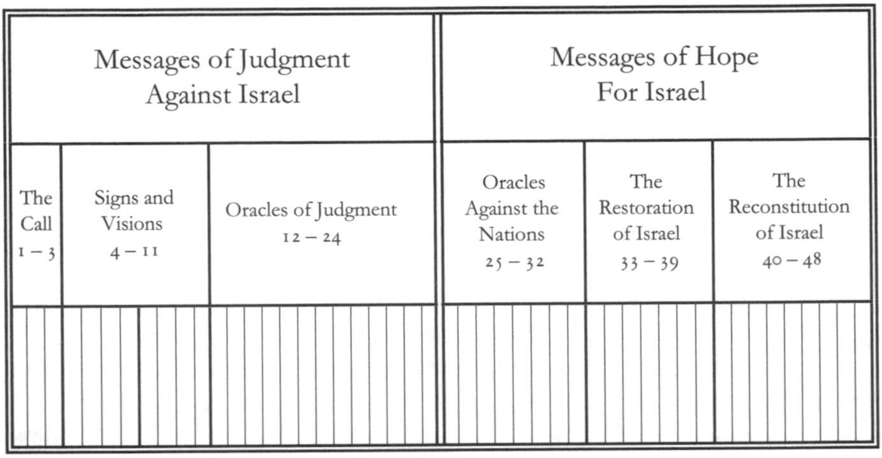

Messages of Judgment Against Israel			Messages of Hope For Israel		
The Call 1–3	Signs and Visions 4–11	Oracles of Judgment 12–24	Oracles Against the Nations 25–32	The Restoration of Israel 33–39	The Reconstitution of Israel 40–48

Figure 1: The Structure of the Book of Ezekiel

(26:1 – 28:19), Sidon (28:20–23) and Egypt (29:1 – 32:32). Seven mini-oracles are incorporated into the first half,[7] and seven oracles against Egypt are preserved in 29:1 – 32:32, signalled by the sevenfold occurrence of the word event formula (29:1, 17; 30:1, 20; 31:1; 32:1, 17). And seven date notices break up the oracles (26:1; 29:1, 17; 30:20; 31:1; 32:1, 17). But there is more. On the basis of the Hebrew verse division, these indirect oracles of hope divide into two virtually equal parts: oracles of judgment against the six (25:1 – 28:23) and oracles of judgment against Egypt (29:1 – 32:32), both made up of ninety-seven verses. But the significance of these oracles against the nations is highlighted by 28:24–26, placed at the precise mid-point and functioning as a fulcrum on which the surrounding oracles balance (see Fig. 2).

Moshe Greenberg noticed some time ago that individual oracles are often deliberately 'halved'. This feature is most striking in the oracle against Gog, which consists of two panels consisting of 38:1–23 (365 words) and 39:1–29 (357 words). Although the word event formula in 38:1 serves as a general heading for both chapters, the intentionality of this division is confirmed by a remarkable correspondence between the respective introductions to each part (38:2–4a; 39:1–2a) (see Fig. 3). These structural features suggest the book is the product of deliberate design, reflecting a concern for precision that many believe characterized priestly scribes.

The second distinctive feature of the book – for which preachers should be

---

7. Egypt is dropped, but compensated for by doubling the oracle(s) against Ammon (25:1–5 and 6–7).

7 Mini Oracles							7 Oracles against Egypt						
A	B	C	D	E	F	G	A	B	C	D	E	F	G

A. Ammon A	25:1–2	A.	29:1–16
B. Ammon B	25:6–7	B.	29:17–21
C. Moab	25:8–11	C.	30:1–19
D. Edom	25:12–14	D.	30:20–26
E. Philistia	25:15–17	E.	31:1–18
F. Tyre	26:1 – 28:19	F.	32:1–16
G. Sidon	28:20–23	G.	32:17–32

Figure 2: The Structure of Ezekiel's Oracles against the Nations

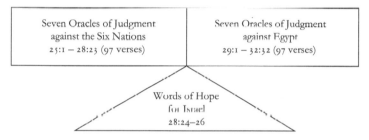

Seven Oracles of Judgment against the Six Nations 25:1 – 28:23 (97 verses)	Seven Oracles of Judgment against Egypt 29:1 – 32:32 (97 verses)

Words of Hope
for Israel
28:24–26

Figure 3: The Place of 28:24–26 in Ezekiel's Oracles against the Nations

grateful—is its clear demarcation of literary units. These are usually signalled by the word event formula, 'The word of Yahweh happened to me, saying. . .' variations of which occur fifty times in the book. This formula perceives the divine word as an almost objective, concrete reality that emanates from Yahweh and confronts the prophet. The boundaries between oracles are seldom blurred.

A third distinctive feature of the book is the care with which many of the oracles are dated.[8] Apart from 1:1, which is enigmatic and general, and 3:16, which is linked to 1:2–3, fourteen oracles are introduced by date notices that tend to be variations of the stereotypical pattern found in 8:1, 'It happened in the sixth year in the sixth [month] on the fifth [day] of the month' (1:2–3; 20:1; 24:1; 26:1; 29:1; 29:17; 30:20; 31:1; 32:1; 32:17; 33:21; 40:1). Although a

---

8. Ezekiel's precision is observable elsewhere only in Zechariah (1:7; 7:1; cf. 1:1) and Haggai (1:1, 15a, 15b; 2:10, 20), undoubtedly under his influence.

Year BC	Biblical Text	Historical Event	Ezekiel's Experience	Cited Date# Yr/mo/day	Modern Equivalent
640	2 Kgs 22:1	Accession of Josiah			
672	Ezek. 1:1		Birth of Ezekiel (623?)		
626		Nabopolassar wins Babylon			
614		Ashur falls to the Medes			
612		Nineveh falls			
609	2 Kgs 23:29–30	Death of Josiah at Megiddo Accession of Jehoahaz			
609/8		Accession of Jehoiakim			
605		Battle of Carchemish: accession of Nebuchadnezzar in Babylon			
604	Dan. 1:1	Daniel and friends are taken to Babylon			
597	2 Kgs 24:10–17	Accession of Jehoiachin Exile of Jehoiachin, Ezekiel and nobility Accession of Zedekiah			
593	1:1 – 3:21	Anti-Babylonian vassals meet in Jerusalem (Jer. 27:1–3) Hananiah prophesies imminent return of exiles (Jer. 28:1–4) Zedekiah visits Babylon (Jer. 51:59)	Ezekiel is called to prophetic ministry	5.4.5	31 July
	3:22–27		Ezekiel is inducted into the prophetic ministry Ezekiel's mouth is closed	One week later	7 August
529	8:1	Unknown	First Temple Vision	6.6.5	18 September
591	20:1	End of Hananiah's two-year prophecy (Jer. 28:1–4)	Elders visit Ezekiel Oracle of Israel's Abominations	7.5.10	14 August
587	24:1	Siege of Jerusalem begins	Ezekiel records the day Ezekiel's wife dies (?)	9[10].10.10	5 January*
	29:1	Pharaoh Hophra attempts to relieve the pressure on Jerusalem	Oracle of Egypt's Doom	10.10.12	7 January
586	30:20	See previous note	Oracle of Egypt's Doom	11.1.7	29 April
	31:1	See previous note	Oracle of Egypt's Doom	11.3.1	21 June
585	33:21	Fugitive announces to Ezekiel, 'The city has fallen!' Ezekiel's mouth is opened		12.10.5	8 January
	26:1	Nebuchadnezzar begins thirteen-year siege of Tyre	Oracle of Tyre's Doom	12.11.1*	3 February
	32:1	Unknown	Oracle of Egypt's Doom	12.12.1	3 March
	32:17	Unknown	Oracle of Egypt's Doom	12.12.15	
573	40:1	Babylonian New Year Festival	The Second Temple Vision	25.1.10	28 April
571	29:17	Nebuchadnezzar's siege of Tyre ends	Oracle of Egypt's Doom	27.1.1	26 April
562		Death of Nebuchadnezzar			
539	Ezra 1:1–4	Cyrus issues decree authorizing the exiles to return to Jerusalem			

Based on Jehoiachin's Exile.

Figure 4: Ezekiel's Dated Oracles in Historical Context

special clustering is evident in the collection of oracles against Egypt (29:1 – 32:32), these date notices are distributed throughout the book, providing a clear chronological and historical framework for Ezekiel's ministry (see Fig. 4).

This interest in chronological precision seems to reflect his awareness of the significance of the events of which he is a part. Israel's history as the nation has known it has come to an end; God must start over again.[9] But the date notices also have an authenticating function. As he edits his oracles, Ezekiel marks the evidence, documenting the fact that Yahweh had given his word long in advance of the events, and even though no-one had paid attention, his word had been fulfilled (12:25, 28; 17:24; 22:14; 36:36; 37:14). These notes invite readers of every age to acknowledge the veracity and power of the divine word, and to recognize in Ezekiel a true prophet of Yahweh (2:5; 12:26–28; 33:33).

Fourth, unlike any other prophetic books, the consistently autobiographical first-person cast of Ezekiel's oracles creates the impression of private memoirs, perhaps his *memorabile*. The I-form is abandoned in favour of the third person only in 1:2–3.[10] Although the oracles are presented in autobiographical narrative style, rarely does the prophet actually admit the reader into his mind. He records his reaction only six times, venting revulsion at what he sees or acknowledging the incomprehensibility of Yahweh's actions (4:14; 9:8; 11:13; 21:5 [20:49]; 24:20; 37:3). In spite of the autobiographic form, one wonders if the real Ezekiel is ever exposed. What we see is a man totally under the control of the spirit of Yahweh; only what God says and does matters.

Proposition 4: In order to preach from Ezekiel with authority and clarity, we need to understand the message that Ezekiel proclaims.

Ezekiel's proclamations represent direct responses to the people's theological delusions. Economically and socially the Judean exiles flourished in Babylon. Probably thanks to the intervention of Daniel, they were settled as a community in favourable circumstances at Tel Abib near the river Kebar (Ezek. 1:1; 3:15), where they were able to maintain their own ethnic identity and social cohesion. Although the exiles from Judah were humiliated by their deportation, in exile they flourished, so that when Cyrus issued his decree in 539 BC permitting the Judeans to return to Jerusalem, many apparently preferred not to go.[11]

---

9. The only date notice in the salvation oracles (40:1) designates the new beginning as *rōʾš haššānâ*, 'the head of the year'. Cf. Exodus 12:1.

10. Other prophets rarely use the first person autobiographical form. But see Amos 7:1–8; 8:1–12; 9:1–4; Hosea 3; Isaiah 6. Jeremiah (1:4, 11, 13; 2:1; etc.) and Zechariah (4:8; 6:9) use the word event person in the first person.

11. Ezra 2 tallies more than 42,000 returnees, but the majority must have remained behind.

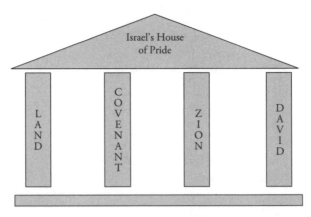

Figure 5: Israel's House of Pride: The Foundations of the Nation's Security

The crises to which Ezekiel responded were not social or economic, but theological. The first half of the book consists of oracles of judgment deliberately aimed at demolishing the pillars on which the exiles' security rested. The theological system may be represented graphically as in Figure 5 above.

Most of the pronouncements address one or more of the four pillars on which their security rested. However, once the city had fallen, Ezekiel's tactic changed. Thereafter he systematically reconstructed the covenantal pillars, demonstrating that Yahweh's promises were indeed eternal. The judgment could not be the last word. On the relationship between specific oracles and the promises, see Figure 6.

While Ezekiel's preaching was firmly grounded in the Scriptures and the traditions of Israel, the goal of his preaching was to change the people's thinking about Yahweh and their disposition towards themselves. The universalism of Isaiah stands in sharpest contrast to the parochialism of Ezekiel. From beginning to end, the God who confronts the reader in this book is the God of Israel, not only passionate about his relationship with his people, but willing to stake his reputation on their fate or fortune. He does indeed sit on his throne in the heavens as cosmic king, and his rule extends to the furthest corners of the earth (1:1–28), but his chosen residence is in Jerusalem,[12] in the land of Canaan/Israel (chs. 4–48), among his own people (48:35). Even in the exercise of his sovereignty over the nations, his agenda is focused on Israel. To Ezekiel, Nebuchadnezzar's place in history is determined by his role as wielder of the

---

12. Compare the departure of Yahweh from the temple in Jerusalem as described in chapters 8–11 with his return to the temple in chapters 40–43.

The Pillar of Orthodox Theology	The Demolition Pronouncements	The Reconstruction Pronouncements
Yahweh has entered into an eternal covenant with his people.	3:16–21; 5:4, 16–17; 6:11–14; 14:1–23; 15:1–8; 16:1–60; 18:1–32; 20:1–44; 23:1–49; 33:1–20; 33:23–29	34:1–31; 36:16–32, 37–38; 37:1–14; 37:15–21; 37:25–28; 39:21–29
Yahweh has given the nation the land of Canaan as their eternal territorial possession.	4:1–3; 4:9–17; 5:5–15; 6:1–7, 11–14; 7:1–27; 11:1–21; 12:17–20; 14:12–23; 15:1–8; 16:1–63; 21:6–22 [1–17]; 21:23–32 [18–27]; 22:1–31; 23:1–49; 24:1–15	34:25–29; 35:1 – 36:16; 36:33–36; 38:1 – 39:20; 47:1 – 48:7, 23–29
Yahweh has chosen Jerusalem as his eternal residence, from which he exercises sovereignty over his people.	7:20–24; 8:1 – 10:22; 11:22–25; 24:16–27	37:26–27; 40:1 – 46:24; 48:8–22, 30–35
Yahweh has promised the Davidic house eternal title to and occupancy of the throne of Israel.	12:1–16; 17:1–24; 19:1 14; 21:30–32 [15–27]	34:23–24; 37:22–25

Figure 6: The Relationship between Ezekiel's Judgment and Salvation Oracles

divine sword directed at Judah and Jerusalem (21:5–37 [1–32]), and as protector of the remnant, so that when the holocaust is over a population (11:14–21) and a scion of David (17:3–4, 22–24) will have survived. While the oracles against the nations (chs. 25 – 32) reflect Yahweh's universal sovereignty, the rise and fall of foreign powers have historical significance primarily as these events affect the fate of Yahweh's people (28:24–26). Gog and his hordes, the archetypical enemies of Israel gathered from the four corners of the earth (chs. 38 – 39), are puppets brought in by Yahweh himself to prove his enduring commitment to his people. By eliminating them he magnifies himself (38:23), makes himself known (38:23) and sets his glory (39:21) among the nations. He is indeed concerned that the whole world recognizes his person and his presence in their affairs, but his agenda is always focused on Israel. Ezekiel's vision of restored Israel has room for non-Israelites, but only as they are integrated into Israelite society and culture (47:21–23).

Space constraints preclude discussion of other theological themes,[13] but we

---

13. For fuller discussion, see Block, *Ezekiel Chapters 1 – 24*, pp. 46–60; and 'Ezekiel: Theology of', in *NIDOTTE*, vol. 4 (Grand Rapids: Zondervan, 1997), pp. 615–628.

may summarize some of these. First, although Ezekiel avoids the expression 'Holy One of Israel', the opening vision and the visions of the temple (chs. 8 – 11, 40 – 46) declare his transcendent holiness and cosmic sovereignty. Second, Yahweh is the gracious covenant-making and covenant-keeping God of Israel (cf. ch. 16). Indeed, both judgment and restoration oracles are based on past covenantal warnings (Lev. 26; Deut. 28) and commitments. Third, more than any other prophet, Ezekiel is a prophet of the Spirit. But he not only spoke of the power of the Spirit, he also embodied the Spirit's power in his own person. Finally, despite the morbid tone of much of Ezekiel's preaching, God is on the side of life, not death. Not only does Ezekiel have a remarkably extensive vocabulary of death, the God who speaks through him has at his disposal a wide range of death-dealing agents – famine, wild animals, pestilence, bloodshed, sword, fire – but through his breath/spirit he brings to life those who have languished under the curse (37:1–14).

If Ezekiel's God is glorious in his transcendence and immanence, his vision of his own people is realistic and sober. His people prided themselves on descent from Abraham and banked on the permanence of the triangular covenantal relationships involving Yahweh, his people and his land.

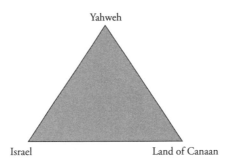

Yahweh

Israel   Land of Canaan

But Ezekiel paints a picture of persistent rebellion, from the beginning of the nation's history to the present. In his revisionist histories (chs. 16, 20, 23) he recalls the abominations of the past. But his view of the people's present is no better. Although his countrymen complain about being punished for sins committed by their predecessors, Ezekiel responds that every generation stands before the divine Judge on its own merits/demerits; no innocent person is punished for the sins of the fathers (18:1–32). But however wicked God's people have been, and however horrendous the judgment – based upon the covenant curses (Lev. 26:14–39 and Deut. 4:25–28; 28:15–68; 29:14–29), so certain is Ezekiel's vision of restoration – based on the covenant promises (Lev. 26:40–46; Deut. 4:30–31; 30:1–10). Indeed, Ezekiel envisions a future when the covenantal triangle that is demolished by the judgment will be completely restored, and the pillars of Israel's security will be restored. Yahweh himself will guarantee the nation's peace and security, with the agency of the David shepherd he installs over his people (34:23–24; 37:24–28). But the restoration presupposes a fundamental transformation of the people themselves, as Yahweh removes their heart of stone and replaces it with a heart of flesh, responsive to his will and resulting in unreserved obedience (36:22–32).

Proposition 5: In order to preach from Ezekiel with authority and clarity, we need to understand Ezekiel's rhetorical and homiletical strategy.

Rhetoric involves communicative strategies employed to break down resistance to the message in the audience and to render the message more persuasive. According to classical definitions, rhetoric involved five elements,[14] each of which is relevant for understanding Ezekiel.

1. Invention – the discovery of relevant materials. Ezekiel received his speeches directly from God by divine inspiration, although consistently in response to the circumstances facing the prophet. I noted earlier that Ezekiel's preaching was firmly grounded in the Scriptures and the traditions of Israel. This is most evident in the links between his pronouncements of judgment and the covenant curses of Leviticus 26 (and to a lesser extent Deut. 28), and his vision of Israel's restoration in 34:25–30 and the covenant blessings in Leviticus 26:4–13. But sometimes Ezekiel's pronouncements go against the grain of Israel's tradition, as in his identification of Jerusalem's/Israel's ancestry in the Amorites and Hittites of Canaan (16:3) rather than Abraham from Ur of the Chaldees, his characterization of Yahweh's ordinances (*ḥuqqîm*) as 'not good' and his laws (*mišpāṭîm*) as not yielding life (20:25), and his introduction of Nebuchadnezzar as the royal figure to whom Genesis 49:10 alludes. But here and elsewhere Ezekiel functions primarily as a rhetorician rather than as a dogmatic theologian or interpreter governed by modern rules of grammatical historical exegesis.

---

14. J. A. Cuddon, *A Dictionary of Literary Terms and Literary Theory*, 3rd rev. ed. (Oxford: Basil Blackwell, 1991), p. 794.

2. Arrangement – the organization of the material into sound structural form. Like the proclamations of other prophets, Ezekiel's pronouncements were crafted according to well-known rhetorical conventions. Based on form-critical considerations alone, this book incorporates a great variety of rhetorical forms: vision reports, dramatic sign acts, disputation speeches, parables and riddles, etc. This variety is evident in both the judgment oracles and the restoration pronouncements.

3. Style – the appropriate manner for the matter communicated and the occasion. Ezekiel's daring style is widely recognized. In chapter 16 alone we find shocking imagery,[15] rare vocabulary, obscure forms and usages, anomalous grammatical forms. Yahweh had warned the prophet at the outset that he will be dealing with a hardened audience, so he pulls no punches in trying to break down that resistance. The abhorrence with which he views the syncretistic ways of his countryfolk is reflected in the strong sexual and faecal language (e.g., chs. 6, 16, 23), which translators tend to soften to accommodate the sensitivities of modern hearers. In fact no other prophet presses the margins of literary propriety as severely as Ezekiel.

4. Memory – guidance on how to remember speeches. While the forms Ezekiel used in the rhetorical situation are striking, his penchant for the number 'seven' (as in the oracles against the nations, chs. 25 – 32) and the 'halving' of texts into panels of roughly equal length will have made his utterances more memorable.

5. Delivery – the technique employed in actually making the speech. For all Yahweh's commands to speak and to act, on only four occasions does he report his rhetorical actions (11:13; 11:25; 24:18–19; 37:7, 10). Ezekiel 12:7 represents the fullest report of actual prophetic performance: 'And I did as I was commanded. I brought out my baggage by day, as baggage for exile, and in the evening I dug through the wall with my own hands. I brought out my baggage at dusk, carrying it on my shoulder in their sight' (ESV). Yahweh's instructions concerning the sign act involving two sticks (37:16–23) anticipate the people asking for clarification, and then prescribe Ezekiel's answer, but all this is contained within the divine

---

15. In chapter 16, flailing about in blood, engaging in harlotry with male images, slaughtering children as food, spreading the legs for every passer-by, pouring out 'your juice', Egypt's swollen member, a bloody victim of wrath and jealousy, hacking in pieces with swords, paying clients to receive her sexual favours.

speech. The text does not say he performed the act, let alone interpreted it. Ezekiel 20:49 [Heb. 21:5] and 33:30–33 suggest that the audience's response varied between annoyance with and being entertained by Ezekiel's performances.

Proposition 6: In order to preach from Ezekiel with authority and clarity, we need to plan carefully.

If a person devoted a sermon to each literary unit in Ezekiel, preaching through the book would take two years. While some congregations would tolerate this strategy for the Gospel of Mark or Paul's epistle to the Romans, none would have the patience for this kind of series on Ezekiel. How then should we proceed?

First, a series on Ezekiel must recognize the pervasive ignorance of Christians with reference to the OT as a whole and this book in particular. People will not recognize the immediate relevance of such a series and they will need a lot of practical guidance along the way. In reality, once we get beyond the first chapter, the book of Ezekiel is no more difficult than Isaiah or Jeremiah or Hosea. But with sound pedagogical wisdom we must move from the known to the unknown. Unless congregations already have great confidence in their pastors, no series on Ezekiel should last longer than twenty-five or thirty weeks. But there should be enough theological and literary variety in this book to sustain interest this long. Through our preaching we should inspire hearers to dare to read obscure texts, and provide guidance in reading those texts.

Second, the selection of texts for a sermon series on Ezekiel should be based on several complementary principles.

1. Include texts with which people are moderately familiar: the opening vision and call (1 – 3), the sermon on sour grapes (18), the good shepherd text (34), the heart transplant text (36:22–32), the resuscitation of the dry bones text (37:1–14).
2. Include texts from every part of the book – not simply the 'good news' texts of chapters 34, 36 and 37.
3. Include texts representing a variety of literary and rhetorical forms. Having selected representative texts from a variety of forms, by explaining typical structures and vocabulary we may encourage the congregation to transfer this information to similar texts and interpret them on their own. (For a classification of texts according to form, see Fig. 7).

Type of Text	Prophecy of Judgment	Prophecy of Restoration
Ezekiel: Call and Commission of the Prophetic Priest	1:1–28a; 1:28b – 3:15	
Ezekiel: Watchman	3:16–21; 6:1–14; 7:1–27; 33:1–9	
Ezekiel: True Prophet	12:21–28; 13:1–23; 14:1–11; 22:23–31; 33:21–22	
Ezekiel: Message Incarnate	3:22–27; 24:15–27; 33:21–22; 33:30–33	
Ezekiel: Visionary	8:1 – 10:22; 11:22–25; 37:1–14	37:1–14; 40:1 – 48:35; 43:1–14
Ezekiel: Dramatist	4:1 – 5:17; 12:1–20; 21:18–27[ET]	37:15–28
Ezekiel: Spinner of Parables, Metaphors and Riddles	17:1–24; 19:1–14; 20:45 – 21:17[ET]; 22:17–22; 27:1–36; 29:1–21	34:1–31; 36:16–38
Ezekiel: Debater	11:1–13; 11:14–21; 12:21–25; 12:26–28; 18:1–32; 24:1–14; 31:10–20; 31:23–33	33:10–20; 33:23–29
Ezekiel: Prosecutor	14:12 – 15:8; 16:1–63; 20:1–44; 22:1–16; 23:1–49	
Ezekiel: Judge of the Nations	25:1–17; 26:1–21; 27:1–36; 28:1–10; 28:11–19; 28:20–23; 29:1–16; 29:17–21; 30:20–26; 31:1–18; 32:1–16; 31:1–18; 35:1–15	30:1–19; 32:17–32
Ezekiel: Messenger of Woe	13:1–16; 13:17–23; 34:1–10	
Ezekiel: Lamenter	19:1–14; 26:1–21; 27:1–36; 28:11–19; 30:1–19; 32:1–16; 32:17–32	
Ezekiel: Miscellaneous Forms	12:17–20; 25:1–7; 25:8–9; 25:12–14; 25:15–17; 28:1–10; 28:20–23; 29:20–26;	36:1–15
Ezekiel: Herald of Good News	6:8–10; 11:14–21; 16:60–63; 28:24–26	34:1–31; 35:1 – 36:15; 36:16–38; 37:1–14
Ezekiel: Literary Cartoonist	38:1 – 39:29	38:1 – 39:29
Ezekiel: A New Moses		40:1 – 48:35

Figure 7: The Message and Method of Ezekiel
(Texts may appear in more than one category)

4. Include judgment and restoration texts that deal with each of the four pillars on which the Israelites based their security (see Fig. 6 above).
5. Be sure that every sermon offers grace to the congregation. Not all texts in the book include notes of grace, but they all assume Israel's past experience of grace and/or anticipate a future work of grace.

Third, prepare the people well for the series and for individual sermons. Invite them during the week to read aloud repeatedly the text to be considered the following Sunday, and introduce them to related texts. Provide helpful notes, explanations and diagrams in church publications.

Fourth, carefully analyse the specific passage selected as the basis for the sermon. This may begin by exploring the genre of the passage and the degree to which it fits idealized genres. Often the distinctive message is discovered in recognizing the deviations from the norm. It will also be helpful to examine inductively the vocabulary and discourse structure of the passage before moving to homiletical considerations, to ensure that the text speaks its message, rather than the message we impose on it (see Fig. 8).

Fifth, in the delivery let the people hear the voice of God by reading entire literary units, not just selected verses, and then develop the theology of the passage. Remind the people often that sermon texts have come to them complete, and then read expositorily, with clarity, appropriate emotion and emphasis, so that in the reading the people hear the voice of God.

Sixth, make appropriate application. Recognize that Ezekiel was not preaching evangelistically to the world, trying to win outsiders to Yahwism; he was preaching to his own people, those who claimed to be the people of God. Herein lies the relevance of his message for our time. Israel was called to be a light to the nations, to embody righteousness and declare by her well-being the glory and the grace of her Redeemer and covenant Lord. In so doing she was to play a paradigmatic role, representing to all nations and peoples the treasure of divine grace and responding with righteous living. Israel was called to bear his name with honour. The message of this prophetic priest was addressed to people who had besmirched the reputation of God, first by their unrighteous living, and second by being in exile. Underlying Ezekiel's preaching is a profound theology that is continuous with the theology of the OT as a whole and the NT as well. Our task as preachers is to establish that theology and translate it into forms that are understandable and relevant in our context. We may do this by asking of each text what it tells us about:

1. God.
2. The world and society in general.

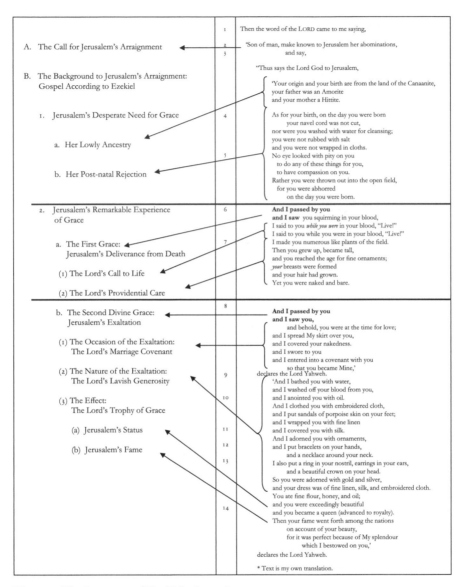

Figure 8: The Structure of Ezekiel 16:1–14*

3. The human condition, the nature of sin, the destiny of humankind.
4. The way God relates to his creation in general and human beings in particular.
5. An appropriate ethical and spiritual response to God's work of grace in our lives.

A test case – Ezekiel 16:1–14: 'The Gospel According to Ezekiel'

How does this strategy work in specific cases? For an example I have selected Ezekiel 16:1–14. This is the opening section of the longest single literary unit in the book. At around 850 words, this chapter alone is longer than half the Minor Prophets (Obadiah, Jonah, Nahum, Habakkuk, Zephaniah, Haggai) and only slightly shorter than Malachi. Within the constraints that govern most pastoral preaching, it is difficult to treat the entire chapter in one sermon, especially if one would read the entire text. Minimally one should treat this text in two or three sessions. The first would involve a dramatic and expository reading of the entire text, concluding with some synthetic comments on the overall theme: 'Trampling under Foot the Grace of God'. The second might focus on verses 1–14, which presents one of the most profound portrayals of the boundless and undeserved love of God in all of Scripture. With this strategy we will confront the congregation with many of the big questions of Scripture: the nature of grace, the innate human condition and our propensity to ingratitude and rebellion, the cause and nature of divine fury, and ultimately the triumph of grace. Beyond these normal theological questions, Ezekiel 16 poses unique hermeneutical, sociological and ethical challenges: What are the boundaries of appropriate rhetoric? What does this text say about gender relations? What are we to make of its portrayal of God? These questions are not easily answered,[16] but texts like this demonstrate that spiritual and theological realities cannot be reduced to formulas, and God himself will not be domesticated.

Generically and structurally, as one of four *rîb* oracles in the book, Ezekiel 16 has a strong legal flavour, as the following broad outline illustrates:

A. The Call for Jerusalem's Arraignment (vv. 1–3a)
B. The Indictment of Jerusalem (vv. 3b–34)
   1. Jerusalem's Lowly Origins (vv. 3b–5)
   2. Jerusalem's Exaltation (vv. 6–14)
   3. Jerusalem's Shamelessness: Her Response to Grace (vv. 15–34)
      a. Her Religious Promiscuity (vv. 15–22)
      b. Her Political Promiscuity (vv. 23–34)
C. The Sentencing of Jerusalem (vv. 35–43)
   1. A Summary of the Charges (vv. 35–36)

---

16. For a brief consideration of factors to consider in dealing with the troubling aspects of texts like Ezekiel 16, see Block, *Ezekiel Chapters 1 – 24*, pp. 467–470.

2.   Yahweh's Response (vv. 37–42)
3.   A Concluding Summary (v. 43)
D.   The Analysis of Jerusalem's Problem (vv. 44–52)
   1.   The Indicting Proverb (v. 44)
   2.   Jerusalem's Family Portrait (vv. 45–46)
   3.   Jerusalem's Shameful Personality (vv. 47–52)
E.   The Double Ray of Hope for Jerusalem (vv. 53–63)
   1.   The Bad Good News: The Qualification for Grace (vv. 53–58)
   2.   The Good Good News: The Triumph of Grace (vv. 59–63)

Our text represents the first half of Jerusalem's indictment in which Ezekiel describes her conduct against the backdrop of divine grace extended to an utterly hopeless city. Jerusalem's roots are in the general human population, represented by her Amorite father and Hittite mother. As a child rejected by mother and father, her doom was certain. But Yahweh came by just in time, rescued her from certain death at the jaws of jackals and beaks of vultures, and caused her to flourish and grow up – that is, survive as a common human being. But then she became vulnerable to human predators, and just in time Yahweh passed by again. With obvious allusions to Sinai, he married her, entering into covenant relationship with her, lavishing on her all his resources and elevating her to the status of his queen.

Although Ezekiel 16 is framed by good news (vv. 1–14 and 60–63), three-fourths of the chapter is taken up with relentless accusation and disturbing pronouncements of the divine response. Not many congregations will endure such proportions in our preaching. I was invited once to preach a four-part series on this text – that was the request. I broke it down into its four constituent parts and delivered four messages with all the enthusiasm I could muster.

A. The Impassioned Love of God (vv. 1–14)
B. The Spurned Love of God (vv. 15–34)
C. The Tough Love of God (vv. 35–43)
D. The Triumphant Love of God (vv. 44–63)

By the time I had finished the third sermon, some had had enough of this brutal image of judgment and did not return for the gospel with which the passage ends.

Like the dry bones in chapter 37, in this text Jerusalem functions paradigmatically. At the literal level this text concerns the fate and fortune of Israel, but at another level the way God deals with his chosen people mirrors the way he deals with humanity. In recounting the OT version of the gospel, Ezekiel has announced all the elements of the gospel that Christians proclaim.

1. God's perspective on the history of his people – including the church universal and local congregations – probably looks quite different from the idealized histories we write. This chapter is not written to the world out there; it is written to those who claim to be God's people. It forces us to ask, 'If God were writing our story, what would it look like?' Have we, like Israel, trampled underfoot his grace, and used all that he has lavished on us for selfish purposes and wicked ends?

2. Like Jerusalem, apart from the intervention of divine grace, all humanity is morally destitute and doomed (Rom. 3:23; Eph. 2:1–3).

3. Apart from common grace, the sentence of physical death hangs over all humanity.[17]

4. Survival does not mean our problems are solved. It is possible to live physically, but still to lack spiritual life, which is possible only through covenant relationship with God.

5. God's grace is the only hope for a lost humanity. By nature destitute, this is the only solution for the human condition.

6. Covenant relationship with God is the highest privilege imaginable.

7. As the objects of God's saving and covenant grace, we have been blessed with every spiritual blessing in Christ Jesus (Eph. 1:14).

8. As the undeserving recipients of God's grace, we are called to joyful and faithful living, as trophies of his grace proclaiming the excellencies of him who has called us out of darkness into his marvellous light (Deut. 26:19; 1 Pet. 2:9–10).

Proposition 7: In order to preach from Ezekiel with authority and clarity for the church, we need to link his message with that of the New Testament responsibly.

There is no need to resort to allegorical methods of interpretation to recognize the Christian gospel in Ezekiel 16. Jerusalem/Judah/Israel does indeed function paradigmatically for all humanity in its lost condition and the church in particular as the object of divine grace. However, we need to remind our people that Yahweh, the God who rescued Israel from her hopeless condition

---

17. Yahweh's first call to Jerusalem to 'Live' holds off the sentence of the fall.

(in Egypt), is incarnate in Jesus the Christ, who saves us from our sin and through whom God the Father lavishes his blessings on us.

Conclusion

It is high time that the church rediscovered the book of Ezekiel and claimed its message as her own. We too have grown complacent, mouthing profound credal statements and for our security banking on the promises of God, when in reality we have abandoned him for all kinds of competing idolatries. For this reason the book is as relevant today as it ever was. May the Lord rekindle in our hearts the passion for God and his people exhibited by Ezekiel, and may he open our eyes to the covenantal faithlessness we demonstrate every day.

Recommended reading

BLOCK, DANIEL I., *Ezekiel Chapters 1 – 24*, NICOT (Grand Rapids: Eerdmans, 1997).
BLOCK, DANIEL I., *Ezekiel Chapters 25 – 48*, NICOT (Grand Rapids: Eerdmans, 1998).

10. PREACHING APOCALYPTIC

Ernest C. Lucas

'Many good and faithful preachers rank preaching on apocalyptic texts along-side handling serpents; they have heard that people do it, but they have no desire to come anywhere near them.'[1] This quotation highlights the sad fact that few preachers choose to preach on apocalyptic texts. One reason for avoiding such texts is that a minority of preachers abuse them. As Thomas Long puts it, 'With their arrogant, glassy-eyed sermons, their endlessly ornate charts of the end times, and their complicated pseudo-mathematics . . . these hawkers of last days superstition keep in perpetual motion a cottage industry of fear, ignorance, and Armageddon anxiety.'[2] A major problem for responsible preachers who do consider preaching on such texts is the diffi-culty of trying to understand their nature in order to be true to them and not abuse them.

---

1. L. P. Jones and J. L. Sumney, *Preaching Apocalyptic Texts* (St Louis, MO: Chalice Press, 1999), p. 1.

2. T. G. Long, 'Preaching Apocalyptic Literature', *Review and Expositor* 90 (1993), pp. 371–381.

What is apocalyptic?

In 1980 Francis Glasson advocated dropping the term 'apocalyptic' from the vocabulary of biblical studies, arguing, 'Apocalyptic has no agreed and recognizable meaning.'[3]

What is an apocalypse?

Until about 1970 much discussion of apocalyptic and apocalypses was indeed confused and confusing because scholars tended to give vague and impressionistic definitions of the terms they were using. K. Koch,[4] in a book whose original German title (*Ratlos vor der Apokalyptik*,[5] 'At a Loss before Apocalyptic') conveys the problem he sought to address, drew attention to the 'cloudiness' of the definitions of apocalyptic in use. He insisted that a distinction must be made between the literary genre 'apocalypse' and the historical 'apocalyptic' movement from which it arose. He also argued that a clear definition of the former must be arrived at before attempting to understand the latter. He listed what he saw as key characteristics of apocalypses:

- Discourse cycles (centred on a vision or audition).
- Description of the seer's spiritual turmoils.
- Exhortatory discourses.
- Pseudonymity.
- Use of symbolic (often mythical) imagery.
- Composite character.

Koch's approach was refined in two directions. P. Hanson[6] made a distinction between apocalypse (the literary genre), apocalyptic eschatology (a religious perspective) and apocalypticism (the symbolic universe of a religio-social movement). A seminar of the Society of Biblical Literature produced a definition of the literary genre 'apocalypse' based on a survey of works from the period 250 BC – AD 250 and normally classed as apocalypses:

> Apocalypse is a genre of revelatory literature with a narrative framework, in which a revelation is mediated by an otherworldly being to a human recipient,

---

3. T. F. Glasson, 'What is Apocalyptic?', *NTS* 27 (1980), pp. 98–105.

4. K. Koch, *The Rediscovery of Apocalyptic* (London: SCM, 1972).

5. Gütersloh, 1970.

6. P. D. Hanson, 'Apocalypticism', *IDB Supplement* (1976), pp. 28–34.

disclosing a transcendent reality which is both temporal, insofar as it envisages eschatological salvation, and spatial, insofar as it involves another, supernatural world.[7]

The seminar also concluded that apocalypses fall into two sub-genres: those with otherworldly journeys and those with a review of history. The definition carries the caveat that its intention is only to mark out the boundaries of the genre and not to give a complete or adequate description of the constituent works that fall within that boundary. It covers only the constant core characteristics of apocalypses. As Koch recognized, most apocalypses are a composite of several types of literature. This definition has found wide, but not universal, acceptance. Some scholars want to add to it a statement about the function of an apocalypse. This is usually along the lines that it provides consolation and encouragement to a group in a crisis situation.[8] The problem is that the function is not usually made explicit within the apocalypse, but has to be deduced from the text, and the argument can become circular.

Daniel 10 – 12 is the one section of the OT which this definition fits well. It is an apocalypse with a review of history. With a bit of a stretch the definition can be taken to encompass the whole of the book of Daniel.

Although Daniel is the only apocalypse in the OT, there are a few other passages that are widely recognized as expressing an apocalyptic eschatology. These are: Isaiah 24 – 27; Joel 2:28 – 3:21 (Heb. 3:1 – 4:21); Zechariah 9 – 14. Some scholars would also include Isaiah 65 – 66. This raises the question of what the distinctive characteristics of apocalyptic eschatology are.

Prophetic and apocalyptic eschatology

The question is usually answered by contrasting the views of history and the end of history (eschatology) found in apocalyptic and in prophecy. However, there is general agreement that, 'The perspective of apocalyptic eschatology can best be understood as an outgrowth from prophetic eschatology.'[9] As a

---

7. J. J. Collins, 'Introduction: towards the Morphology of a Genre', *Semeia* 14 (1979), pp. 1–20. The definition is on p. 9.

8. For example: D. Hellholm, 'The Problem of Apocalyptic Genre', *Semeia* 36 (1986), pp. 13–64.

9. P. D. Hanson, 'Apocalyptic Eschatology', *ABD*, vol. 1 (New York: Bantam Doubleday Dell, 1992), p. 281a.

result the dividing line between the two is fuzzy, with the classification of some passages in the OT Prophets, such as Isaiah 65 – 66, being debatable. What follows is a typical list of the major contrasts between prophetic and apocalyptic eschatology.[10]

1. The prophets expose the sinfulness of those to whom their oracles are addressed – often God's people but sometimes the other nations. Apocalyptists generally assume that those whom they address are themselves upset, even angry, with the evil that they see around them and are anxious for God to do something about it.
2. The prophets urge their hearers to acknowledge their wickedness and to repent. Apocalyptists assert that wickedness has passed the point of no return. Judgment is now inevitable.
3. The prophets call the people of God back to the covenant and obedience to God. Apocalyptists call upon the few remaining faithful within the people of God to persevere to the end despite the difficulties that face them.
4. When the prophets announce that God is going to judge sin and offer salvation, this is usually seen as being accomplished through human agents and natural means. Apocalyptists announce that God is going to intervene directly and effect judgment and salvation through supernatural means.
5. The prophets are usually speaking of an imminent act of judgment and salvation, although this may sometimes be seen as also having a distant reference also. Apocalyptists seem to be envisaging a final solution.
6. The prophets' focus is on a particular historical situation. They use end-of-the-world language of crises within history (Isa. 13:9–22; 34:4–5). They announce the end of an era in the life of a nation or the end of a particular world order within history. The apocalyptists have a cosmic outlook and speak of the end of history.
7. Prophetic eschatology has little, if anything, to say about a meaningful afterlife, whereas this is a feature of apocalyptic eschatology.

---

10. Compare the list in D. B. Sandy, *Plowshares and Pruning Hooks: Rethinking the Language of Biblical Prophecy and Apocalyptic* (Leicester: Inter-Varsity Press, 2002), p. 107.

Preaching apocalyptic texts: the challenge

Among the plethora of literature on preaching there are relatively few books and articles which deal with preaching apocalyptic texts. In part this reflects the fact that such texts are rare in the lectionaries which influence what is preached on in many Christian traditions. Much of the literature on preaching apocalyptic texts concentrates on the book of Revelation. Although some of this is applicable to apocalyptic texts in general, much of it concentrates on matters specific to Revelation itself. A survey of the existing literature reveals a number of challenges which face those who want to preach responsibly from these texts.

Their symbolic imagery

An obvious characteristic of apocalypses is their use of symbolic images, which are sometimes quite weird, even bizarre, as in Daniel 7. The imagery could be quite unprecedented, but it is more likely that it was familiar to the author – whether it came out of his mind as a genuine vision or as a purely literary creation. If the imagery was meant to convey something to the original readers, it would do that more effectively if it was imagery that they shared with the author. There is good reason to believe that in most cases the imagery has its origin in the culture shared by the author and readers and the problem that confronts modern preachers is that they do not share that cultural background.

As a Briton newly arrived in the USA, I was puzzled by the appearance of elephants and donkeys in certain newspaper cartoons. In my cultural background the elephant symbolized a prodigious memory and the donkey symbolized stupidity. That did not seem to make sense of the cartoons. All became clear when I was told that the animals were the traditional symbols of the two main political parties. Cartoons can be quite complex in their use of symbols. I remember one from that period which depicted the Statue of Liberty chained to a rock and menaced by a sea monster with the face of the incumbent president of the USA (Richard Nixon), with a knight in armour, who had the face of the presidential candidate of the other party (George McGovern), charging to the rescue on a donkey. There are allusions here to the Greek story of Andromeda and Perseus and to the story of St George and the dragon. That cartoon would seem bizarre and opaque to anyone who knew nothing of the Statue of Liberty, who could not identify the two faces, or who lacked the classical education to be able to spot the allusions to Perseus and St George. So it is not surprising that the imagery in apocalypses seems bizarre and opaque to those lacking the necessary cultural background.

Much of the imagery in OT apocalyptic texts has its roots in cultural imagery that was widespread in the Ancient Near East. Preachers who do not do their homework may miss, or misunderstand, the significance of this imagery. For example, Zechariah 14:10–11 paints the image of much of Judah becoming a plain with Jerusalem remaining 'aloft on its site'. Behind this imagery lies the idea that the gods dwell upon a high mountain. In Ugaritic texts the throne of the gods is on Mount Zaphon. Zechariah is not making a geographical statement, but a theological one: Jerusalem, not Mount Zaphon or any other mountain, is the dwelling place of God. This imagery is also behind the evocation of Jerusalem in Psalm 48:1, although some English translations obscure this.[11]

Another example is the description of Leviathan in Isaiah 27:1. Nicolas Wyatt comments that the description of the serpent Lītān/Lôtān in the Ugaritic text about Baal and Mot is 'remarkably close to the Heb. text of Isa. 27:1'.[12] The significance of Baal's conflict with that serpent is unclear. In the Ugaritic text Lītān/Lôtān has many heads, as does Leviathan in Psalm 74:14. In Psalm 74:12–19 Leviathan and the dragon appear together, having their heads crushed by Yahweh, in the context of Yahweh's creation of the world. This suggests allusion to a creation story like that in Babylon, where Marduk does battle with the forces of chaos, depicted as bizarre sea monsters, and defeats them before creating the world. So, with this background, Isaiah 27:1 speaks of Yahweh eventually destroying all that is chaotic and disruptive in the world.

There is a widespread consensus that the Babylonian creation story lies behind the imagery in the vision of the four beasts from the sea in Daniel 7. The story would be known to the Jews in exile in Babylon because it was read, or re-enacted, each New Year's Day. It is important to recognize the cultural roots of this imagery, because this is what gives it evocative power. This can be illustrated by comparing two different actions.[13] Suppose someone took an old bed sheet into a public place, doused it with petrol and set it on fire. The action might evoke curiosity and puzzlement in any bystanders. However, if instead of a bed sheet the action involved a national flag, the reaction would be very different, possibly violent – because a national flag is a cultural symbol

---

11. P. C. Craigie, *Psalms 1 – 50* (Waco, TX: Word Books, 1983), p. 353.

12. N. Wyatt, *Religious Texts from Ugarit* (Sheffield: Sheffield Academic Press, 1998), p. 115.

13. The example is taken from D. S. Jacobsen, *Preaching in the New Creation: The Promise of New Testament Apocalyptic Texts* (Louisville, KY: Westminster John Knox, 1999), pp. 60–61.

which evokes passions in a way that other pieces of cloth do not. One of the challenges for preachers of apocalyptic texts is to find ways of helping their congregations to understand, and ideally feel, the passions that the symbolic imagery in their texts would have evoked.

David Jacobsen points out two ways in which symbolic language and imagery tends to get misused today.[14] One is to regard it as having simply an objective reference. So Daniel's four beasts are taken to refer simply to four successive empires and all that is needed is to 'crack the code'. Do they stand for Babylon, Media, Persia, Greece? Or Babylon, Medo-Persia, Greece, Rome? Or the Third Reich, the USSR, America, China? The vision has become a cipher to be decoded instead of being a symbolic vision that expresses, and evokes, the anxiety that chaos threatens to destroy God's purpose for his creation. As a cipher the vision can have only one referent and getting the correct set of empires is what preoccupies the interpreter. As a symbolic vision it can speak to various situations where chaos seems to threaten to overwhelm God's purposes.

The other misuse of which Jacobsen speaks is to retreat into personal subjectivity – a move which Jacobsen sees influenced by both Freudian psychotherapy and Bultmannian 'demythologizing' of the Bible and 're-mythologizing' it in terms of existentialist philosophy. I have not seen it, but maybe someone has interpreted the vision in Daniel 7 in terms of the seer's inner struggles between his Ego and Superego as he seeks to live in obedience to God as an exile in a pagan land. The more general point here is the tendency of much modern preaching to personalize and individualize the message of any biblical text.

Their use of history

Some apocalypses contain a survey of history. What many commentators and preachers fail to recognize is that these surveys are also a form of symbolic literature. To 'objectify' them and treat them as primarily chronological accounts of history such as we expect in modern 'scientific history' is to miss their point. They are better regarded as what Lester Grabbe calls 'chronography',[15] a symbolic scheme of history which is intended to interpret the meaning and significance of major events in it, not to provide a means of predicting when they will happen.

---

14. ibid., pp. 54–60.

15. L. L. Grabbe, 'Chronography in Hellenistic Jewish Histography', *SBLSP* 17 (1979), pp. 43–68.

The most striking example of this is the 'seventy weeks' scheme of Daniel 9:24–27. James Montgomery described this passage as 'the Dismal Swamp of O.T. criticism',[16] because there have been so many unsatisfactory attempts to 'decode' it, assuming that it is meant to be treated as chronology. I have argued elsewhere[17] that the seventy weeks pattern makes use of the symbolism of the sabbatical and jubilee cycles of Leviticus 25. The effect of the use of the symbolism of cycles of sabbatical years and jubilees is to evoke trust in Yahweh as the God who redeems his people from oppression. In this case a cultural practice enjoined in the Mosaic law is the basis of the symbolism used to provide a way of understanding a period of history.

There is a less obvious symbolic patterning of history in the surveys of Daniel 8 and Daniel 11:2 – 12:4. In Daniel 8:1 the mention of Belshazzar does not only provide a dating. It invites a comparison between the story in Daniel 5 and this vision. To some extent Belshazzar is a pale foreshadowing of the little horn. He desecrated the vessels from the temple (8:11–12) and his fate was sealed by a hand sent from heaven (8:25c). The repetition of words and phrases creates a clear pattern in the careers of the ram, the goat and the little horn. They each become great (8:4c, 8a, 9a), the power of each is stressed (vv. 4b, 7b–8, 24), and the end of each is expressed in terms of being broken (vv. 7a, 8b, 25c). The purpose of the patterning is to assure those who suffer at the hand of the little horn that although he seems to tower over the land and be invincible, his power will collapse.

The careers of four particular kings stand out in Daniel 11:2 – 12:4: the 'warrior king' (11:3–4), the 'king of the north' (vv. 10–19), the king of verse 20, and the 'contemptible person' (vv. 21–45). The space given to the last figure indicates that he is the focus of the survey. Some aspects of his career are foreshadowed by those of the earlier kings. Like the warrior king and previous king of the north, he is able to 'do as he pleases' (vv. 3b, 16, 36a). Like the king of the north, he invades 'the Beautiful Land' (vv. 16, 41 NIV) and gains some support there (vv. 14, 30b, 32a). Both make treacherous agreements (vv. 17, 23) and meet a check during their rise to power (vv. 18b, 30a). The king of the north shows a hint of the hubris of the contemptible person (vv. 12a, 36a, 37b). Like the king of verse 20, the contemptible person is concerned with exacting tribute and amassing wealth (vv. 28, 43). The fact that the careers of the earlier kings foreshadow that of the contemptible person prepares the reader for the fact that, despite his much greater success, his career, like theirs, will come to an

---

16. J. A. Montgomery, *The Book of Daniel*, ICC (Edinburgh: T. & T. Clark, 1927), p. 400.

17. E. C. Lucas, *Daniel*, AOTC (Leicester: Apollos, 2002), pp. 245–248.

untimely end (vv. 4a, 19, 20b). This patterning assures those who are suffering under him that his rule is limited and will meet an untimely end.

The patterns in Daniel 8 and 11 are not simply imposed on history – they are recognized in it and drawn out of it. There is similarity here with the work of the wisdom teachers in ancient Israel. They looked for such patterns at various levels of experience and expressed them in proverbs. One pattern was, 'Pride goes before destruction, a haughty spirit before a fall' (Prov. 16:18 NIV). The author of Daniel sees this pattern writ large on the stage of international politics. The arrogance that might come with success and power can lead rulers and nations to overreach themselves in various ways that contribute to their downfall.

Just as it is the symbolic meaning of apocalyptic images that enables them to apply to various situations, so it is with the symbolic meaning of the surveys of history revealed by these patterns. If the surveys are read as chronologies, referring to simply one period of history, then the preacher struggles to find a message for today. However, read as chronography, the preacher is challenged to ask whether and where the pattern presented is to be seen today.

Talk of patterns in history does not sit easily in a postmodern environment. Postmodern people are averse to meta-narratives, overarching stories which integrate and give meaning to the smaller narratives within history. There are at least two reasons for this. One is the suspicion that the meta-narratives are not real, but simply imposed on history. Readers of the Bible are free to judge for themselves the validity of its meta-narratives. Professor Paul Kennedy of Yale University, writing from a totally secular perspective, discerned a pattern in history much like that in Daniel and describes it at length in his book *The Rise and Fall of the Great Powers: Economic and Military Conflict from 1500 to 2000*. Despite its title, the book was published in 1988. Writing in 1985/6, Kennedy was so sure of the pattern he had discerned that he predicted that the USSR would not survive very far into the twenty-first century. He overestimated its lifespan. As we know, it collapsed in 1989. He sees this as the result of impersonal economic, political and social forces. I think we are justified in seeing the hand of God at work in them.

The other reason for the postmodern aversion to meta-narratives is the claim that they are 'oppressive'. Those in power use them to impose their views and ways of doing things on other people. This does not fit the meta-narratives in biblical apocalyptic texts. These present a view from the 'underside'. They are a challenge to the meta-narrative of those who are the oppressors, whose meta-narratives are exposed as mere arrogant boasting which will end in their downfall. The challenge for preachers is to expose current false meta-narratives and their oppressive effects. However, instead of dismissing all meta-narratives, they must then catch the hearers' imagination with an alternative, real, liberating Christian meta-narrative.

Another challenge for preachers is that the apocalyptists look at history on the large scale. Daniel, Isaiah, Joel and Zechariah all deal with what God is doing with and to whole communities and nations. What Charles Campbell says of the book of Revelation also applies to these texts.

> John . . . was not concerned primarily with individual sins, but with these enormous forces which threaten and seduce the people of God into the ways of death . . . the focus of John's testimony is not on individuals, but on the *community* of faith. His purpose is not to address individual pastoral or therapeutic issues that persons in the congregation may be facing. Rather he seeks to build up the church as a community with the resources of faith and hope required to resist the threats and seductions of the principalities and powers . . . Revelation is not a book for therapeutic preachers who wish to address the needs and problems of individual congregation members. It is a book that invites preachers into the public, political arena . . . That fact, even more than the bizarre imagery and obscure metaphors, may present the greatest challenge to Christian preachers today.[18]

Their dualism

The definition of an apocalypse quoted at the start of this paper highlighted two kinds of dualism which appear in apocalyptic texts. There is a 'spatial' dualism in the contrast between the visible world and a supernatural reality, and there is also the 'temporal' dualism in the contrast between 'now' and 'that day', 'the Day of the Lord' or 'the end'. Both of these present something of a challenge to the modern Western worldview, but there are ways by which the preacher can help people take these dualisms seriously.

When I was at Sunday school we used to sing that hymn which includes the lines, 'There's a home for little children, above the bright blue sky.' Such imagery became obsolete with the advent of space flight. When my children were young and asked, 'Where is heaven?' my answer was, 'Heaven is where God is.' Tom Wright says the same, although he puts it in rather more sophisticated theological language. He says, '"Heaven" is God's dimension of present reality.'[19] He explains what he means by reference to the story in 2

---

18. C. L. Campbell, 'Apocalyse Now: Preaching Revelation as Narrative', in J. B. Green and M. Pasquarello III (eds.), *Narrative Reading, Narrative Preaching* (Grand Rapids: Baker Academic, 2003), pp. 151–175. The quotes are from pp. 156–157.

19. N. T. Wright, *New Heavens, New Earth* (Cambridge: Grove Books, 1999), p. 14.

Kings 6:15–19 in which Elisha and his servant are surrounded by the Syrian army. The servant says, 'Alas, master, what shall we do?' Elisha tells him not to be afraid and prays, 'Lord, open the young man's eyes.' The Lord opens his eyes and he sees the mountain full of horses and chariots of fire round about Elisha. What had happened was a sudden unveiling of a dimension of reality that was there all along, but normally unseen. God does not exist in a totally separate reality from ours. Rather his *immediate presence*, as distinct from his *mediated presence*, which is what we normally experience, exists in a normally unseen dimension of our reality. This idea of heaven as 'God's dimension of present reality' which is an unseen part of our reality should not seem strange to us, since cosmologists have talked for the last twenty years about String Theory in which there are at least ten dimensions of reality, of which six are 'compactified' ('rolled up') so that we are unaware of them – not that I am suggesting that heaven is in one of those hypothetical dimensions. The idea of different dimensions of reality, and moving between them, is common in science fiction literature and films.

From time to time possible 'end of the world' scenarios break into the modern mind: nuclear holocaust, global environmental disaster, asteroid impact. It is questionable how helpful it is to relate any of these to the apocalyptic scenario. However, they can be used to awaken people to the vulnerability of human existence on planet earth and to the fact that human sinfulness (desire for power, aggression, selfishness, greed) exacerbates this.

There is also a strong ethical dualism in apocalyptic thought that challenges the modern Western mindset which gives a prime place to tolerance based on relativism. This ethical dualism has to be treated with care by the preacher. It can too easily degenerate into a spiritual witch-hunting or demon-spotting. However, it does challenge us to take seriously the truth that evil rarely makes itself plain, and sometimes takes on the appearance of something good. Subprime mortgages, defended as a way of making home ownership available to poorer people, become part of financial packages invented by greedy financial traders to line their pockets and fuel a lavish lifestyle. Satan can masquerade as an angel of light. This makes it all too possible for those in the church, as well as those outside, to become complicit with evil. Part of the 'unveiling' work of apocalyptic which preachers of apocalyptic often miss in their desire to unveil the future is the unveiling of evil at work now in the church and the world. This does not make for popular preaching to congregations of people who have at least some wealth, some power and some degree of control over their life choices, all of which gives them some vested interest in the economic and political status quo.

Preaching apocalyptic texts: the message

Having considered what practitioners and teachers of preaching regard as some of the major challenges involved in preaching from apocalyptic texts, it is time to outline briefly some of their main theological themes.

God is the Lord of history

The Hebrew prophets saw the hand of Yahweh at work in the history of his people, even using the great powers which surrounded them as agents of his purposes. This theme comes out even more strongly in apocalyptic thought. Behind the surveys of history and their patterns is the belief that God is in control. In particular God will bring history to the climax he has planned for it. This is expressed powerfully in the vision of the Ancient of Days on the judgment throne in Daniel 7:9–10. Yet this conviction does not make history nothing more than the run-through of a pre-scripted play with all the actors simply having to fulfil the roles set for them. The kings in Daniel 11 have some freedom to do as they please. The Prince of Persia can oppose and delay what God intends. Daniel's prayer has some influence on events. People are held to account for their actions, implying some moral responsibility for them. The impression given is of a synergy between what happens in the spiritual realm and in human history, not that actions in the one simply determine what happens in the other. Moreover, God's control of history is not presented as something that is plainly evident. He works behind the scenes. This is why what happens can be perplexing to the faithful, but they are assured that he is nonetheless in control and his good purposes will be achieved.

Evil is rampant in the world but will be overcome

The apocalyptists took the reality of evil very seriously. The wickedness of humanity and its effect is graphically summed up in Isaiah 24:5–6a (NRSV):

> The earth lies polluted
> under its inhabitants;
> for they have transgressed laws,
> violated the statutes,
> broken the everlasting covenant.
> Therefore a curse devours the earth,
> and its inhabitants suffer for their guilt.

The primordial sin of seeking to be God is exemplified in the 'little horn' and 'the contemptible person' in Daniel 7 – 12.

A particular emphasis of the apocalyptists is that evil is not seen simply in terms of individual acts of sinning. The use of the imagery of the chaos monsters in Isaiah 27:1 and Daniel 7 implies that there is an endemic evil that is not limited to humans and what they do, although they play their part in it. Isaiah 24:21 implies the existence of evil spiritual powers in heaven when it declares, 'On that day the LORD will punish the host of heaven in heaven and on earth the kings of the earth' (NRSV).

OT apocalyptic texts do not provide any explanation for the origin and existence of evil. They do promise that God will overcome it. There will be a final Day of the Lord when the wicked will be judged and evil eradicated from God's creation. Leviathan will be punished with a 'cruel and great and strong sword', the dragon killed (Isa. 27:1 NRSV), the beast put to death and burned (Dan. 7:11).

The Lord will reign

Although seemingly pessimistic because of its depiction of evil rampant on the earth, the message of apocalyptic eschatology is ultimately one of hope. The Day of the Lord brings salvation for the faithful. This is depicted by various images: a great feast of rich food (Isa. 25:6); the removal of death and the replacement of tears by gladness (Isa. 25:7–9), a fruitful plant (Isa. 27:6), a fruitful land (Joel 3:18).

The most pervasive image is that of God establishing his rule:

- Isaiah 24:23: 'The LORD of hosts will reign on Mount Zion and in Jerusalem' (NRSV).
- Zechariah 14:9: 'The LORD will become king over all the earth; on that day the LORD will be one and his name one' (NRSV).
- Zechariah 9:9–10 has the picture of the victorious king coming to Jerusalem to establish peace among the nations and to rule to the ends of the earth.

Further, in Daniel 7:13–14, after the judgment of the beasts 'one like a human being' (NRSV) receives 'dominion and glory and a kingdom, that all peoples, nations and languages should serve him' (ESV). This takes on a particular significance in view of the creation imagery of the vision of the beasts. What is being depicted is the fulfilment of God's purpose when he created the earth, that humans made in his image and likeness should have dominion over it and rule it as his representatives. The understanding of salvation here goes beyond saving individual people to include the whole creation. This is also the understanding in the 'new heaven and new earth' passages in Isaiah 65 and 66.

The salvation of the individual is not neglected. It is in apocalyptic eschatology that there is the first clear promise of resurrection to either everlasting life or everlasting contempt (Dan. 12:2).

A call to remain faithful

The overall message of apocalyptic encourages the faithful to endure and to remain faithful to the end, whether that is death or the Day of the Lord. With its ethical dualism it rejects relativism and compromise and calls the faithful to remain righteous. This is the logic of the link between the stories of Daniel 1 – 6 and the apocalyptic visions of Daniel 7 – 12. The stories are a challenge to live a life faithful to the Lord in a pagan world where the beasts are on the rampage. The visions provide the motivation for this. The beasts will be judged and destroyed, the rule of God will be established on the earth and the faithful will be raised to share in it.

Preaching Christ from apocalyptic texts

The NT gives Christian preachers several leads for relating these texts to the person and work of Christ.

Jesus frequently referred to himself as 'the Son of Man'. This is due, at least in part, to seeing himself as the one who was bringing in the rule of God and the fulfilment of God's purpose in creating the world. Hebrews 2:1–9 also throws light on this understanding of Daniel 7. It makes clear that Jesus, through whom the world was created and of which he is the heir (Heb. 1:2), came not just to save individual humans, but to accomplish God's original purpose when he created the world and created humans in his image to have dominion over it. His defeat of the devil (Heb. 2:14–15) means that we can be restored to true humanness and exercise our dominion in a proper way. There are clear implications here regarding our care of creation.

The 'one like a son of man' in Daniel 7:13 (NIV) represents 'the saints of the Most High' who are spoken of later in that chapter. They have to endure suffering before receiving the kingdom. This may have been an element in Jesus' understanding of his suffering, and in particular that the kingdom of God can only be brought in through those who are willing to suffer in the struggle with evil. This is an important theme in the NT's teaching about discipleship (Mark 8:34–38; 1 Pet. 3:13–17; 4:12–19).

Jesus is the 'first-fruits' of the resurrection that is promised in Daniel 12:2–3. His resurrection gives assurance to those who suffer, even to the point of death, that theirs is not a lost cause, but their suffering will lead to glory. This leads to Paul's exhortation in 1 Corinthians 15:58 to be steadfast in working for Christ, knowing that our work will not be pointless.

In his entry into Jerusalem Jesus acts out Zechariah's picture of the king who comes to establish a universal rule of peace. John 19:37 sees a partial fulfilment of Zechariah 12:10 in the crucifixion of Jesus. Ultimate, lasting peace comes through humility and suffering, not violence.

At Pentecost Peter declares that the gift of the Holy Spirit as the climax of Jesus' ministry, death, resurrection and ascension is the fulfilment of what Joel 2:28–29 promised. However, Pentecost is only a foretaste of the end envisioned by the apocalyptists. It signals the 'beginning of the end'. We live in an 'overlap' of the ages: 'this age' and 'the age to come'. This is something not clearly seen in the vision of the OT apocalyptic texts. It is an important NT contribution to understanding how we should approach living in the light of these texts.

The banishment of death promised in Isaiah 25:8 is achieved by the death and resurrection of Jesus, as Paul makes clear in 1 Corinthians 15:54, where 'Death is swallowed up in victory' is probably a free quotation of the verse in Isaiah. Christ's victory gives us added assurance of God's ultimate victory over evil that is proclaimed in the apocalyptic texts.

The picture in Isaiah 26:17–18 of God's people as a woman in birth pangs who cannot produce a child is no doubt one of the roots of the image in Revelation 12:1–6 where the child is born and is the Messiah. The imagery of John's vision is also based on the Apollo myth and makes the claim that Jesus, not the Emperor, is the true Saviour.

Sermon outline on Daniel 7:1–22 and Revelation 5:1–10: 'Trusting God's Purposes'

Daniel 7 – 12 is an example of apocalyptic literature, a type of literature which abounds in imagery. The book of Revelation is another example. Their imagery was not meant to hide the message and provide experts in prophetic literature with puzzles to solve. It was used because it communicated powerfully in the culture from which it came. Our problem is that we come from a different culture.

The world can be a frightening place

The weird imagery of Daniel 7 was fairly commonplace to people living in Babylon in Daniel's day, including exiled Jews. They would have linked it with two features of Babylonian culture.

Omens

The Babylonians believed that unusual happenings foreshadowed important events. One form of omen divination concerned the malformed naturally aborted foetuses of domestic animals. The Babylonian omen priests saw all kinds of weird creatures in these misshapen foetuses.

Birth omens affected Babylonian art, in which bizarre creatures are depicted (project pictures). So it would have been clear to the readers of Daniel 7 that the vision concerned important future events. However, Daniel did not rely on Babylonian birth omens. He received a revelation from Israel's God concerning the rise and fall of great empires. God used Babylonian cultural imagery because that was a powerful way to communicate to those he addressed.

The New Year festival

This was *the* major Babylonian festival. It included acting out their creation story with a battle between the Babylonian god Marduk and the forces of chaos – depicted as a raging sea full of monsters. Only after Marduk subdued the forces of chaos could he create an ordered cosmos. Babylonians had a constant fear that the cosmos would collapse back into chaos.

So often there seems to be a real possibility of a collapse into chaos: nuclear proliferation, international terrorism, economic chaos. Daniel's vision says graphically that the world can be a frightening place, even for the godly person.

God is still in control

The vision shifts at verse 9. Daniel sees that, despite the apparent ascendancy of the beasts of chaos on earth, God is still on the throne of the cosmos. He is the King and Judge, the sovereign Lord of history.

It is an OT theme that God's purpose can be achieved even through earthly powers as they rampage about (Isa. 10:5; 45:1). This is hard to understand. Isaiah cries out, 'Strange is his deed! . . . alien is his work!' (Isa. 28:21 NRSV). Hard though this truth is to grasp, it has been a great source of encouragement and strength to God's people down the centuries.

Daniel sees God judging the beasts. They are deprived of power and the 'dominion and glory and kingdom' is given to 'one like a son of man'.

God's people will suffer

Following this assurance of God's control of history and the triumph of his kingdom, the scene shifts again. We are back with the fourth, fearsome beast (v. 19ff.) and are told that the ruler it represents 'made war with the saints, and prevailed over them' (v. 21 ESV), and that he 'shall wear out the saints of the

Most High . . . and they shall be given into his hand' (v. 25 ESV) before he is finally destroyed.

God's faithful people are not promised immunity from the hardship and suffering that the beasts cause. The initial fulfilment of Daniel 7:25b was the terrible persecution which the Jews suffered under Antiochus Epiphanes in 167–164 BC. Jesus reapplied some of the prophecies of Daniel to the sufferings which Jews and Christians had to endure as a result of the Roman destruction of Jerusalem in AD 70. Revelation 13 reapplies Daniel 7 to the persecution of Christians by Roman emperors – and so it has gone on through history. Suffering is inevitable if we are faithful to God in a faithless world (1 Pet. 4:12).

God's purpose will be achieved

However, Daniel 7 encourages us to stand firm and not lose hope. God is still on the throne. God's purpose will be achieved and his people will share in this final triumph.

The fact that the imagery of Daniel 7:13–14 stands in parallel with verses 26–27 makes clear that the giving of the kingdom to 'the saints of the Most High' in verse 27 is depicted in verses 13–14 by the giving of kingship to 'one like a son of man', that is to 'a human figure'. Here God's purposes in creation and redemption reach a common goal. Humans were created in God's image to have dominion on earth. When we rebel and reject God we become less than what we should be, less than truly human. Hence the rebellious earthly powers are depicted as beasts. God's redemptive purpose is to restore us, and all his creation, to what he originally intended: in our case, to make us truly human.

Daniel's vision assured his readers that God's purposes will triumph. We have an additional assurance – the death and resurrection of Jesus. He called himself 'the Son of Man'. This identified him with the suffering saints of God, and also as the one through whom God's purposes will be achieved. This meant suffering for Jesus. He was trampled by the beasts, caught between Jewish nationalism and Roman imperialism. They crucified him. But he rose again victorious and now rules from heaven as the Lamb who has been slain.

Conclusion

This chapter teaches fundamental truths about living in our world.

- We may be confronted by fearsome powers and be affected by the chaos they cause, *but* we can be confident that God is still on the throne.

• We may suffer for our faith, *but* God's purpose will prevail and we shall share in his triumph, achieved through the suffering and resurrection of Jesus.

So, when we wonder whether it is worth facing up to the challenge to stand firm for God in a pagan world and bear faithful witness to his kingdom, we can draw encouragement and strength from Daniel's vision of the assured triumph of his purposes.

Further reading

JONES, L. P. and J. L. SUMNEY, *Preaching Apocalyptic Texts* (St Louis, MO: Chalice Press, 1999).

LUCAS, E. C., *Decoding Daniel: Reclaiming the Visions of Daniel 7 – 11* (Cambridge: Grove Books, 2000).

SANDY, D. B., *Plowshares and Pruning Hooks: Rethinking the Language of Biblical Prophecy and Apocalyptic* (Leicester: Inter-Varsity Press, 2002).

11. PREACHING THE MINOR PROPHETS

Alison Lo

The Minor Prophets are remarkably contemporary in the sense that the themes of social justice, religious corruption, financial impropriety and social and political unrest are highly analogous to our world and today's church. Despite their brevity, they are considered as 'the most heterogeneous'[1] books in the Jewish and Christian canon. The issues addressed in these books certainly provide inexhaustible preaching material, which is still highly relevant to us. With interpretative and preaching skills, preachers will find preaching the Minor Prophets most rewarding. This chapter, therefore, seeks to discuss the basic principles of preaching the Minor Prophets. In particular, it proceeds to apply those principles by using the book of Zephaniah as an example. For illustrative purposes, an extended sermon outline will be given at the end of the chapter. First, the seven principles:

1. Briefly explain historical-cultural context

God speaks to the peoples of Israel and Judah through the prophets in specific periods of history. An understanding of the historical circumstances can

---

1. H. Marks, 'The Twelve Prophets', in R. Alter and F. Kermode (eds.), *Literary Guide to the Bible* (Cambridge, Mass.: Belknap Press of Harvard University Press, 1987), p. 207.

provide essential clues to the meaning of these texts. Preachers have to take this first step seriously when preparing to preach from the Minor Prophets. The heading of the book may well inform the reader about its setting (e.g. Hos. 1:1; Amos 1:1; Mic. 1:1, etc). Where this is absent, the text itself may give clues about its historical context.

In the eighth century BC Hosea and Amos in Israel, and Micah in Judah, witnessed the destruction of Israel by Assyria (in 722 BC). Nahum, Habakkuk and Zephaniah were active towards the seventh century BC, when the Assyrian Empire was declining and the Babylonian Empire ascending. The Babylonians destroyed Judah in 587 BC, resulting in the exile. Obadiah 11 – 14 perhaps reflects the situation in 587 BC when Edom joined in the destruction of Judah by the Babylonians. When Haggai, Zechariah and Malachi prophesied, the Babylonian Empire had been defeated by the Persians, who allowed the Jews to return home (538 BC) and rebuild their temple in Jerusalem. This began the post-exilic period. Inspired by Haggai and Zechariah, the temple was completed in 515 BC. There is no common consensus regarding the dates of Joel and Jonah's ministries. Joel is generally considered post-exilic. The allusion in 2 Kings 14:25 suggests that Jonah might be an Israelite prophet during the reign of Jeroboam II, but his story is sometimes considered fictional. The historical background of the Minor Prophets can be found in most commentaries.

A brief introduction to the historical contexts in the sermon can save the audience from anachronism. They will then know what to expect from an eighth-century prophet, or from an exilic or post-exilic prophet. With this historical knowledge, for instance, the audience can figure out why Hosea is so different from Amos, even though both were eighth-century prophets. The former saw Israel from the perspective of a native, while the latter perceived Israel with Judean eyes. Moreover, the knowledge of historical background can open up possibilities for application. For instance, if Amos, as a shepherd and dresser of sycamore trees, was sent by God from Judah to take up an unpopular ministry in Israel, some in the church today may also be called by God to a challenging mission or ministry where they may face opposition and adversity.

2. Consider genres and literary features

Preachers need to identify the genres and literary features of the text. The Minor Prophets utilize a variety of genres, for instance, symbolic actions (Hos. 1:2–11), vision reports (Amos 7:1–8; Zech. 1:8–17), judgment oracles (Obad. 15 – 16), salvation oracles (Amos 9:11–15; Mic. 4:1–4), woe oracles (Nah.

3; Hab. 2:6–19), oracles against the nations (Zeph. 2:4–15; Amos 1:1 – 2:3), lawsuits (Mic. 1:2–7), dirges (Amos 5:1–3; Mic. 1:8–16), etc. Most of these forms are explained in *The Forms of Old Testament Literature: Isaiah 1 – 39* (vol. 16) which has an introduction to the prophetic literature (pp. 1–30) and a glossary of genres (pp. 512–547).[2] Special attention should be paid to other literary features too, such as repetition, parallelism, chiasm, *inclusio*, wordplay (pun), rhetorical question, doubling, contrast, contradiction, metaphor and so on.

In the preparation of a sermon, knowing the genres and literary features is crucial for unit demarcation and exegetical analysis. Take Amos 5:1–17 as an example. This passage can be broken into smaller units according to their genres:

> A Lament the death of the nation (vv. 1–3)
> B Call to seek God and live (vv. 4–6)
> C Accusation of injustice (v. 7)
> D Hymn to Yahweh (vv. 8–9)
> C' Accusation of injustice (vv. 10–13)
> B' Call to seek God and live (vv. 14–15)
> A' Lament the death of the nation (vv. 16–17)

Amos 5:1–3 and 5:16–17 are dirges, 5:4–6 and 5:14–15 are calls to repentance; and 5:7 and 5:10–13 are accusations of no justice. In the centre stands the hymn to Yahweh (5:8–9). This passage neatly displays a chiastic structure: A–B–C–D–C'–B'–A'. The key message usually lies in the middle of a chiasm, i.e. the hymn to Yahweh (5:8–9), which highlights God's sovereign power over the future of the nation.

Preachers should know how a dirge was used in ancient Israel. It was usually sung to mourn the loss of the deceased and to describe their merits during the funeral. Very often prophets used the dirge mockingly to proclaim the approaching doom of a king or personified nation. Here Amos is bewailing the nearly dead nation of Israel (5:1–3, 16–17). Israel is doomed to destruction because she fails to do justice (5:7, 10–13). In such a situation Amos calls for repentance, and urges the Israelites to seek God and live (5:4–6, 14–15). Confronting the people with the question of death and life, Amos spurs them on to return to God – the One who determines their destiny (5:8–9). Compared to Amos' painful agony for Israel's fate, how much does the church

---

2. M. Sweeney, *The Forms of Old Testament Literature: Isaiah 1 – 39* (Grand Rapids: Eerdmans, 1996).

today lament the lost of the world, who will suffer the punishment of eternal death?

This example demonstrates how genres and literary features give clues to unit demarcation, exegetical analysis and even application of the text. More importantly, the sermon outline is derived from the form of biblical texts. This will be explored below using Zephaniah as an example.

3. Highlight the central theme of each book

There is so much that could be preached on in the Minor Prophets, but too much information will put people off. Therefore, it is better to echo the central message of each prophet. Due to the constraints of length, we only pick up Hosea for discussion in this section. How one establishes the theme of a book will be demonstrated in the example of Zephaniah below.

Whereas his contemporary Amos has other nations in mind, Hosea's main concern is Israel as a chosen people. Therefore preachers must be aware that Hosea speaks within the context of the covenant relationship between Israel and Yahweh. The portrayal of Yahweh as a husband and a father to Israel demonstrates God's covenantal love to his people, a love that tolerates no rivals. 'The knowledge of God' (6:6)[3] and 'steadfast love/faithfulness' (4:1; 6:6; 12:6) are the qualities of covenant loyalty.

Take Hosea 2:14–23 as an example. Here God acts to restore the relationship with Israel. When Hosea speaks of God wooing Israel again, he reminds us of God's intimate relationship with Israel in the old days of exodus (vv. 14–15). Now God promises to help Israel turn away from Baal. After restoring the broken relationship, God will become her husband again (vv. 16–18). In this exclusive covenantal relationship, God will betroth Israel in righteousness, justice, steadfast love, mercy and faithfulness that Israel may know him (vv. 19–20). Finally the names of Hosea's children are reversed from images of judgment to images of hope (vv. 21–23). Now 'Jezreel' fulfils its true meaning 'God sows' (vv. 22, 23a; cf. 1:4, 11); 'No mercy' becomes 'I shall have mercy' (v.23b; cf. 1:6); and 'Not my people' becomes 'You are my people' (v. 23c; cf. 1:9). The name 'My people' alludes to the Sinai tradition, in which Yahweh called Israel 'my people' (Exod. 6:7; 3:7, 10). Hosea 2:14–23 demonstrates how Hosea should be read in the light of covenant theology.

---

3. Bible quotations in this chapter are taken from ESV, unless otherwise identified.

4. Trace thematic coherence among the books

Recent scholars tend to read the Minor Prophets as one whole 'Book of the Twelve', which presupposes the inner coherence of the books. The analysis of the thematic thread helps sketch the bigger picture of the Minor Prophets. Preachers need to be aware of the catchwords, repetition, verbatim, *inclusio*, contrast, contradiction and so on when finding the linkage between these books.

This section demonstrates how the first four books (Hosea – Obadiah) are united by the key theme of the 'Day of the Lord'. Hosea uses the images of marriage and father-son relationship to describe the broken covenant relationship between God and Israel. The book calls for Israel's repentance and return to God, who is in great dilemma between love and judgment for his people. Standing as the first book of the Twelve, Hosea sets the stage for the rest, highlighting the common Israelite problem of covenant infidelity. Hosea also brings out another key theme of the Twelve – the Day of the Lord. Both positive and negative sides of the Day are clearly indicated in this book. On that Day, God will bring about the unification of Israel and Judah (1:11) and the restored relationships between Yahweh and Israel (2:16–20) and Israel and the animal realm (2:21–23). On the other hand, it will herald 'the days of punishment' and 'the days of retributions' (9:7–9).

'The day of the LORD' (1:15; 2:1, 2, 11, 29, 31; 3:1, 14, 18) is the main concern in Joel, which extends Hosea's emphasis on both positive and negative sides of God's intervention. In face of the impending disaster, Joel calls for repentance. Similarly to Hosea 9:7–9, Joel warns that an army will come to attack Jerusalem and Judah (1:15 – 2:11). If their repentance is accepted (1:2–14; 2:12–17), there will be an outpouring of Yahweh's spirit (2:28–29), deliverance on the day of universal judgment, and judgment of the nations (3:1–21). Joel quotes Hosea 2:22 (Joel 2:19), highlighting God's promise of sending grain, new wine and oil. Picking up where Hosea leaves off, Joel develops a more complex picture of the Day of the Lord, and moves to Amos.

Hosea ends with a call to repentance for the Northern Kingdom, whereas Joel begins with a call to repentance for Judah and Jerusalem before the Day of the Lord arrives. Amos pronounces the Day of the Lord towards the Northern Kingdom (Amos 5:18–20) and it presumes that the calamity results from Israel's refusal to return to Yahweh (Amos 4:6, 8, 9, 10, 11). The day of judgment will bring an end to Israel (Amos 8:3). Amos' description of the calamity of the Day is similar to Joel's depiction (Amos 5:18; Joel 1:15; 2:1–2, 11). They both underscore the military destruction on that Day. The remnant theme in Amos 5:14–15, which highlights the survivors' salvation on the Day of the Lord's wrath, also echoes Joel 2:32. Amos 9:11–15 positively brings out God's future restoration, in which the restoration of the Davidic kingdom resonates with Hosea 1:11 (Amos 9:11) and the agricultural abundance – 'the mountains shall drip sweet wine' – parallels Joel 3:18 (Amos 9:13). Moving forward, Amos 9:12 sums up Obadiah's message, announcing Edom's destruction (Obad. 1–15) and the restoration of the Davidic kingdom (Obad. 18) as it repossesses Edom and the surrounding territory (Obad. 19–21). Again the theme of the Day of the Lord runs through Hosea, Joel and Amos to Obadiah (Obad. 8, 11–14, 15). The motif of God's judgment against the nations is reiterated in Obadiah by announcing the doom of Edom, which well represents all the nations (Obad. 15).

Alongside the recent trend of scholarship, preaching a series on the Minor Prophets is more palatable nowadays. No matter whether preaching a series on the books or focusing on one individual book, preachers need to find out the thematic thread, which knits all the books together and gives a sense of unity and purpose. Mentioning thematic coherence in the sermon helps the audience understand the interrelationships between these books. Preachers can demonstrate to the audience how exegesis is done in a broader context. We believe preaching is a great opportunity for educating the congregation – not only edifying them through the message, but also modelling to them how to expound a text carefully across the boundary of a single book.

5. Keep a balance with other Minor Prophets

Joel 3:16, 'The LORD roars from Zion', is duplicated in Amos 1:2. When Joel said this, he was pointing to Yahweh's restoration of Judah and his judgment on the nations. The ending of Joel becomes a shocking contrast at the beginning of Amos, where the message is totally reversed because it does not declare the salvation, but rather the judgment of Judah and Israel alongside other nations. In Amos the judgment on the nations precedes the condemnation of Judah and Israel, whereas in Joel the punishment of the nations comes before the restoration of Judah and Israel. The juxtaposition of the verbatim (Joel 3:16; Amos 1:2) in these two adjacent books appears to bring powerful rhetorical impacts upon their audience – giving a shock to the Israelites because of their false expectation about Yahweh's roaring from Zion. Explaining this interlink, preachers powerfully demonstrate to the congregation how verbatim in different contexts can mean different things. They can even apply the text by relating the shock of Amos's readers to the contemporary audience, to whom the message of the sermon is actually pointing.

In Joel, Yahweh challenges the nations to 'beat ploughshares into swords and pruning hooks into spears' for war with his warriors (Joel 3:10) and he will defeat Israel's enemies. However, the images are reversed in Micah. Now the nations are drawn to Zion and 'they shall beat their swords into ploughshares, and their spears into pruning hooks' (Mic. 4:3; cf. Isa. 2:4). Obviously, the restoration of the nations and a new age of international peace are anticipated in Micah. This reversal of images reveals the different perspectives of the same God, who judges the nations out of his divine justice and also restores the nations out of his steadfast love.

A balanced view of God's character can be perceived when Jonah and Nahum are read side by side. God's forgiveness and compassion to Nineveh is vividly depicted when he passionately said, 'And should not I pity Nineveh, that great city, in which there are more than 120,000 persons who do not know their right hand from their left, and also much cattle?' (Jon. 4:11). However, God's vengeance and wrath on Nineveh is expressed in diametrically opposite terms when he said in fury, 'Behold, I am against you . . . I will burn your chariots in smoke, and the sword shall devour your young lions; I will cut off your prey from the earth . . . Woe to the bloody city, all full of lies and plunder – no end to the prey!' (Nah. 2:13 – 3:1). When Jonah preached repentance, the Ninevites responded and were spared, whereas when Nahum preached a century later, Nineveh did not repent and thus faced God's judgment. Despite the fact that sinful people deserve a penalty, God is still willing to change his mind because of human repentance.

The messages of 'perhaps' and 'who knows?' echo each other in Joel, Amos, Jonah and Zephaniah. By using 'perhaps', Amos and Zephaniah urge their people to seek Yahweh. Nevertheless, neither righteousness nor humility can guarantee one's safety on the Day of the Lord (Amos 5:15; Zeph. 2:3). It is all in God's hands. To the Ninevites, 'who knows?' is what they think of their salvation when God's message to them is only destruction (Jon. 3:9). God's judgment of destruction is just, but his compassion may prevail. Similarly in Joel, 'who knows?' indicates God's freedom and sovereignty (2:14). Human repentance cannot manipulate God. People may hope for his forgiveness and compassion, but they cannot command it. The note of 'perhaps' and 'who knows?' serves as an ongoing counterbalance throughout the Minor Prophets regarding the issue of divine sovereignty and human deeds.

Reading the Minor Prophets as a book, therefore, can provide different angles in expounding the texts, because each single book portrays God from a particular perspective. The church congregation needs to have a balanced theology. Therefore, it is essential for preachers to keep other prophetic books in mind when preaching any particular Minor Prophet.

6. Preach Christ from the Minor Prophets

Like other prophetic literature, the Minor Prophets must be interpreted in light of the history of redemption, which reveals God's plan for all the nations through his covenant promises to Abraham. God promises to send a Redeemer to save Israel, and all humankind through Israel. Being the Redeemer, Jesus is the fulfilment of the 'promises'. It is not difficult to preach Christ from the Minor Prophets, because the covenant promises are seen as fulfilled in Jesus Christ.

It is noteworthy that prophecy very often carries multiple fulfilments, which continue to be fulfilled until it is completely fulfilled throughout the redemptive history. Some prophecies do not end at certain historical events, but point towards the first and second coming of Jesus Christ. The gift of Jesus' Spirit to his church (Acts 2:17–36; 1 Cor. 2:6–13) is a fulfilment of God's promise to pour out his Spirit on all flesh (Joel 2:28–29). Not only will salvation be available to all who have faith in God, but God's Spirit will be available to them regardless of their age, gender or social status (Rom. 10:12–13; Titus 3:6). Concerning the prediction in Joel 2:31, 'The sun shall be turned to darkness, and the moon to blood, before the great and awesome day of the LORD comes', Matthew, Mark and Luke all quote this verse to refer to the signs that precede Christ's return with great power and glory (Matt. 24:29–30; Mark 13:24–25; Luke 21:25–27). The complete realization of this promise still lies in the future.

Micah 4:9 – 5:4 is another example demonstrating the progressive fulfilment of God's words in different times of history. Some years after Micah's prophecy, Judah was captured by the Babylonians and the Israelites were exiled to Babylon (4:10a). After nearly seventy years' exile, a portion of the Jewish exiles returned to their homeland (4:10b; 5:3). Some seven hundred years after Micah's prophecy, Matthew quotes 5:2 in reference to Jesus' birth as a king of Israel in Bethlehem, where the line of David began (Matt. 2:6). In Jesus' time many Jews in Palestine saw themselves as still in exile because 'the prophecies of restoration had not yet come true'.[4] Furthermore, the complete fulfilment of God's universal rule over the whole earth in Micah 5:4 is still longingly awaited.

Even though the Minor Prophets provide ample material for preaching Christ, preachers should avoid doing this too quickly. One must first discover what the message was for its original readers, and then move step by step towards the NT. Then they need to investigate how and whether the prophecy

---

4. N. T. Wright, *Jesus and the Victory of God*, vol. 2 (London: SPCK, 1996), p. 126.

has been fulfilled throughout history (before, during and after Jesus' day). In order to expound the texts correctly, preachers have to move cautiously back and forth between the two testaments.

7. Preach to individuals, society and the world

There is a continuity and parallel 'between what God is and does for Israel, teaches Israel, or demands of Israel, and what God in Christ is and does for the church, teaches the church, or demands of the church'.[5] Preachers can thus use analogy to preach the Minor Prophets in our time.

The issues of social injustice, religious formalism, corrupt leadership, dishonest trade, violence, war crime, military armament and slave trafficking in the Minor Prophets are not that different in our modern world. Some people may therefore think that the major concern of the Minor Prophets is calling for social reforms and eliciting political changes in society. However, the Minor Prophets very often speak to individuals. When Zephaniah urged the Israelites to seek God, righteousness and humility (Zeph. 2:3), it was individuals who needed to respond. When Haggai rebuked people for living in 'panelled houses' while the temple remained in ruins (Hag. 1:4), he was calling individuals to repent and take action – to build the temple.

While most of the Minor Prophets are focused on the covenant community, they do so with an external/outward focus in mind. Consequently, it is necessary to draw out the missional and worldwide visions of the Minor Prophets, because they and their internal covenant community bear witness to the watching world. That is what the book of Jonah is all about. It is important for preachers to keep 'the individuals, society and the world' in mind when preaching the Minor Prophets in order to have a balanced application of the texts.

Take Amos 1 – 2 as an example. The sovereign God judges both the nations (1:1 – 2:3) and his people (2:4–16) because of their sins of violence, oppression, human trafficking and social injustice. To preach this passage, preachers need to sort out whether injustice exists within the church, such as the overdominance of the wealthy, racial discrimination, sexual inequality, abuse of power, sexual abuse, financial fraud, adultery and so on. At the same time, the worldwide vision has to be kept in mind too. The world issues in

---

5. S. Greidanus, *Preaching Christ from the Old Testament: A Contemporary Hermeneutical Method* (Grand Rapids: Eerdmans, 1999), p. 263.

the twenty-first century like the slave trade, unlawful military invasion, inhumane treatment of war criminals, overdominance of the world's superpowers and deprivation of third-world countries are our prime concern. Just as the individuals who were challenged by Amos to seek the Lord (5:4–6), hate evil, love good and establish justice in the gate (5:14–15), Christians today are also individually called to live out justice in our daily life, faith community, nation and wider world community.

What can ordinary Christians do about these huge global evils? Preachers require pastoral wisdom to challenge the congregation to break their bonds of ignorance, silence and complacency. In what way are we calling individuals to respond to the slave trade? Responses may include: praying for the situation, educating the public, buying traffic-free products, joining campaigns, raising funds, ministering to the slaves, intervening on government policies, and so on. Individual believers are actually in the forefront, guiding our communities towards eliminating injustices in every corner of the world. It starts with the transformation of each individual's life, which can then infiltrate into our families, churches, work, nation and the world. It will be even more fruitful if community, state, national or international leaders are in the congregation, because they make policies.

Having discussed the seven principles above, we now proceed to explore how these principles can be applied as we look at Zephaniah 1 – 3.

Application: the book of Zephaniah

1. Historical-cultural context
According to the superscription, Zephaniah's genealogy goes back to Hezekiah. Whether the prophet was a prince (son of Hezekiah) or of African descent (son of Cushi) is debatable. Zephaniah ministered during the reign of Josiah (640–609 BC). It is widely accepted that Zephaniah might have prophesied before Josiah's reforms (621 BC) because he condemned Judah's syncretistic practices, Baal worship and child sacrifice (1:4–9, 11–12; 3:1–4), which were prevalent during the reigns of Josiah's predecessors Manasseh and Amon. Zephaniah's familiarity with Jerusalem suggests that he probably prophesied in the capital city. The book anticipated the fall of Nineveh in 612 BC (2:13–15) and the imminent destruction of Jerusalem (1:4, 10–11; 2:1; 3:1–4). Despite the fact that Zephaniah never mentioned who would be the agent used by God to punish his people, the historical records show that the Chaldeans were most likely the agent because they attacked Jerusalem in 597 BC and finally destroyed the Southern Kingdom in 587 BC.

The social, economic, political and religious situations at Zephaniah's time can be traced through the prophet's accusations of his people. As mentioned above, idolatry was one of the major problems at that time (1:4–6, 9). Trust in themselves and their wealth (1:10–12) led to their pride and arrogance. The corrupt leaders (the officials and princes) had caused God to proclaim the advent of the Day of the Lord's sacrifice (1:7–8).

2. Central voice of Zephaniah

Repetitions in the texts provide us with important clues to the main theme of the book. 'The day of the LORD' appears three times (1:7, 8, 14). Elsewhere in the book, it is expressed as 'the great day of the LORD' (1:14), 'the day of the wrath of the LORD' (1:18), 'the day of the anger of the LORD' (2:1, 3), 'a day of wrath' (1:15), 'a day of distress and anguish' (1:15), 'a day of ruin and devastation' (1:15), 'a day of darkness and gloom' (1:15), etc. Its many occurrences strongly suggest that it is the major theme of the book.

The sheer scale of judgment on that day is vividly described by the echoes of Zephaniah 1:2–3, 18 and 3:8, which reiterate that all the earth shall be consumed in the fire of God's jealousy. The repetition of 'wrath' (1:15, 18) and 'anger' (2:2 [x2]; 2:3; 3:8) reflects God's fury over the sins of Judah and other nations, which lead to the universal destruction on the Day of the Lord. On the other hand, God's compassion for his people is clearly shown by the 'remnant'/'survivors' motif (2:7, 9; 3:9–10, 12–13) and the conversion of the nations (2:11; 3:9–10) which surface in the midst of the judgment oracles against Judah and the nations.

Compared with other Minor Prophets, Zephaniah gives a more balanced view of the Day of the Lord, which reflects these two perspectives: (1) the judgment upon Judah and other nations (1:1 – 3:8), and (2) the salvation of Judah and other nations (3:9 20). The prophetic message is more balanced in the sense that it contains both judgment and restoration, and it also involves both Judah and the Gentiles.

3. Textual analysis of Zephaniah 1 – 3

Zephaniah 1 focuses on the coming judgment on Judah. The imminence of the Day of the Lord is emphasized through repetition in Zephaniah 1:7 and 1:14. Zephaniah 1:18 echoes Zephaniah 1:2–3. They form an *inclusio*, which highlights the universal destruction when the Day of the Lord comes. This chapter gives a long list of the reasons for God's wrath upon Judah (1:4–13): (a) syncretistic worship (vv. 4–6), (b) corruption of leadership (vv. 8–9), (c) trust in commerce and wealth (vv. 10–11), and (d) complacency of the people (vv. 12–13). Then it proceeds to describe the terrible consequences of the Day of the Lord (1:14–18). The structure of chapter 1 is as follows:

1:1	Superscription
1:2–3	Introduction – Universal Judgment of God
1:4–13	Sources of God's Wrath – Sins of Judah
	• Syncretistic Worship (vv. 4–6)
	• Corrupt Leadership (vv. 7–9)
	• Dependence on Commerce and Wealth (vv. 10–11)
	• Complacency (vv. 12–13)
1:14–18	Consequences of God's Wrath
	• Day of the Lord (vv. 14–17)
	• Universal Judgment of God (v. 18)

The main concern of Zephaniah 2 is the sweeping away of all the nations (Judah's enemies) from the land so that it can be possessed by the humble and faithful remnant of Judah. Zephaniah first summons the humble people in Judah to seek the Lord in the hope that they might be hidden from God's wrath on the Day of the Lord (2:1–3), and he declares that the remnant will live in the land again because the Lord will restore their fortune (2:7, 9, 11; cf. 3:10–13). The rest of the chapter underscores the destruction of other nations in all directions during the violent Day of the Lord (2:4–15).

vv. 4–7	West [Seacoast]: Gaza, Ashkelon, Ashdod, Ekron, Chereth, Canaan
vv. 8–11	East: Moab, Ammon
v. 12	South: Cush
vv. 13–15	North: Assyria

Basically, these nations will be punished because of their pride and arrogance. The Moabites and Ammonites insult and boast against God's people (2:8, 10). The Ninevites say proudly in their heart, 'I am, and there is no one else' (2:15a). Compared to the absolute statements of sheer judgment (e.g. 'I will utterly sweep away'; 'I will stretch out my hand'; 'I will cut off'; 'I will punish'; 'I will bring distress', etc.) in Zephaniah 1, the tone of announcement is so much softened in Zephaniah 2. Amid the gloomy darkness of doom, it opens up the possibility of salvation, which gives God's humble people a glimmer of light and hope during their time of hardship. The structure of Zephaniah 2 is as follows:

2:1–3	Call for a Humble Remnant to Seek the Lord
2:4–15	Judgment upon Other Nations
	• West (vv. 4–7)
	• East (vv. 8–11)
	• South (v. 12)
	• North (vv. 13–15)
	Reasons for Punishing the Nations
	• God intends to restore Judah's fortune (2:7, 9)
	• They insult God's people (2:8, 10)
	• They are arrogant (2:10)

Zephaniah 3:1–8 draws a conclusion to Zephaniah 1 – 2 regarding God's judgment on Judah (3:1–5) and on the nations (3:6–8). Zephaniah 3:8b echoes 1:18, summarizing God's strong determination for universal destruction – 'for in the fire of my jealousy all the earth shall be consumed' (3:8b; 1:18). Then finally the book is brought to its climax, which highlights the conversions of the nations (3:9) and the restoration of Judah (3:10–20).

3:1–8	Conclusion God's Universal Judgment
	• On Judah (vv. 1–5)
	• On the Nations (vv. 6–8)
3:9–20	Climax – God's Universal Salvation
	To the nations (v. 9)
	To Judah (vv. 10–20)
	• God will reserve a remnant (vv. 10–13)
	• God will rejoice with his people (vv. 14–17)
	• God will gather the remnant home (vv. 18–20)

The analysis above shows that the prophetic form of judgment and salvation in Zephaniah shapes the structure of the book. How this textual form affects the sermonic form will be demonstrated later in the sermon outline.

4. Preaching Christ from Zephaniah

Preachers will find many significant linkages between Zephaniah and the NT. This provides a good opportunity for preaching Christ through Zephaniah. For instance, Zephaniah's prophecy of the Day of the Lord does not end with the destruction of Jerusalem in 587 BC. It is open to further interpretations in different historical epochs. Zephaniah mentions that God will utterly sweep away everything from the face of the earth (1:2) and in the fire of his jealousy, all the earth shall be consumed (1:18; 3:8). The language of the universal judgment (1:2–3, 18; 3:8) sounds as if it is pointing to an eschatological application. This is closely linked to the final Day of Judgment in the NT, where Jesus spoke of it: 'For then there will be great tribulation, such as has not been from the beginning of the world until now, no, and never will be' (Matt. 24:21; cf. Mark 13:19). The early church also awaited its arrival (Acts 2:20; Rom. 2:2–9; 2 Pet. 3:10; Rev. 6:17, etc). Peter describes this vividly, 'But the day of the Lord will come like a thief, and then the heavens will pass away with a roar, and the heavenly bodies will be burned up and dissolved, and the earth and the works that are done on it will be exposed' (2 Pet. 3:10). Christians today are still looking forward to the advent of this Day.

Regarding the Day of the Lord's wrath, Paul picks up the language of God's wrath and anger from Zephaniah when he gives severe warnings to the Christians in Rome (Rom. 1:18; 2:2–3, 5, 8–9). Paul warns that those who indulge in those sins listed in Romans 1:21 – 2:1 will face God's wrath as would the people in Zephaniah's time. Zephaniah 3:15, 'The King of Israel, the LORD, is in your midst; you shall never again fear evil', finds an echo in John 12:13–15 (cf. Zech. 9:9), where John describes Jesus' royal entry into Jerusalem, with the big crowd in the palm procession shouting, 'Hosanna! Blessed is he who comes in the name of the Lord, even the King of Israel!' Jesus is the one fulfilling Zephaniah's prophecy about the 'King of Israel'.

Zephaniah 3:17 describes God's rejoicing over the salvation of his people, echoing Luke 15:11–32, where a father rejoices over the return of his prodigal son. It also parallels Isaiah 62:5, which depicts God's rejoicing over his people as the bridegroom over the bride. Zephaniah 3:18–20 highlights God's promise of gathering his remnant home. This concept of 'homecoming' is reiterated in the NT. Jesus spoke of gathering his elect from the four winds, when he (the Son of Man) comes again in great glory (Matt. 24:31–32). Jesus went to his Father in order to prepare for us a place with many rooms. More importantly, he promised to come again and bring us home (John 14:1–6). Preachers can find an analogy between gathering the 'remnant' and our 'homecoming' when preaching the book of Zephaniah.

5. Knowing the audience

The book of Zephaniah can be addressed to various audiences. Preachers should know to whom their message is delivered. The sermon outline in this section will be particularly designed for the needs of a regular church congregation. As analysed above, the universal judgment on the Day of Yahweh described by Zephaniah is devastating in its totality. However, the big challenge facing Christians today is the attitude towards God's wrath over our sins. Many of us feel 'numb' about the judgment oracles in Zephaniah despite its terrifying description of sheer destruction. Very often we are impressed by Jesus' love, death and forgiveness, but lack a sense of awe and reverence towards God's anger. Many of us admit that we are all sinners, but we are surely not as bad as we could be. After all, Jesus has included us in salvation and we are not afraid of losing it. That is why many Christians find the message of universal judgment in Zephaniah irrelevant to them.

To address the above-mentioned issue, three passages are chosen for a three-point sermon – Zephaniah 1:1–18; 2:1–3 (with special reference to 2:7, 9; 3:12); and 3:14–17. The development of these points will be discussed later in the next section. The aim of this sermon is to challenge the congregation to care how God feels about us. If we care how God feels about us, we care how we live.

6. Sermon development

Based on Zephaniah 1, the first point – God's wrath over our sins – is introduced. After pointing out the reasons for God's anger (1:4–13) and the consequences of his wrath (1:2–3, 14–18) in chapter 1, the preacher can then point out the contemporary parallels to Judah's sins. Take syncretistic worship as an example. Some Christians may worship their modern idols – money, materialism, consumerism, fame, power, self-ambition, success, addicted hobbies and so on – alongside God. What is 'complacency' in a modern sense? Many Christians in affluent Western countries are reluctant to leave their comfort zone and go out to minister to the needy in third-world countries. The MP expense scandals in recent months, which have made the British people furious, are vivid examples of corrupted political leadership. In addition, the audience's attitude towards God's judgment – their 'numbness' – can be challenged too. Even the slightest sins matter to God. Sproul points out the deeper implication of the slightest sins: 'It is an act of supreme ingratitude toward the One to whom we owe everything, to the One who has given us life itself . . . When we sin as the image-bearers of God, it is an insult to His Holiness and we become false witnesses to God.'[6] This implication makes the message of Zephaniah relevant even to those who think they are behaving well (committing only the slightest sins). The preacher can then challenge the congregation with how much we care about God's wrath over our sins.

---

6. R. C. Sproul, *The Holiness of God* (Wheaton: Tyndale House Publishers, 1985), pp. 151–152.

The second point is about God's compassion over our punishment (2:1–3). God's compassionate love is clearly seen when he exhorts the humble and obedient to seek the Lord, seek righteousness and seek humility (2:3). 'Perhaps' they may be sheltered on the day of Yahweh's anger. The adverb 'perhaps' indicates a possibility of salvation, which becomes an assurance of deliverance later in 2:7, 9 and 3:12, where God promises to reserve a humble remnant during the judgment. An illustration can be added to highlight God's compassion. For example, parents often get hurt when their misbehaving children need to be disciplined. Then the preacher should proceed to challenge the audience as to how much we care about God's compassion for us.

The third point brings out God's great joy over our salvation (3:14–17), where the sermon reaches its climax. Remarkable parallels can be found in Isaiah 62:5 and Luke 15:11–32. God's joyful cheers (Zeph. 3:17) echo those of the remnant when they are delivered in Zephaniah 3:14. What a God, who shares the same emotions with us! When we sin, he feels angry with us. When we get hurt in our punishment, he feels compassion for us. When we rejoice over our salvation, he bursts into joyful cheers with us. Martin Luther examined the Great Commandment: 'Love the Lord your God with all your heart and all your soul and all your mind and all your strength, and your neighbour as yourself.' Then he asked himself, 'What is the Great Transgression?' You may say, 'Murder, adultery, blasphemy, unbelief or all the sins mentioned in Zephaniah.' Luther disagreed. He said, 'If the Great Commandment was to love God with all your heart, the Great Transgression was to fail to love God with all your heart.'[7] None of us can keep the Great Commandment even for five minutes. If we love someone, we will certainly care how he or she feels. Finally the preacher can challenge the congregation as to how much we care about God's feelings for us.

To sum up, the example of Zephaniah demonstrates how preachers can apply the suggested principles to prepare for their sermons on the Minor Prophets. According to the analysis above, an extended sermon outline is provided below. It is not difficult to find out that the sermonic form is derived from the textual form (cf. 'Textual analysis of Zephaniah 1 – 3' above).

Sermon outline on the book of Zephaniah

Selected texts
Zephaniah 1:1–18; 2:1–3 (cf. 2:7, 9; 3:12); 3:14–17.

---

7. ibid., pp. 116–117.

Proposition
Zephaniah reminds us how God feels about us. If we care how God feels about us, we will care how we live.[8]

Background

1. Historical context of the book (1:1)
2. Key theme – Day of the Lord

A. God's wrath over our sins (Zeph. 1:1–18)

1. Sources of God's wrath (1:4–13)
   (a) Syncretistic worship (vv. 4–6)
   (b) Corrupt leadership (vv. 7–9)
   (c) Trust in commerce and wealth (vv. 10–11)
   (d) Complacency (vv. 12–13)
2. Consequences of God's wrath (1:2–3, 14–18)
   (a) Imminence of the Day of the Lord (vv. 14–17)
   (b) Universal destruction (vv. 2–3, 18)
   Link with the severe warnings in Romans 2:2–9; 2 Peter 3:10; Acts 2:20; Revelation 6:17
3. Contemporary application
   (a) Contemporary parallels to Judah's sins
   (b) 'Numb' feeling towards God's wrath and his judgment
   (c) Greater implication of our slightest sins
   (d) Challenge: How much do we care about God's anger over our sins?

B. God's compassion over our punishment (Zeph. 2:1–3, 7, 9; 3:12)

1. A possibility of salvation (2:1–3)
   (a) Seeking God, righteousness and humility (vv. 1–3ab)
   (b) Perhaps they may be saved on the Day of the Lord (v. 3c)
   Link with Romans 11:5–6 (being chosen by grace, not by work)

---

8. The proposition of a sermon highlights why the message is so important to the audience. It needs to be repeated throughout the sermon in order to draw the congregation's attention to the issue. In this sermon outline the proposition surfaces again as a challenge to the audience at the end of each key point.

2. An assurance of deliverance (2:7, 9; 3:12)
   (a) The remnant will possess the lands of their enemies (2:7, 9)
   (b) The move from the possibility of salvation (2:3) to the assurance of deliverance (3:12) shows God's compassion over his people
3. Contemporary application
   (a) An illustration: a mother's tears when she is disciplining her misbehaving child. God feels our hurt during our punishment.
   (b) Challenge: How much do we care about God's compassion for our punishment?

C. God's joy over our salvation (Zeph. 3:14–17)

1. The humble remnant rejoices for their salvation (v. 14)
2. God rejoices over his people's salvation (v. 17)
   Link with Isaiah 62:5; 65:17–19 (as the bridegroom rejoicing over the bride) and Luke 15:11–32 (the prodigal son's returning home)
3. Contemporary application
   (a) Martin Luther's question about the Great Commandment and the Great Transgression
   (b) God feels angry about our sins; he feels compassionate over our punishment; he shares our joy over our salvation
   (c) Challenge: How much do we care about his feelings over us? If we care how God feels about us, we will care how we live.

Recommended further reading

BERLIN, ADELE, *Zephaniah*, Anchor Bible Commentary 25A (New Haven: Yale University Press, 1994).

REDDITT, PAUL L. and AARON SCHART, *Thematic Threads in the Book of the Twelve* (Berlin: Walter de Gruyter, 2003).

SWEENEY, MARVIN A., *The Twelve Prophets*, 2 vols., Berit Olam (Collegeville: The Liturgical Press, 2000).

12. PREACHING FROM DIFFICULT TEXTS

Gordon J. Wenham

Introduction

Writing this chapter, I have often thought of the old joke. A tourist asked an Irishman the way to Dublin. He replied, 'If I were going to Dublin, I wouldn't start from here!' If I were going to preach on the difficult texts from the OT, I certainly would not start with them. In many circles, including the churches, the OT has such a bad reputation, as cruel, violent and obsolete, that a preacher will have a job to make people listen to its message. Those churches which follow a lectionary which prescribes an OT reading each week may have a slightly easier task, as the lectionary rarely includes the most awkward passages. But this is to evade the problem rather than deal with it.

Nevertheless, it seems to me fundamental that pastors should not walk too far ahead of their flock, or the sheep will soon drop away and cease to follow. How, or even whether, one tackles the difficult passages from the OT must depend very much on the spiritual maturity and understanding of the congregation. If they are well versed in the Bible and are sympathetic to its authority, one may well dare to preach on the difficult passages as long as one is not the new raw curate in the parish. I would suggest that a much-loved established vicar is much more likely to be listened to as he explains the value of such passages than someone without that personal following. So anyone contemplating preaching on these texts should carefully consider his own standing with regard to the flock and reflect on how to treat the text in a way that will not ruffle their feathers unhelpfully. This issue of tact is not unique to the OT, of course: there are plenty of topics in the NT – wealth, divorce, hell, pluralism, and so on – that require prudent exposition from the pulpit.

So what are the difficult parts of the OT for the modern reader and preacher? Genesis 1 offers us an account of creation in six days that conflicts with modern science. Genesis 5, 10, 11, 36 and 1 Chronicles 1 – 9 consist of genealogies that bore modern readers as well as surprising them by the age of the patriarchs. Genesis 22 shocks moderns by God's demand for human sacrifice. Exodus presents its own problems: the hardening of Pharaoh's heart, the plagues, slavery laws and the rule of talion. Leviticus's preoccupation with sacrifice and uncleanness excites few Western readers. The belligerence of Deuteronomy demanding the ethnic cleansing of the Canaanites strikes many as obscene. Warfare continues to dominate the pages of Joshua to Kings: can it really be that God approves of all this bloodshed? Then in the Psalms and Prophets there are some vicious prayers invoking God's vengeance on Israel's enemies. Can all this, as St Paul said, be 'written for our instruction' (Rom. 15:4)?[1]

To tackle all these issues thoroughly would require a lengthy book. Here I will just offer a few observations that may alleviate the problems. I think they fall into two main categories: misunderstandings of OT customs, and clashes between the biblical outlook and the modern world.

Genealogies

Genealogies, for example, bore the modern reader, because our ancestry is comparatively unimportant for us, unless it is a hobby. What our parents or grandparents did for a living rarely determines our occupation or place of residence today. But in biblical times your genealogy was all-important, especially for the male. It determined where you lived, as you would normally inherit your father's land or his business. So a man's career was determined by his family background. If you were a Judean, you would live in Judah, or if your father were a priest, you would become a priest. In other words, your genealogy defined your identity. Not to be able to prove your pedigree was therefore serious: priests who returned from the exile but could not prove their

---

1. Biblical quotations are from ESV, unless otherwise indicated.

ancestry were excluded from the priesthood (Ezra 2:62; Neh. 7:64). The NT also underlines the importance of one's forefathers by giving two genealogies of our Lord (Matt. 1:1–18; Luke 3:23–38).

Sacrifice

Sacrifice is another no-go area for moderns. It seems to them primitive, barbarous and irrelevant. But these reactions are again based on ignorance and a failure to note the parallels in our social practice to ancient sacrifice. If one considers the constituents of a major sacrifice, meat, flour and wine, it is apparent that they reflect what made and makes a lavish meal (Gen. 18:1–8). The basic metaphor of sacrifice is that of treating God as you would a most honoured guest. Those who enjoy barbecues in the summer should thoroughly appreciate the imagery of sacrifice.

If preachers can first make their congregation see the relevance of sacrifice, it then becomes possible to introduce its deeper significance and the differences between different types of sacrifice.[2] Why are different animals prescribed? Why is blood thrown, smeared and sprinkled in different places? What is meant by atonement? How does blood effect purification, and so on? As the preacher explores these issues, he needs to point out how they inform the NT teaching about the death of Christ and its atoning significance. This should convince the Marcionite tendency in the congregation that perhaps Leviticus should remain part of Christian Scripture after all.

Western preachers of Leviticus face a problem in that most of their hearers have never seen a sacrifice and therefore find it extremely difficult to visualize what it involves. Discussion of the different functions of the burnt offering and the sin offering will hardly register if one's listeners do not appreciate the different rituals involved. So in this situation it would be worth considering how the rites might be illustrated first, before an exposition of their theology is attempted. Perhaps a sacrifice could be acted out as the children's talk, or PowerPoint diagrams could be used.

---

2. For detailed discussions, see John E. Hartley, *Leviticus* (Dallas: Word, 1992); Jacob Milgrom, *Leviticus 1 – 16* (New York: Doubleday, 1991); Rolf Rendtorff, *Leviticus 1 – 10* (Neukirchen, Neukirchener Verlag, 2004). For a more popular discussion, see my NICOT commentary, *The Book of Leviticus* (Grand Rapids: Eerdmans, 1979), and for an analysis of the interpretative issues, see Leigh Trevaskis, *Holiness, Ethics and Ritual in the Book of Leviticus* (Sheffield: Phoenix, forthcoming).

Slavery

Another difficulty that arises from misunderstanding or inept translation is that of slavery. The very benevolent attitude that informs the laws on slavery in Exodus 21, Leviticus 25 and Deuteronomy 15 is obscured by the vocabulary of slavery. If, instead of, 'When you buy a Hebrew slave, he shall serve six years, and in the seventh he shall go out free, for nothing', Exodus 21:2 were translated, 'When you hire a Hebrew worker, he shall work for six years, and in the seventh he shall go out free, for nothing', one would see more easily the nature of biblical slavery and the intention of the laws. In biblical times every family in Israel was supposed to have its own plot of land on which to grow its crops and raise its herds. Every family ran its own farm and thus could in modern parlance be called self-employed. In good times, when the rains came and the family was healthy, this arrangement was fine. But what happened in times of drought, famine or other disaster? Families could run out of food and even seed to sow next year's crops. What was to be done then?

The pentateuchal laws prescribe that in this situation wealthier landowners should take on their impoverished neighbours as their employees or 'slaves'. This was viewed as an act of kindness to the destitute. When Joseph made the Egyptians lifelong slaves of the Pharaoh, they exclaimed, 'You have saved our lives; may it please my lord, we will be servants to Pharaoh' (Gen. 47:25). The main thrust of the laws in the Pentateuch is to limit the period of service, but it is recognized that some 'slaves' may find the security of employment so appealing that they elect to become permanent slaves of their master (Exod. 21:5–6; Deut. 15:16–17). Even today there are those who prefer the status of employee to being self-employed. But it is in poor countries that one sees the advantages of the biblical slave laws most clearly. In these societies destitute peasants migrate to the towns and there eke out a pitiful existence in the slums.[3] The biblical slave laws kept them on the land, provided them with work and food, and gave them the opportunity to return to their own land after six years.[4] And finally it encouraged the rich to be generous: as Deuteronomy 15:18 puts it, 'At half the cost of a hired servant he has served you six years.' Our modern welfare provision might learn a few lessons from the biblical system.

---

3. For a graphic account of the consequences of this process, see D. Lapierre, *The City of Joy* (London: Arrow, 1986).

4. For a fuller discussion of the laws including the Jubilee (Lev. 25), see G. C. Chirichigno, *Debt-Slavery in Israel and the Ancient Near East, JSOT* Sup. 141 (Sheffield: JSOT Press, 1993).

Talion

The law of talion, 'eye for eye, tooth for tooth', is another pentateuchal principle (Exod 21:23–25; Lev. 24:17–21; Deut. 19:21) that is frequently misunderstood. It is decried as a cruel expression of vengeance that is contrary to Christian attitudes of forgiveness. The problem arises from the Bible's preference for vivid metaphors instead of long-winded abstraction. Few people would dissent from the principle that at law the punishment should be proportionate to the offence, that, as we say, 'the punishment should fit the crime'. And this is precisely what the talion formula is asserting.

Unless this principle is acknowledged, disputes may spiral into ongoing feuds, and the strong will take out their vengeance on the weak, as Lamech did:

> Lamech said to his wives:
> 'Adah and Zillah, hear my voice;
> you wives of Lamech, listen to what I say:
> I have killed a man for wounding me,
> a young man for striking me.
> If Cain's revenge is sevenfold,
> then Lamech's is seventy-sevenfold.'
> (Gen. 4:23–24)

The law of talion limits the right of compensation to one for one, not seventy-seven for one: one eye for one eye, one tooth for one tooth, and so on. It is a rule to cap violence, not to legitimate it. It was a maximum, not a minimum penalty. In Bible times the law operated like our civil law, not our criminal law. If an offence was committed, you did not call the police (there were none), but you or your relative brought the offender to the elders at the city gate, who decided if he was guilty. If the offender was convicted, negotiation between him and the injured party would follow and compensation would be agreed. 'You have knocked out my tooth, I am entitled to knock out yours, unless you give me X shekels.' For example, a slave might be given his freedom if he lost an eye or a tooth (Exod. 21:26–27). Exodus 21:30–31 mentions the negotiations that would ensue if a bull gored someone to death. Proverbs 6:32–35 warns would-be adulterers not to count on the offended husband accepting compensation instead of the death penalty.[5] So far from talion

---

5. The death penalty was standard punishment for adultery across the ancient world.' For further discussion of the principles of talion, see R. Westbrook, *Studies in*

being barbarous and primitive, it is the very heart of justice, the quintessence of fairness. Far from perpetuating violence, it is designed to bring a quick and fair resolution to disputes.

Genesis 1

Anyone starting to preach on the OT today runs into problems in the very first chapter. Creation in six days does not seem to be compatible with Darwin. The following chapters 2 – 11 also present problems to the modern preacher. I do not intend to discuss those here, but the observations I make about chapter 1 also have relevance to the ensuing chapters.

Fundamentally this is another case of modern readers misunderstanding ancient idiom, or, more precisely, the genre of Genesis 1 – 11. It is not a scientific description of creation, for how would people of earlier times have understood such an account? One might be tempted to describe it as a myth, for in many respects it has similarities with the accounts of world origins from the Ancient Near East that are usually called myths. But however apt a genre description myth might be, I would never use it in the pulpit. Myth's first meaning to the modern ear is untruth, error; and if one uses this term as a description of Genesis 1 some will be very upset and others will think they can dismiss this fundamental account of biblical theology as of no value.

Instead I tell them bits of the great Mesopotamian stories of origins, such as the Atrahasis epic. I point out some of the similarities between these stories and Genesis, so that modern listeners grasp that we are dealing with the same sort of tale, without ever using the dreaded word 'myth'. I tell them that the ancients would have believed these stories with the same conviction that we believe the theory of evolution. But what would really strike a visitor from ancient Babylon or Egypt visiting Jerusalem and hearing the Genesis version of world origins is not the similarity with his Babylonian version, but the differences. There is only one God. There is no theogony, with gods and goddesses marrying and having children. The sun and moon are created objects, not gods. Mankind is the climax of God's creation, not an afterthought necessitated by a strike by the lesser gods. God provides mankind with food, not the other way round as the Atrahasis epic relates.

Footnote 5 (*continued*)

Biblical and Cuneiform Law (Paris: Gabalda, 1988); and 'Lex Talionis and Exodus 21, 22 – 25', *Revue Biblique* 93 (1986), pp. 52–69.

Genesis, I say, is putting a new spin on old tales. The outline of events from creation to flood may be the same in Mesopotamian and Israelite accounts of world origins, but the theology taught by the rival versions is quite different. Genesis affirms monotheism, the sovereignty of God who brings things into being by his word, the place of mankind in the divine plan, and God's solicitude for man's well-being. More points along these lines may be made by comparing the genealogies with the Sumerian King List and the Genesis flood story with the Gilgamesh epic. One should go on to point out that the emphases of Genesis 1 – 11, when contrasted with Near Eastern parallels, are some of the central affirmations of the Bible and the Christian faith: for example, the unity of God (Mark 12:29), divine sovereignty (John 1:3), mankind as God's image (1 Cor. 11:7), God's love for man (John 3:16). The opening chapters of Genesis provide us with the spectacles to read the rest of Scripture with the right presuppositions.[6]

When handled this way, the opening chapters of the Bible no longer seem an obstacle to faith, but a support for the foundational truths of the faith. I sometimes go on to suggest that we take a leaf out of Moses' (or whoever wrote Genesis) book and take the modern scientific cosmology, from big bang to evolution, and retell it from a perspective of a belief in God the Creator. 'Moses' retold the ancient oriental story of origins from the perspective of a mankind-friendly monotheism and thereby taught in this narrative what God was really like. Our vision of time and the universe is so much greater and richer than that of the ancients that to hold that there is a God who designed and upholds it explodes our imagination and demands our worship. As he said to Job:

Where were you when I laid the foundation of the earth?
Tell me, if you have understanding.
(Job 38:4)

We can only join with the psalmist and say:

When I look at your heavens, the work of your fingers,
the moon and the stars, which you have set in place,
what is man that you are mindful of him,
and the son of man that you care for him?
(Psalm 8:3–4)

---

6. For further elaboration, see G. J. Wenham, *Genesis 1 – 15* (Waco: Word, 1987); E. C. Lucas, *Can We Believe Genesis Today?* (Leicester: Inter-Varsity Press, 2000).

This approach has worked well with me. Not only do I think it is the correct approach to Genesis 1, but congregations find it helpful. However, I once overstepped the mark. Preaching in a local Baptist congregation with a good sprinkling of younger people, I thought I would go a bit further and explain why I thought the days should be regarded as 'days' in the life of God, not twenty-four-hour human days. I pointed to the fact that the sun, which makes our day and night, was not created until the fourth day. Anyway, this was too much. A member of the congregation got up and started heckling me. He then walked out! So I would suggest it is better to leave such controversial points out and just leave people to draw their own conclusions or let them ask you at the end of the service.

Violence

The issue of violence is one of the most pervasive for any preacher on the OT, and it is of course one of those most often raised by unbelievers. Here it is partially misunderstanding and partially a rejection of biblical theology that is to blame. We would not suppose that because a newspaper described a massacre in Darfur or a murder in Manchester that the journalist responsible approved of these events. But that is often the way biblical accounts of warfare are handled. When Scripture is read more carefully, it is clear that most violence is not approved of.

If one allows Genesis 1 – 11 to colour one's reading of the whole book, if not the whole of Scripture, it is patent that violence is seen as a catastrophic irruption into God's good creation. Genesis 1 gives a picture of perfect harmony in the newly created cosmos. Both animals and humans are vegetarian: they do not hunt and kill each other. According to Isaiah 11:1–9 and 65:25, this pacific state will characterize the new creation too. But in chapter 3 the descent into chaos begins with animosity between mankind and the snake.[7]

> I will put enmity between you and the woman,
> and between your offspring and her offspring;
> he shall bruise your head,
> and you shall bruise his heel.
> (Gen. 3:15)

---

7. This understanding of Genesis 3:15 does not exclude it being also the Protevangelium: see Wenham, *Genesis 1 – 15*, pp. 79–81.

Violence grows in chapter 4, with Cain slaying his brother and his descendant Lamech threatening seventy-sevenfold violence (4:8, 24). Genesis 6:5 declares, 'The LORD saw that the wickedness of man was great in the earth, and that every intention of the thoughts of his heart was only evil continually.' Soon after we read that 'the earth was filled with violence' (6:11) and God decrees, 'I have determined to make an end of all flesh, for the earth is filled with violence through them. Behold, I will destroy them with the earth' (Gen. 6:13). In other words, the flood was sent as a punishment on human and animal ('all flesh') violence.[8] This is very different from the Atrahasis explanation, where the flood is prompted by population growth.

This rejection of violence and its corresponding desire for peace informs many of the later stories in Genesis. Abraham is implicitly commended for his peaceable dealings with Lot and Abimelech, an attitude perpetuated by his son Isaac, whereas Jacob's sons' slaughter of the Shechemites is cursed by Jacob:

> Cursed be their anger, for it is fierce,
> and their wrath, for it is cruel!
> (Gen. 49:7)

One of the bloodiest books of the Bible is Judges. Battles, assassinations, massacres and civil war seem to be its dominant themes. Overall the book portrays Israel's decline into chaos, a chaos caused by their disloyalty to God. Violence is here depicted as the consequence of sin, not a good to be applauded or imitated.[9] Against this ever-darkening background, the heroic deeds of the judges themselves stand out: they are examples of bravery and faith in action in the direst situations. But this does not mean that fighting is inherently good. It may be necessary to prevent worse evils, but the goal is a sin-free society where there is no violence. The book hints that monarchy might bring Israel nearer that ideal: 'In those days there was no king in Israel. Everyone did what was right in his own eyes' (Judg. 21:25).

The ambivalence towards violence, which can be sensed in Judges, emerges earlier in Genesis. As already mentioned, the flood was prompted by mankind's thoughts being 'only evil continually' and consequently the earth being full of violence (Gen. 6:5, 11, 13). But after the purging of the earth by the flood, the problem of the human heart still remained: 'man's heart is evil from his youth'

---

8. See ibid., p. 171.

9. For further discussion, see G. J. Wenham, *Story as Torah* (Edinburgh: T. & T. Clark, 2000), pp. 45–71; R. Ryan, *Judges* (Sheffield: Sheffield Phoenix Press, 2007).

(8:21). Sacrifice may persuade God not to send another flood, but how is man's propensity for violence to be curbed? Genesis 9:5–6 gives an answer:

> And for your lifeblood I will require a reckoning: from every beast I will require it and from man. From his fellow man I will require a reckoning for the life of man.
> 'Whoever sheds the blood of man,
> by man shall his blood be shed,
> for God made man in his own image.'

The death penalty for murder is an application of the talion principle discussed earlier. But this text points to its paradoxical nature. Homicide is an assault on God's image, man, and therefore must be punished, even though to take a second human life assaults another example of that image. But this is better, the text implies, than the whole earth being filled with violence and being wiped out in another divine judgment.

Genesis 9:6 is the first passage in the OT in the form of a case law, that is a law that determines what should be done when an offence has been committed.[10] Case law does not set out moral ideals (such as 'You shall not steal'), but defines what should be done when these ideals have been broken (e.g. the penalties for theft). So here, the ideal is the preservation of human life, but the loss of a second life in the execution of the murderer is better than a blood feud that may never end or may develop into the situation described in Judges 19 – 21.

This desire for peace and the aversion to violence must therefore be seen as the basic presupposition underlying all biblical descriptions of war and homicide. This is illustrated by the laws on warfare in Deuteronomy 20. These laws form part of Deuteronomy's exposition of the Decalogue: chapters 19 – 21 apply 'You shall not murder' to various situations. Deuteronomy 19:1–13 deals with the cities of refuge to which a homicide may flee if he has killed someone accidentally, and verses 15–21 set out what should be done to someone who falsely accuses another of a capital crime. Then, after the laws on war, 21:1–9 deals with the ceremony to purge the land of the guilt of an unsolved murder. The laws on war in chapter 20 are thus put under the general heading 'You shall not murder' and sandwiched between laws intent on enforcing that principle justly.

The laws on war are themselves remarkable. They begin with a long preamble allowing all sorts of men to opt out of being called up, new homeowners,

---

10. Exodus 21 – 22 contains many case laws.

new vineyard growers, newly married and the fearful. The priority of peace at home rather than fighting abroad could hardly be clearer. This long-term vision is reinforced by the conclusion which prohibits fruit trees from being cut down in a siege, which is justified by the rhetorical question, 'Are the trees in the field human, that they should be besieged by you?' (Deut. 20:19). Then within this peace-loving, eco-friendly section come the rules relating to the enemy. This covers three scenarios of siege warfare.

1. Enemy city offered peace and accepts: enemy does forced labour (vv. 10–11).
2. Enemy city outside Canaan rejects peace: all enemy males killed (vv. 12–15).
3. Enemy city inside Canaan rejects peace: all enemy killed (vv. 16–18).

On this understanding, every city attacked by the Israelites, whether inside the land or outside, was given the option of surrender.[11] If they refused, they faced very harsh treatment – death of all, or at least all males. One may be shocked at this threat: maybe it was designed to encourage a quick surrender and shorten the campaign, but we do not really know.

What really shocks the modern Christian is the command to kill all the inhabitants in Canaanite cities which do not surrender. It looks like ethnic cleansing. But this is not accurate: it is religious cleansing that Deuteronomy is concerned with. The Canaanites must not be allowed to live, 'that they may not teach you to do according to all their abominable practices that they have done for their gods, and so you sin against the LORD your God' (Deut. 20:18).

This is the reason given in chapter 7 when the rationale for complete destruction is set out. In this passage the command does sound like hyperbolic exaggeration, for it continues by forbidding intermarriage with the Canaanites.

You shall not intermarry with them, giving your daughters to their sons or taking their daughters for your sons, for they would turn away your sons from following me,

---

11. The view of Maimonides (so Jeffrey H. Tigay, *Deuteronomy*, Philadelphia: Jewish Publication Society, 1996, p. 472) and more recently Norbert Lohfink, 'ḥāram', in *TDOT* V (Grand Rapids: Eerdmans, 1986), p. 197. Most commentators suppose the option to surrender applied only to cities outside the land, but Deuteronomy 20:10, 'When you draw near to a city to fight against it, offer terms of peace to it', makes no such restriction.

to serve other gods. Then the anger of the LORD would be kindled against you, and he would destroy you quickly. (Deut. 7:3–4)

A prohibition of intermarriage would be quite redundant if all the Canaanites were to be destroyed. But if some had surrendered and were working for the Israelites, the temptation to marry them and adopt their religion would be real. The only passage where extermination of idolaters is unequivocally required concerns an *Israelite* town, whose inhabitants have turned to other gods (Deut. 13:12–18). Not only are all its inhabitants to be put to the sword, but the town itself is to be burnt down and never rebuilt.

Deuteronomy's concern is not racist, but religious. Moses is demanding total fidelity to the Lord in the Lord's land. But it must be admitted that to modern ears this is almost as bad. Pluralism and toleration are values that modern secular society loves to applaud, although it becomes rather less tolerant if you do not hold to this belief and affirm there is only one way to God. It is therefore a very hard truth to convince people of, especially in a short sermon. All a preacher's rhetorical skills will be necessary. It is essential to show that the NT, especially Jesus, taught the same. The congregation needs to be reminded of texts such as Acts 4:12, 'And there is salvation in no one else, for there is no other name under heaven given among men by which we must be saved', and John 14:6, 'Jesus said to him, "I am the way, and the truth, and the life. No one comes to the Father except through me."'

This practice of backing up hard messages from the OT by appeal to the NT is, I think, vital, if one is to make people take it seriously. I think the OT comes lowest in congregational esteem, St Paul may be respected a little more, the other apostles more still, and finally Jesus and his teaching command most respect: even if they have forgotten or have ignored Christ's teaching, most churchgoers will take him seriously. This must be borne in mind when preaching on the OT. One must back up its awkward teaching by appeal to the NT and especially the Gospels.

The imprecatory psalms

The Psalms are the most loved and most used part of the OT for very obvious reasons. But they also contain some of the fiercest expressions of hate towards enemies that are found anywhere in Scripture, and many commentators even of quite conservative disposition have lamented the psalmists' lapse from grace. Churches have directed that some whole psalms and parts of others should not be sung. C. S. Lewis, for example, called them 'terrible' and 'contemptible',[12] Kirkpatrick said they were 'barbarous and revolting',[13] and Oesterley 'vindictive' and 'a disgrace to human nature'.[14] Even Derek Kidner thought that Christians could not use these psalms as their own.[15]

In more recent years there has been a change of mood towards these psalms. It is argued by various scholars that the failure to use the lament psalms, of which the imprecatory psalms are a subset, has greatly impoverished Christian worship. Life for many people is not a bed of roses, and therefore they need the opportunity to express their fears, frustrations and complaints to God in worship. A diet of upbeat songs and positive testimonies does not meet the needs of those suffering disappointment, ill health or persecution. As the laments constitute the largest group of psalms in the Psalter, it is a great mistake to leave them out.

Yet does this justify asking God to wreak vengeance on one's enemies? Among others, D. G. Firth,[16] J. C. McCann[17] and E. Zenger[18] have tackled this issue head on, and their works should be required reading for every ordinand. Here we can give only a brief summary of their approach.

The first point to note is that the psalmists' prayer is that God will treat their enemies as they have treated the psalmists. It is putting into prayer the principle of talion that we discussed earlier. In Psalm 109:

The psalmist's request is in accordance with what most persons, then and now, would say is only fair – the punishment should fit the crime (Deut. 19:18–21). In particular, the enemy deserves no kindness (v. 12, or 'steadfast love'), because he showed no kindness (v. 16). The enemy deserves to be impoverished (vv. 8–11), because he mistreated the poor and the needy (v. 16; see Ps. 10:2). The enemy

12. C. S. Lewis, *Reflections on the Psalms* (London: Collins, 1961), p. 24.

13. A. F. Kirkpatrick, *The Book of Psalms* (Cambridge: Cambridge University Press, 1902), p. xciii.

14. W. O. E. Oesterley, *The Psalms II* (London: SPCK, 1939), pp. 458, 548.

15. D. Kidner, *Psalms 1 – 72* (London: Inter-Varsity Press,1973), p. 32.

16. D. G. Firth, *Surrendering Retribution in the Psalms* (Milton Keynes: Paternoster, 2005).

17. e.g. in J. C. McCann, *A Theological Introduction to the Book of the Psalms* (Nashville: Abingdon, 1993).

18. E. Zenger, *A God of Vengeance?* (Louisville: Westminster John Knox Press, 1996).

deserves to be cursed, because he cursed others (vv. 17–19, 28–29; see Ps. 62:4). In short, the enemy deserves to die (v. 8), because he pursued others to their death (vv. 16, 31).[19]

Second, the psalmists never suggest that they will do this themselves: they leave the punishment to God. In Psalm 38, for example:

[T]here is no attempt to personally retaliate for the violence received. Although vindication is sought . . . it is sought only in a context of confession (verse 19), and a desire that Yahweh should be the source of redemption. Personal violence is thus rejected because the expectation of deliverance from sickness and persecution is found only in waiting on Yahweh.[20]

Third, the psalmists pray for God to take action against the wicked not simply for the sake of justice, but for the sake of his reputation. By punishing the wicked he demonstrates his power and his care for the poor and oppressed. Divine inaction is construed by the wicked as proof that he does not care, or cannot act, or even that he does not exist. It is vital that such ideas be scotched.

As poetic prayers, the psalms of vengeance are a passionate clinging to God when everything really speaks *against* God. For that reason they can rightly be called *psalms of zeal*, to the extent that in them passion for God is aflame in the midst of the ashes of doubt about God and despair over human beings. These psalms are the expression of a longing that evil, and evil people, may not have the last word in history, for this world and its history belong to God.[21]

But why should modern worshippers use these prayers today, if they have not been persecuted or otherwise ill treated? Praying these prayers teaches us to sympathize with those who suffer: it puts their feelings into our mouth. More than that, however, praying these psalms teaches us to hate injustice and violence. McCann writes:

In the face of monstrous evil, the worst possible response is to feel *nothing*. What *must* be felt is grief, rage, outrage. In their absence, evil becomes an acceptable

---

19. J. C. McCann, *NIB* IV (Nashville: Abingdon, 1996), p. 1126.
20. Firth, *Surrendering Retribution*, p. 124.
21. Zenger, *A God of Vengeance?*, p. 79.

commonplace. To forget is to submit to evil, to wither and die: to remember is to resist, be faithful, and live again.[22]

Furthermore:

As we pray and reflect upon Psalm 137, we remember and are retaught the pain of exile, the horror of war, the terror of despair and death, the loneliness of a cross.[23]

Zenger suggests another benefit of praying these psalms: they can teach their users to reflect on their own responsibility for oppression and involvement with evil. Psalm 139, after expressing the psalmist's hatred of the wicked, goes on:

Oh that you would slay the wicked, O God!
O men of blood, depart from me!
(v. 19)

It ends:

Search me, O God, and know my heart!
Try me and know my thoughts!
And see if there be any grievous way in me,
and lead me in the way everlasting!
(vv. 23–24)

Zenger suggests that many who pray the psalms may themselves be guilty of violence and oppression. 'Those who pray them are inevitably faced with the question of *their own* complicity in the web of violence.'[24]

To sum up, these appeals for divine intervention, often dubbed the imprecatory psalms, are much more than curses parading as prayers. They are undergirded by the conviction that God is both sovereign and just – indeed, that he cares about the injustice suffered by the poor and downtrodden. The psalmists cry out that God will treat the wrongdoers as they have treated others. In situations where faith in God's goodness seems to be disproved, they reassert that faith, and trust God to vindicate them rather than take revenge themselves.

---

22. McCann, *A Theological Introduction*, p. 119.

23. ibid., p. 121.

24. Zenger, *A God of Vengeance?*, p. 76.

Those who pray these psalms today may be taken aback by their directness, but that may reflect our own sheltered existence and the blandness of the piety with which we have been brought up. These psalms shatter our illusions, make us face life in the raw and make us ask whether we really believe in a sovereign loving God. Zenger comments, 'Any kind of trust in God or mysticism that is blind to social injustice or does not want to dirty its hands with such things is, in fact, a form of cynicism.'[25] The cry of the poor resounding from one end of the Psalter to the other[26] reaches its highest pitch in these psalms and challenges all who take them on their lips to identify with them and with their Creator.

I fear, though, that some of our listeners to a sermon along these lines may still object that Jesus said, 'Father, forgive them, for they know not what they do.' He told us to love our enemies and pray for those who persecute us. It is overlooked that his prayer at the crucifixion was for the soldiers, not for those who had betrayed him and tried him. Of Judas he said, 'Woe to that man by whom the Son of Man is betrayed! It would have been better for that man if he had not been born' (Matt. 26:24). Interestingly, Psalm 69 is the second most quoted psalm in the NT, which applies it directly to Judas's career. And then there is Matthew 23, which I suspect is rarely read in churches, with its string of woes against the scribes and Pharisees, culminating in the prediction that on them will come 'all the righteous blood shed on earth' (23:35). These emphases must form part of our picture of Jesus' teaching, not just his calls for forgiveness.

However we react as individuals when we are unjustly treated (and in such situations we may well feel these psalms are highly apposite), we should surely pray them for fellow Christians enduring suffering that God will deliver them from evil. We may leave this vague, whereas the psalms are more realistic in what is required. Finally we can remind our listeners that when we pray 'Thy kingdom come', we are praying for Christ's second coming, otherwise known as the Last Judgment, at which the goats will be told, 'Depart from me, you cursed, into the eternal fire prepared for the devil and his angels' (Matt. 25:41). The imprecatory psalms seem mild in comparison.

All Saints, Worcester, Sermon on Genesis 22 (4 September 2005)

Recently, coming in to land at Heathrow, our plane lurched to the left and went into a dive. Some people screamed; others held their breath and prayed. As you

---

25. ibid., p. 33.

26. So Jean-Luc Vesco, *Le psautier de David* (Paris: Cerf, 2006), p. 154.

now realize, we did land safely, but at the time it was really scary. The silence of the captain and the reticence of the crew to explain what had happened made me conclude we had a near miss. Most of us, I suppose, can recall our own brushes with death.

But ours are quite different from that experienced by Abraham and Isaac in this morning's reading. This story from Genesis 22 is not only one of the most brilliant in all literature, but it is of central significance in both Jewish and Christian theology. So let us reflect on it for a few minutes today.

Whereas our near misses usually happen almost before we realize it, and are often the result of human error, this was certainly not the case with Abraham and Isaac. Abraham at least had a long time to ponder God's command to slaughter his only remaining son.

He had already suffered the loss of his older boy Ishmael some years earlier, a matter of great grief to him. Now his sole surviving heir was apparently to be sacrificed. So awful was this idea that Abraham said nothing to his wife about it before he left home. He put his servants off the scent, when he told them, 'I and the boy will go and worship and we shall come again to you.' On their three-day trek to the mountain, Isaac asked his father, 'Where is the lamb for a burnt offering?' Yet again Abraham disguised the fearful truth by saying, 'God will provide the lamb for a burnt offering, my son.'

Parents everywhere will identify with Abraham's distress. Our children's happiness is one of our deepest desires. What would it be like to have to slaughter your only child with your own hand?

But it was not only his love for his son that Abraham was being asked to deny, it was his whole life's work.

Many years earlier Abraham had been told to leave home with the words, 'Go from your country to the land I will show you.' Now he has been told, 'Go to one of the mountains of which I shall tell you.' God's first call to Abraham is echoed in this last call. Abraham obeyed that first call. It led him from Iraq to the land of Israel and eventually to the birth of his precious son Isaac. It was Isaac's descendants who had been promised the land and who would bring blessing to all the nations. But now very old, Abraham is told to slay his dear son, on whom all his hopes rested.

We, the readers of Genesis, have been told that this command was only a test, but for Abraham and Isaac it was totally real. Abraham's career had been built on faith in God's promises and obedience to God's commands: how will he react now to this ultimate test of his character?

We too are called to imitate Abraham in faith and obedience: we must be ready to give to God what we hold most dear: our home, our possessions, our career, our children. He calls us, like Abraham, to make sacrifices both early in life and in our later years. It is not easy when one is young; it is no easier when one is older. As Jesus said, 'Whoever would be my disciple must take up his cross daily and follow me.'

The NT sees Abraham's willingness to sacrifice his son Isaac as prefiguring God's love to the world in sending his own Son to us. To make this point, John 3:16 borrows the phraseology of this story, 'For God so loved the world that he gave his only Son, that whoever believes in him should not perish but have eternal life.'

Christ's obedience brought life to the world. The obedience of Abraham and Isaac led to God making an oath that 'in your offspring (that is in Christ) all the nations will be blessed'. Four thousand years later we can look back and see the fulfilment of this promise in the growth of the worldwide church to over a billion members. This growing church in Worcester shows that God still honours his promise where people and clergy are ready to make sacrifices and to follow his call 'to go to the mountain I will tell you'. May we all be ready to heed that call whenever it comes to us, however disturbing it may be.

Amen.

Further reading

FIRTH, DAVID G., *Surrendering Retribution in the Psalms* (Milton Keynes: Paternoster, 2005).

LUCAS, ERNEST C., *Can We Believe Genesis Today?* (Leicester: Inter-Varsity Press, 2000).

McCANN, J. CLINTON, *A Theological Introduction to the Book of the Psalms* (Nashville: Abingdon, 1993).

ZENGER, ERICH, *A God of Vengeance?* (Louisville: Westminster John Knox Press, 1996.

13. PREACHING CHRIST FROM THE OLD TESTAMENT

R. W. L. Moberly

The question of how best to read the OT in relation to Jesus Christ is a perennial issue for Christian faith. Many major Christian theologians, be it Origen and Augustine in antiquity, Luther and Calvin at the Reformation, or Barth and de Lubac in the twentieth century, offer weighty accounts, and it would be straightforward to devote this paper to reviewing some of them and reflecting on what in them is of enduring significance. Nonetheless, despite the resources within such theologians, I propose to offer my own outline account, as someone who in recent years has been trying to hold together the disciplines of biblical and theological studies. I will do this through reflecting on some general hermeneutical issues that help constitute a frame of reference, and briefly offering a worked example.

I am assuming for present purposes that reading and preaching are in principle closely related activities, where preaching essentially seeks to communicate and give specific application to the results of one's reading.[1] To be

---

1. This is, of course, an oversimplification! David Tracy's proposal for the different roles of theologian and preacher is helpfully suggestive of greater depth in this whole area: 'The theologian, in principle, need show only that the world of meaning and truth is a genuinely *possible* one for human beings (and thus "applicable" to the human situation). The preacher needs to do more: concretely to

sure, this may not apply to every kind of reading of the OT, but I have in mind what is conveniently called a 'canonical approach'.[2] Reading the OT within a canonical frame of reference seeks to shift the focus of interpretative interest from the questions characteristic of a 'historical-critical approach' (which sometimes give the impression that the main issue about the OT is the extent to which it is or is not a kind of ancient history *manqué*) to questions about how the OT can best be understood and appropriated within a Christian frame of reference.

Context and recontextualizations

Although one of the first rules one learns in biblical study is the importance of interpreting a text 'in context', this rule is of limited value unless one also addresses the questions of 'which context?' and/or 'whose context?' My impression is that 'interpretation in context' was considered to be self-evident as long as the implicit axiom was that 'context' meant 'context of origin' (whatever the problems in determining what that might be). Yet as soon as we take seriously the phenomenon of recontextualization already within the OT canon, never mind when that canon is itself recontextualized in Jewish and Christian frames of reference, we see that 'context' is itself a complex and variable notion.

One of the most significant contributions to this area can be found in essays by Jon Levenson, who articulates within a Jewish frame of reference concerns that apply also in a Christian frame of reference.[3] Among other things, Levenson develops the significance of differing contexts for interpretation. He

---

Footnote 1 *(continued)*

apply it now *in order to interpret it*' (*The Analogical Imagination*, New York: Crossroad, 1981, p. 136).

2. For a valuable discussion of the relationship between a canonical approach and classic evangelical approaches, see Stephen B. Chapman, 'Reclaiming Inspiration for the Bible', in Craig Bartholomew et al. (eds.), *Canon and Biblical Interpretation*, Scripture and Hermeneutics Series, vol. 7 (Milton Keynes: Paternoster, 2006), pp. 167–206.

3. Although all the essays in his groundbreaking *The Hebrew Bible, the Old Testament, and Historical Criticism: Jews and Christians in Biblical Studies* (Louisville: Westminster John Knox, 1993) are important, for present purposes there is particular significance in 'The Eighth Principle of Judaism and the Literary Simultaneity of Scripture'

has no doubts as to the value of rigorous historical work; yet historical context is not the only context. There is also a context constituted by the formation of the literature into a larger whole, a context that is literary and/or canonical:

> The problem is that by making *historical* context sovereign and regulative, historical criticism destroys the *literary* context that is the Bible (either Jewish or Christian) as a whole and often even the smaller literary context that is the book, the chapter, or whatever.[4]

Moreover, Levenson valuably (and sharply) recasts the familiar preoccupation of biblical scholars, concerning the difference between what the text meant in its ancient context and how it is to be understood now, into the issue of differing contextualizations of the biblical text. This leads to a restatement of the classic understanding that Scripture has more than one sense:

> Just as in medieval Europe there could be interreligious agreement on the *sensus literalis*, so in modern biblical criticism there will continue to be a broad base for agreement on the meaning of textual units in their most limited literary or historical settings. But when we come to 'the final literary setting' and even more so to 'the context of the canon', we [sc. Jews and Christians] must part company, for *there is no non-particularistic access to these larger contexts*, and no decision on these issues, even when made for secular purposes, can be neutral between Judaism and Christianity. Jews and Christians can, of course, study each other's Bible and even identify analogically or empathetically with the interpretations that the other's traditional context warrants, growing in discernment and self-understanding as a consequence. For the normative theological task, however, a choice must be made: Does the canonical context of the Abraham story, for example, include the Abraham material in Galatians and Romans or not? For Christians it must; for Jews it must not.[5]

Or, in a related formulation:

> In the realm of historical criticism, pleas for a 'Jewish biblical scholarship' or a 'Christian biblical scholarship' are senseless and reactionary. Practicing Jews and Christians will differ from uncompromising historicists, however, in affirming the

---

(pp. 62–81) and 'Theological Consensus or Historicist Evasion? Jews and Christians in Biblical Studies' (pp. 82–105).

4. ibid., p. 100.

5. ibid., pp. 80–81.

meaningfulness and interpretive relevance of larger contexts that homogenize the literatures of different periods to one degree or another. Just as text has more than one context, and biblical studies more than one method, so scripture has more than one sense, as the medievals knew and Tyndale, Spinoza, Jowett, and most other moderns have forgotten.[6]

All this helps in various ways to establish a frame of reference for our concern with preaching Christ from the OT. The inherent depth of specific biblical texts is intrinsically open to fruitful realization through the phenomenon of canon and varying recontextualizations.

First, it is important to see that the phenomenon of textual depth, resonance and plurality of senses is not in the first instance something peculiar to Scripture that needs to be justified by appeal to theological notions of inspiration and/or *sensus plenior* (notions which of course have their place but which, I suggest, best function otherwise – although that is an essay for another day!). One might compare the comment of the literary critic F. R. Leavis on the impact of Jane Austen within what he calls the 'great tradition' in English literature:

> She not only makes tradition for those coming after, but her achievement has for us a retroactive effect: as we look back beyond her we see in what goes before, and see because of her, potentialities and significances brought out in such a way that, for us, she creates the tradition we see leading down to her. Her work, like the work of all great creative writers, gives a meaning to the past.[7]

If Jane Austen can give meaning to the English literature of the eighteenth century that nourished and helped form her, so too Jesus Christ can give meaning to the scriptures of Israel that nourished and helped form him. A mature distillate and enhancement of a tradition constitutes a privileged vantage point for the deeper comprehension of that tradition.

Second, the potential impact of canonical placement upon particular texts is suggestively illuminated by David Steinmetz via an analogy with detective stories.[8] Characteristically in such stories there is a 'first narrative', that is the

---

6. ibid., p. 104.

7. F. R. Leavis, *The Great Tradition* (Harmondsworth: Penguin/Pelican, 1972; repr. of 1948 ed.), p. 14.

8. David Steinmetz, 'Uncovering a Second Narrative: Detective Fiction and the Construction of Historical Method', in Ellen F. Davis and Richard B. Hays (eds.), *The Art of Reading Scripture* (Grand Rapids: Eerdmans, 2003), pp. 54–65.

sequential unfolding of the story, which contains, among other things, clues, intelligent guesses, false leads and puzzlement. However, there is also a 'second narrative, one that is invariably recited by the principal investigator in the last or nearly last chapter':

> This narrative is crisp and clear and explains in considerable detail what was really occurring while the larger narrative was unfolding. The cogency of this narrative is not in the least undermined by the fact that none of the characters except the perpetrator of the crime and, until the very end of the story, the principal investigator himself or herself had any clear notion what the story was really about. . .
>
> It is important to understand that this second narrative is not a subplot, even though it is short. It is the disclosure of the architectonic structure of the whole story. Therefore, the second narrative quickly overpowers the first in the mind of the reader, who can no longer read the story as though ignorant of its plot and form. The second narrative is identical in substance to the first and therefore replaces it, not as an extraneous addition superimposed on the story or read back into it, but as a compelling and persuasive disclosure of what the story was about all along.[9]

The analogy is simple:

> Traditional Christian exegesis reads the Bible very much in this way – not exactly in this way, of course, but close enough to provide useful points of comparison. Early Christians believed that what had occurred in the life, death, and resurrection of Jesus Christ was of such importance that it had transformed the entire story of Israel and, through Israel, of the world. The long, ramshackle narrative of Israel with its promising starts and unexpected twists, with its ecstasies and betrayals, its laws, its learning, its wisdom, its martyred prophets – this long narrative is retold and reevaluated in the light of what early Christians regarded as the concluding chapter God had written in Jesus Christ.[10]

Steinmetz's thesis is straightforward: this analogy can help Christians recover a way of reading and understanding the Bible that has been marginalized under the impact of historical criticism's concern to understand texts in their originating contexts. After relating the notion of a second narrative to the patristic conception of a rule of faith, developing a further analogy between the construction of a second narrative and the work of a historian (Steinmetz's

---

9. ibid., p. 55.
10. ibid., p. 56.

own professional role), and considering various difficulties and objections, Steinmetz concludes:

> I am inclined to think that biblical scholars who are also Christian theologians should worry less about anachronism and more about the quality of the second narratives they have constructed. I can well understand why biblical scholars are wary of a traditional exegesis that ascribes to characters in the Bible, especially characters in the Old Testament, an explicit knowledge of the finer points of Christian theology. Such explicit knowledge would have been impossible for them at the time. But I do not have to believe that Second Isaiah had an explicit knowledge of the crucifixion of Jesus of Nazareth to believe that he was part of a larger narrative that finds its final, though not its sole, meaning in Christ. Like many of the characters in a mystery novel, Isaiah had something else on his mind. But the meaning of his work cannot be limited to the narrow boundaries of his explicit intention. Viewed from the perspective of the way things turned out, his oracles were revealed to have added dimensions of significance that no one could have guessed at the time. It is not anachronistic to believe such added dimensions of meaning exist. It is only good exegesis.[11]

Third, another analogy that can be helpful for understanding the implications of canonical context is that between the Bible and the American constitution, an analogy touched on by Steinmetz,[12] and developed more fully by Jaroslav Pelikan.[13] The importance of the analogy is that in each case you have a text

---

11. ibid., p. 65. The tradition of ascribing knowledge of Christian theology to OT characters does, however, continue among certain evangelical scholars, although whether it is appropriate is open to question. Thus Gleason L. Archer comments with reference to Genesis 3:21, 'Since Genesis 3:15 contains the first announcement of the coming of the Savior . . . it seems logical to conclude that at the time God clothed the nakedness of Adam and Eve, He also instructed them in the significance of the atoning blood of the substitute sacrifice. Adam then doubtless passed on to his sons his understanding of the blood-sacrifice atonement; for it is clear that Abel, Adam's second son, was a true believer and was well instructed about substitutionary atonement, symbolized by his sacrifice of an innocent lamb on the altar (Gen. 4:4)' (Gleason L. Archer, *Encyclopedia of Bible Difficulties*, Grand Rapids: Zondervan, 1982, p. 76).

12. Steinmetz, 'Uncovering a Second Narrative', p. 62.

13. Jaroslav Pelikan, *Interpreting the Bible and the Constitution* (New Haven and London: Yale University Press, 2004).

whose enduring significance is inseparable from its relation to a continuing community of people (although, of course, the Bible, unlike the constitution, cannot be amended). Both the Bible and the American constitution can legitimately and valuably be studied in relation to their meaning in their originating contexts. Yet what makes both important, and generates most of the study that is given to them, is the fact that they continue to matter for how people are to live their lives in settings and circumstances which may differ more or less from those originating contexts. Contexts of reception are not contexts of origin, and it is the contemporary context of reception that poses the question of how best to understand and appropriate the foundational text.

This generates a never-to-be-finally-resolved dialectic. On the one hand, the intrinsic meaning of the authoritative document matters; the community is bound to, and constrained by, the meaning of its foundational charter, which outlines its basic character and its *raison d'être*; without fidelity to this document, the community ceases to be what it is meant to be. On the other hand, life goes on, things change, and one cannot remain in the founding context. So there must necessarily be some kind of *development* in relation to the authoritative charter, development which is characteristically expressed in terms of realizing the *implications* of the original, or else of determining what is *compatible* with it. All of this requires the continuing interpretative activity on the part of the community as a whole, and of its recognized representatives, to explore, via both argument and practice, what does and does not constitute a good implication or an appropriate compatibility. The community must both attend to and be constrained by the original meaning, and also not be restricted by original meaning and be able to move beyond it.

It is because the continuing significance of the Bible is realized supremely in the continuing life of the church, just as the continuing significance of the American constitution is realized in the continuing life of the American people, that study of original meaning is both necessary but not necessarily determinative. Academic study of the Bible, by the very act of removing the Bible from its prime life setting within the church, can achieve analytical clarity about origins and development at the same time that it risks obscuring the dynamics that actually pertain when the Bible is seen to matter for life now, and decisions need to be taken as to its appropriation now.

It is therefore clear, I hope, in at least a preliminary way, that the phenomenon of biblical canonization intrinsically brings about recontextualizations which show that as context varies so do the sense and use of the OT vary. The challenge for Christian preachers of the OT is to combine historical respect for the distinctive biblical voices with a robust Christian understanding of

God in Christ as the frame of reference within which the OT witness is now to be appropriated.

Engaging with the subject matter

The importance of seriously engaging with the content, the subject matter, of Scripture was forcefully reintroduced into biblical scholarship by Karl Barth. In the preface to the second edition of his Romans commentary, Barth famously (whether or not entirely fairly) complains that the kind of historical work characteristic of mainstream biblical scholarship does not move beyond prolegomena to the real work of interpretation. In order genuinely to understand Paul there must be a 'reconsideration of what is set out in the Epistle, until the actual meaning of it is disclosed'. To illustrate, Barth appeals to Calvin:

> How energetically Calvin, having first established what stands in the text, sets himself to re-think the whole material and to wrestle with it, till the walls which separate the sixteenth century from the first become transparent! Paul speaks, and the man of the sixteenth century hears. The conversation between the original record and the reader moves round the subject-matter, until a distinction between yesterday and today becomes impossible.[14]

Barth's concern has been mediated within OT scholarship notably by Brevard Childs, not least in his *Biblical Theology of the Old and New Testaments*.[15] Childs argues that biblical theology should necessarily move 'from a description of the biblical witnesses to the object toward which these witnesses point, that is, to their subject matter, substance, or *res*'.[16] Fundamentally, this subject matter is the reality of God as known in Jesus Christ, and the context from which this reality is approached is the life of the church:

> [T]he heart of the enterprise [i.e. of biblical theology] is christological; its content is Jesus Christ and not its own self-understanding or identity. Therefore the aim of the enterprise involves the classic movement of faith seeking knowledge, of those who confess Christ struggling to understand the nature and will of the One who

---

14. Karl Barth, *The Epistle to the Romans*, trans. Edwyn C. Hoskyns (Oxford University Press: 1933, 1968), p. 7.
15. Brevard Childs, *Biblical Theology of the Old and New Testaments* (London: SCM, 1992).
16. ibid., p. 80.

has already been revealed as Lord. The true expositor of the Christian scriptures
is the one who awaits in anticipation toward becoming the interpreted rather than
the interpreter. The very divine reality which the interpreter strives to grasp, is the
very One who grasps the interpreter. The Christian doctrine of the role of the
Holy Spirit is not a hermeneutical principle, but that divine reality itself who makes
understanding of God possible.[17]

Moreover, Childs is clear that there should be a dialectical interplay between
the interpreter's own theological understanding and the specifics of the
biblical text. That is,

> there is an important function of hearing the whole of Christian scripture in the light
> of the full reality of God in Jesus Christ. In other words, there is a legitimate place
> for a move from a fully developed Christian theological reflection back to the biblical
> texts of both testaments.

To make this final move should not flatten or impose upon the biblical text, or
imply that 'the Old Testament's hidden agenda was always Jesus Christ':

> It rather has to do with the ability of biblical language to resonate in a new and
> creative fashion when read from the vantage point of a fuller understanding of
> Christian truth. Such a reading is not intended to threaten the *sensus literalis* of the
> text, but to extend through figuration a reality which has been only partially heard.[18]

Although I think that Childs's actual practice can be disappointing in relation
to his principle, his principle remains compelling. If the God who is known
supremely and definitively in Jesus Christ, and the many and varied dynamics
of life with this God, is the real subject matter of Scripture, then the serious
reader faces a never-ending challenge to engage more fully with that subject
matter.

On using the imagination

One heritage of the Enlightenment was a certain suspicion of the imagination, on the basis that the imagination, unlike reason, is in essence a vehicle for

---

17. ibid., pp. 86–87.

18. ibid., p. 87.

fantasy or illusion. In biblical scholarship this has generally showed itself in a preference for philological work and for evidential approaches to historical reconstruction, alongside a suspicion of other interpretative approaches that could appear to be merely subjective. Nonetheless, a striking aspect of recent work in theology and philosophy has been a recovery of the importance of the imagination.

Nicholas Lash, for example, in the context of critiquing the limited intellectual categories of the contributors to *The Myth of God Incarnate*,[19] utilizes the concept of imagination to indicate an alternative interpretative strategy to assumptions concerning rationality and objectivity which he considers highly questionable. He sees the failure of the contributors to *The Myth* as supremely an imaginative failure. Constructively, he sketches out the significance of the imagination thus:

> [T]he appropriate exercise of imagination is, as every novelist knows, as strenuous, costly and ascetic an enterprise as is any other intellectually and morally responsible use of the human mind. The poet is as impatient of imprecision, as constrained by that of which he seeks to speak, as is the historian or the physicist. In every field of discourse, practical or theoretical, literary or scientific, the quest for appropriate speech is a quest for precision that is fearful of illusion. . .
>
> Instead of contrasting 'reason' and 'imagination', I should prefer to suggest that *imagination is the intellect in quest of appropriate precision.* The function of 'appropriate', in that definition, is to serve as a reminder that types of human discourse are bewilderingly and irreducibly various, and that what is to count as 'precision', in any particular field of discourse, cannot be precisely stipulated in advance, but will emerge in the course of enquiry, discussion, and critical reflection.[20]

From the specific perspective of biblical studies, Walter Brueggemann, among OT scholars, has argued extensively for the centrality of imagination to biblical interpretation,[21] while A. K. M. Adam sounds comparable notes in a NT context. Adam, speaking generally about biblical interpretation, argues that contemporary culture opens up ways of re-engaging with the biblical text that

---

19. Nicholas Lash, 'Interpretation and Imagination', in Michael Goulder (ed.), *Incarnation and Myth: The Debate Continued* (London: SCM, 1979), pp. 19–28.

20. ibid., pp. 21–22.

21. Brueggemann sums up key aspects of his own work in his recent *Redescribing Reality: What We Do When We Read the Bible* (London: SCM, 2009). For the centrality of imagination, see pp. xx, 28, 32.

stand in real continuity (while allowing of course for differences) with characteristic premodern approaches:

> For the past two centuries, interpreters' imaginations have been policed by criteria native to the discipline of historical analysis; other approaches have been permitted to extend the range of biblical interpretation, to add a second interpretive dimension, only so long as they orient themselves toward the pole-star of historical soundness. [22]

However:

> Imaginations informed by cybermedia will not sit still for the ponderous police of historical authentication. New media will oblige interpreters to extend the range of their interpretive and critical faculties.[23]

Moreover, these new media can lead interpreters in directions not dissimilar to those of premodern and allegorical interpretation, as represented by the fifteenth-century *Pauper's Bible*:

> [A]s the *Pauper's Bible* reminds us that the work of biblical interpretation has in past times communicated well in images, so the allegorical imagination that funded the *Pauper's Bible* can provide clues for the directions that critical interpretation may take in new media . . . [T]he fourfold approach to allegorical interpretation was not a license to permit imaginations to run wild but a set of channels to guide interpretive imaginations. Those channels rely for their cogency not on intrinsic properties of words but on an aptitude for drawing correlations, *confections*, that satisfy the imaginations of their readers. The allegorical criteria . . . honor the inevitability that interpretations will go divergent directions without necessarily diverging from legitimacy.[24]

What is at stake is a shift of intellectual culture, a shift that should be congenial to Christian concerns to appropriate the OT as Christian scripture:

---

22. A. K. M. Adam, 'This is not a Bible: Dispelling the Mystique of Words for the Future of Biblical Interpretation', in Robert Fowler et al. (eds.), *New Paradigms for Biblical Study: The Bible in the Third Millennium* (New York/London: T. & T. Clark International, 2004), pp. 1–20 (p. 16).
23. ibid., p. 17.
24. ibid.

Scholars unfamiliar with construing biblical texts on any basis other than that of historical accuracy fumble and grope as they reach beyond the boundaries of their familiar practices. When academicians eventually become habituated to thinking aesthetically or ethically or politically about their interpretations, these modes of interpretation will seem no more subjective than interpretations based on varying assessments of historical probability.[25]

Much more could be said. My present concern is briefly to indicate something of the resources available for a richer, more wide-ranging and more robust use of the intellect in biblical interpretation than has often been characteristic of modern biblical scholarship, and to utilize these as providing a frame of reference for thinking about Christ in relation to the OT.

An example: Isaiah 49:14–16

I will conclude with a brief worked example, which is, I think, constructively controversial in a way that may be helpful in focusing our thinking as to what are, and are not, appropriate moves to make in relating Christ and the OT.

The OT passage, Isaiah 49:14–16, reads thus (in the NRSV):

> But Zion said, 'The LORD has forsaken me,
> my Lord has forgotten me.'
> Can a woman forget her nursing-child,
> or show no compassion for the child of her womb?
> Even these may forget,
> yet I will not forget you.
> See, I have inscribed you on the palms of my hands;
> your walls are continually before me.

This stands at the beginning of a section which speaks extensively of God restoring and repopulating Zion, and turning the tables on her enemies (49:14–26). When Zion speaks lamentingly (v. 14), as Jacob has spoken earlier (40:27) – although verse 14 can also be read as a response to Lamentations 5:20 – there is a response of deep reassurance: stronger than the maternal attachment which is famously unreserved and self-giving is the Lord's attachment to Zion (v. 15). This is then further supported by a picture of reassurance

---

25. ibid., p. 15.

(v. 16), whose general tenor (the Lord's unfailing awareness of Zion, because he is constantly reminded of her) is clear even while its precise imagery is unclear.

Many preachers today might focus upon the feminine imagery used to depict God's care (v. 15), since sensitivity to gender issues, not least in relation to language about God, is a widespread characteristic of our contemporary context. Moreover, it is worth remembering that long before gendered language became a lively issue, one of England's most famous spiritual writers, Julian of Norwich in the late fourteenth century, spoke devotionally of the Motherhood of God; as had done previously St Anselm in the late eleventh century.[26] Julian develops the theme in chapters 58–63 of her *Revelations of Divine Love*, where she says, for example:

> Our Mother in nature, our Mother in grace [sc. Jesus], because he wanted altogether to become our Mother in all things, made the foundation of his work most humbly and most mildly in the maiden's womb . . . The mother's service is nearest, readiest and surest . . . We know that all our mothers bear us for pain and for death . . . [b]ut our true Mother Jesus, he alone bears us for joy and for endless life, blessed may he be . . . The mother can give her child to suck of her milk, but our precious Mother Jesus can feed us with himself, and does, most courteously and most tenderly, with the blessed sacrament, which is the precious food of true life.[27]

So there would be good precedent for a preacher to dwell imaginatively on possible implications of the imagery of verse 15.

Nonetheless, I want to take a different tack and focus rather upon the possible implications of the imagery of verse 16. Here there is an initial exegetical question as to what is envisaged by the Lord's inscribing/engraving (*ḥāqaq*) upon the palms of his hands. This is something without clear analogy in the OT. Conceptually, the best OT parallel is probably the command to Israel to bind the words of the Shema 'as a sign upon your hand', where the point appears to be that a wristband with the all-important words written upon it would serve as a constant reminder (analogous to looking at a wristwatch). Most commentators mention, and many opt for, some kind of tattooing (with general uncertainty as to whether the prohibition of bodily incisions in

---

26. See Dom André Cabassut, 'Une dévotion médiévale peu connue: la dévotion à Jésus "notre mère"', in *Révue d'Ascétique et de Mystique*, 99–100 (1949), pp. 234–245.

27. Julian of Norwich, *Showings*, ch. 60, *Long Text*, Classics of Western Spirituality, trans. and ed. Edmund Colledge and James Walsh (New York: Paulist, 1978), pp. 297–298.

Lev. 19:28 should have any bearing on the idea of tattooing here).[28] Klaus Baltzer even ingeniously suggests 'that it is the lines on the palm that are meant, lines in which people thought they could discern the plan of Jerusalem'.[29] And some scholars simply consider such discussion misplaced: 'The prophet is undoubtedly using here a long-familiar figure of speech, this and nothing more.'[30]

Standard ancient resources are interesting in their own right, although limited in the help they offer. The Septuagint modifies the imagery by rendering 'inscribe' with 'paint',[31] and takes 'walls' as the object of this verb, rather than as the subject of the next clause: 'See, I have painted your walls on my hands, and you are continually before me.'[32] Beyond the OT, there is a much-cited Ancient Near Eastern analogy: 'There is a remarkable parallel in an extant statue of Gudea, Sumerian ruler of Lagash c. 2100 BC, holding in his lap the plan of a city of which he was presumably reckoned to be the architect'[33] – although the analogy is surely not in fact remarkable, precisely because an architect holding a plan in his lap sheds no light on how we are to envisage what is specifically on the Lord's hands.

In terms of historical argument and imagination in relation to verse 16a, therefore, we have not advanced, and probably cannot advance, beyond Bishop Robert Lowth's eighteenth-century comment:

> This is certainly an allusion to some practice, common among the Jews at that time, of making marks on their hands or arms by punctures on the skin, with some sort of sign or representation of the City or Temple, to shew their affection and zeal for it.[34]

---

28. The Hebrew preposition makes tattooing unlikely. Leviticus 19:28 uses *bĕ*, as is appropriate for something *in* one's bodily flesh, whereas Isaiah 49:16, like Deuteronomy 6:8, uses *'al*, which envisages something being located *upon* one's hand/wrist.

29. Klaus Baltzer, *Deutero-Isaiah*, trans. Margaret Kohl (Minneapolis: Fortress, 2001), p. 323.

30. C. C. Torrey, *The Second Isaiah* (Edinburgh: T. & T. Clark, 1928), p. 386.

31. Similarly the Vulgate, *descripsi te*, i.e. 'I have depicted you'.

32. This is the rendering in Albert Pietersma and Benjamin Wright (eds.), *New English Translation of the Septuagint* (Oxford University Press: 2007), p. 863.

33. R. N. Whybray, *Isaiah 40 – 66*, NCB (London: MMS, 1975), p. 144.

34. Robert Lowth, *Isaiah. A New Translation; With a Preliminary Dissertation, and Notes Critical, Philological, and Explanatory*, vol. II, 5th ed. (Edinburgh: Caw, 1807), p. 305. Lowth also adduces then-contemporary pilgrim practices in support.

It is the imprecise 'some practice' that we cannot get beyond. What does seem clear, however, is that, by analogy, a human practice is envisaged on the part of God himself, rather as elsewhere the OT depicts God as reminded by the sign of the rainbow in a way analogous to Israel being reminded by fringes on their garments (Gen. 9:8–17; Num. 15:37–41).

What difference, however, might it make when Isaiah is contextualized in a Christian frame of reference? There is one rather obvious and major imaginative resonance. As Michael Thompson puts it, 'Christians can hardly fail to see the parallel with the wound marks of Christ, indelible evidence of divine love.'[35] Nonetheless, the contention that 'Christians can hardly fail to see the parallel' is hardly borne out by the evidence. Christian scholars, even when commenting for an ecclesial and not primarily (if at all) academic audience, generally make no mention of the parallel,[36] although it appears occasionally.[37] Even leading advocates and practitioners of a canonical approach, Brevard Childs and Christopher Seitz, make no reference to it in their commentaries.[38]

How therefore might one evaluate a reference in this context to the wounds of Christ? Is it more than, or even as much as, the famous analogy between Isaac carrying the wood of the sacrifice to Moriah and Jesus carrying his cross

---

35. Michael E. W. Thompson, *Isaiah 40 – 66* (London: Epworth Press, 2001), p. 81.

36. I can find no mention in, for example, G. W. Grogan, 'Isaiah', in Frank Gaebelein (ed.), *The Expositor's Bible Commentary*, vol. 6 (Grand Rapids: Zondervan, 1986), p. 286; Paul Hanson, *Isaiah 40 – 66*, IBCTP (Louisville: Westminster John Knox, 1995), p. 134; Barry Webb, *The Message of Isaiah*, BST (Leicester: Inter-Varsity Press, 1996), p. 196; Walter Brueggemann, *Isaiah 40 – 66*, WBC (Louisville: Westminster John Knox, 1998), p. 116; John Goldingay, *Isaiah*, NIBC (Peabody: Hendrickson/ Carlisle: Paternoster, 2001), p. 285; John Oswalt, *The Book of Isaiah: Chapters 40 – 66*, NICOT (Grand Rapids: Eerdmans, 1998), p. 306.

37. For example, Alec Motyer, *The Prophecy of Isaiah* (Leicester: Inter-Varsity Press, 1993), p. 394: 'When the Servant's sufferings are reviewed (50:6, 53:4ff) his hands are not mentioned; that is reserved for a later date (Jn. 20:19–20)'; and John Oswalt's second commentary, *The NIV Application Commentary: Isaiah* (Grand Rapids: Zondervan, 2003), p. 558: 'when he speaks of our names as being "engraved . . . on the palms of my hands" (49:16), we think of the nail scars in the hands of God's Son. When he has done that for us, how could he forget us?'

38. Brevard Childs, *Isaiah*, OTL (Louisville: Westminster John Knox, 2001), p. 391; Christopher Seitz, 'Isaiah 40 – 66', in Leander Keck et al. (eds.), *NIB*, vol. 6 (Nashville: Abingdon, 2001), pp. 307–552 (pp. 431–434).

to Golgotha which, while suggestive, does not substantively contribute to engagement with the subject matter either of Genesis 22 or of the crucifixion narratives?[39] Is it other than a fortuitous imaginative association, which may be initially striking but which, if one stays with it, will most likely distract from the Isaianic picture of the rebuilding and repopulating of Zion? Should one make more of it than perhaps an elegant reference in passing, in the mode of Christopher North: 'Yahweh's "stigmata" are sketches of the city he loves and of which he is reminded whenever he looks at his hands'?[40]

I briefly offer three reflections in response to this question. First, the situation with regard to contemporary Isaiah commentaries is, as far as I can see, mirrored in the history of Christian interpretation: this Christological resonance is known, but appears only intermittently. If one consults Robert Wilken's valuable recent compilation of patristic and medieval commentators on Isaiah, one finds Jerome and Ambrose on 49:16, with no apparent reference to Christ's passion;[41] and, of course, if, like the Fathers, one is reading Isaiah in Greek, where Zion is painted, rather than incised, on the hands, an imaginative link to the passion may be less apparent. Moreover, neither Luther nor Calvin make mention.[42]

Yet the seventeenth-century Jesuit commentator, Cornelius à Lapide, gives a rather different picture. His commentary on 49:16 starts with a series of suggestions as to the historical practice envisaged, but then continues:

> Secondly, the real meaning is that Christ depicted the Church, his spouse, and his faithful individual people, in the scars of his wounds which he received in his hands for them, and which he will bear always, to eternity. For there he depicted them not with ink, but with his blood; not with a pen, but with nails and marks (*stigmata*); not in the skin, but in the flesh, so deeply that neither time nor eternity should ever erase them. For thence shall flow the gifts of grace, the Sacraments of the Church, and all good spiritual qualities, by which He protects and strengthens the walls of the Church

---

39. I have argued this in my *The Bible, Theology, and Faith: A Study of Abraham and Jesus*, CSCD (Cambridge University Press: 2000), esp. pp. 133–134.

40. Christopher North, *The Second Isaiah* (Oxford: Clarendon, 1964), p. 195.

41. *Isaiah: Interpreted by Early Christian and Medieval Commentators*, The Church's Bible (Grand Rapids: Eerdmans, 2007), pp. 376–378.

42. *Luther's Works, Vol. 17: Lectures on Isaiah, Chapters 40 – 66*, ed. Hilton Oswald (St Louis: Concordia, 1972), pp. 184–185; John Calvin, *Commentary on the Book of the Prophet Isaiah*, vol. 4 (Grand Rapids: Baker, 2005; repr. of ET by William Pringle in Calvin Translation Society), p. 31.

for ever. Thus St Ambrose . . . Whence St Cyril observes that by 'on the hands' is designated strength and power, and so on the hands of Christ the unconquerable strength of the Church is founded. For he says this: 'The passion of Christ, and the precious cross, and the nailing of his hands, have been security and an unbreachable wall.' So the wounds of Christ are a sure and safe refuge and sanctuary for all the faithful in any persecution or tribulation. So take refuge here, any who are worried, sad or afflicted. St Augustine prayerfully says (*Soliloquies*, Ch.2): 'Your hands, Lord, have made me and have formed me: those hands, indeed, which were fastened by nails for me. Lord, do not disdain the work of your hands; I pray you to look upon the wounds of your hands. Behold, on your hands, Lord God, you have depicted me; read that writing (*scripturam*), and save me. . .'[43]

Here we have a potent linkage between Isaiah 49:16 and John 20:20, 27. Although some Fathers see 'on your hands' solely as an image of strength and support, it is when Jesus' showing of his wounds is linked with the writing/depicting of the beloved in the Isaiah text that we have the imaginative scenario that Lapide himself finely expounds at the outset, and that Augustine deeply appropriates ('on your hands you have depicted me; read that writing and save me').

Second, there is no doubt that one can become so immersed in the imagery of *our* names on Christ's nail-torn hands that Isaiah's own context and concerns can recede from view. And perhaps some sermons might be none the worse for that. Nonetheless, this is not a necessary consequence. Especially if one takes the point of the risen Jesus showing his wounds to his disciples to be a matter not of 'proving' his resurrection, but rather of establishing his identity as the risen one – that the risen one is only and always the one who suffered and died for his own on the cross – then one can return to Isaiah's own context with a Christian construal of the identity of this God who rebuilds Zion. The divine compassion which here involves rebuilding leads in due course to unreserved self-giving. That is, the depth of the divine care for Zion, which surpasses maternal love and is displayed in the coming restoration which is to be envisaged with eyes of faith and hope (49:18), is understood to be given its deepest content by Christ's self-giving which for Christians defines the identity of God. This would not have been the prophet's own understanding of what he says about God, but it becomes a reasonable way of appropriating the text within a Christian frame of reference.

---

43. *Commentaria in Quatuor Prophetas Maiores: In Isaiam* (Antwerp: Martin Nutius, 1622), p. 440 (my translation).

Finally, I recognize that this particular linkage between Isaiah and Jesus is likely to vary in its appeal. I suspect that Nicholas Lash might have reservations about this use of the imagination, even while A. K. M. Adam might welcome it. But then not all sermons speak equally to all those who listen. Put differently, theological interpretation and the preaching of the OT can be done in more than one way, and is a task constantly to be renewed, as we make our journeys of faith with Scripture alongside. Especially when it comes to preaching, one needs to make decisions about the nature of one's hearers and the kind of message that seems right for the occasion. My general remarks about context, subject matter and imagination do not require a Christological reading of the engraving upon the divine hands in Isaiah 49:16. Nonetheless, I have tried to show how this time-honoured, though regularly neglected, construal may be a meaningful and legitimate way of appropriating the OT text and of preaching Christ through it.[44]

Further reading

DAVIS, ELLEN F., *Wondrous Depth: Preaching the Old Testament* (Louisville: Westminster John Knox, 2005).

FERGUSON, SINCLAIR B., *Preaching Christ from the Old Testament* (London: Proclamation Trust, 2002).

MOBERLY, R. W. L., *The Bible, Theology, and Faith* (Cambridge University Press: 2000).

© R. W. L. Moberly, 2010

---

44. I am grateful to Richard Briggs and my wife Jenny for helpful comments on a first draft.

INDEX OF SCRIPTURE REFERENCES